Routledge Transnational Perspectives on American Literature

EDITED BY SUSAN CASTILLO, *King's College London*

American Utopia and
Social Engineering
in
Literature, Social Thought,
and Political History

American Utopia and Social Engineering in Literature, Social Thought, and Political History

Peter Swirski

Routledge
Taylor & Francis Group
New York   London

First published 2011
by Routledge
711 Third Avenue, New York, NY 10017

Simultaneously published in the UK
by Routledge
2 Park Square, Milton Park, Abingdon, Oxon OX14 4RN

Routledge is an imprint of the Taylor & Francis Group, an informa business

Typeset in Sabon by IBT Global.
Printed and bound in the United States of America on acid-free paper by IBT Global.

Library of Congress Cataloging-in-Publication Data
Swirski, Peter, 1963–
  American utopia and social engineering in literature, social thought, and political history / by Peter Swirski.
    p. cm. — (Routledge transnational perspectives on American literature ; 15)
  Includes bibliographical references and index.
  1. American fiction—20th century—History and criticism. 2. Political fiction, American—History and criticism. 3. Utopias in literature. 4. Social control in literature. 5. National characteristics, American, in literature. 6. Exceptionalism—United States. 7. Social engineering—United States—History—20th century. 8. Political culture—United States—History—20th century. 9. Literature and society—United States—History—20th century. 10. Politics and literature—United States—History—20th century. I. Title.
  PS374.U8S85 2011
  813'.5409355—dc22
  2010046678

ISBN13: 978-0-415-89192-9 (hbk)
ISBN13: 978-0-203-81661-5 (ebk)

This book is dedicated to
Tse Ka Lai

Contents

Any satirist who had invented Reagan during the Eisenhower years would have been accused of perpetrating a piece of crude, contemptible, adolescent, anti-American wickedness, when, in fact, he would have succeeded, as prophetic sentry, just where Orwell failed; he would have seen that the grotesquery to be visited upon the English-speaking world would not be an extension of the repressive Eastern totalitarian nightmare but a proliferation of the Western farce of media stupidity and cynical commercialism—American-style philistinism run amok.

Philip Roth

Figures

Chapter 1

Chapter 2

Chapter 3

Chapter 4

Chapter 5

Introduction
Life Is More Important Than Art
or
Social Engineering, Eutopia, and Evolution

A LAND OF MILK AND HONEY

> Whether written to inform, edify, or entertain, literary works harbour a great variety of hypotheses about the world: tacit and overt, particular and general, testable and not, field-specific and interdisciplinary.
>
> Peter Swirski, *Between Literature and Science*

In 1972, after a reading at the University of Oregon, Bernard Malamud attended a dinner reception thrown by the English Department in his honour. Also attending was a doctoral candidate whose thesis was on Malamud and Wright. At one point during the party her supervisor found out from her husband that she was pregnant. As all good supervisors are wont to, he began to worry how it was going to affect the completion of her thesis. Suddenly a voice spoke up. "Life is more important than art," pronounced Malamud before warmly congratulating the student and her husband.[1]

Life *is* more important than art. And yet we value art precisely because it enriches our lives, holds a mirror to our experience, and imbues it with meaning. Art, someone else might point out, is no less valuable as a social barometer and a cultural diagnostic tool. It identifies social trends and cultural patterns and weaves elaborate counterfactuals—literary fictions—that hang human faces on large-scale abstractions such as society and culture. In the end, we value art precisely because nothing will ever be more important to any human being than society and culture. They are, after all, our only sources of meaning in a meaningless universe.

American Utopia and Social Engineering is a book about contemporary American society and culture. It seeks to understand the United States during the post-World War II era which took such a heavy toll on its institutional policies and ideals. But far from subscribing to American exceptionalism, it seeks larger truths. It seeks to draw from the American experience lessons that hold no less for other societies and other cultures. As such, even as it remains a book of literary scholarship, it is also a book of science—analytical rather than experimental, but science none the less.

American Utopia and Social Engineering is constructed around a series of interlocking critiques of sociopolitical policies of the last six decades. Chapter by chapter it revisits the theory and the history of campaigns to engineer a better America and the setbacks that habitually beset them. In the process it takes stock of several natural experiments—historical experiment-like variations in social life—which, although uncontrolled, are replete with heuristic value. Coupled with a neo-Darwinian orientation, this diagnostic perspective sets *American Eutopia and Social Engineering* apart from studies of never-never utopian republics.

The United States was created by revolution, only to be engineered by the founding fathers so that political rebellion could not take root again. Nothing puts it in sharper relief than the consternation over the French Revolution which, like the American Revolution barely thirteen years earlier, got rid monarchy in the name of people's power. Even as Jefferson and Franklin cheered the insurgents, Hamilton and the Federalists were aghast at the spectre of this popular political uprising spreading to America and jeopardizing their plans to engineer the newly united states into a continental capitalist corporation.

Today we live in Hamilton's utopia. The problem is, much like the myths of American democracy, the myths of American capitalism are often the opposite of reality. Political propaganda makes out the United States to be a promised land for the average Joe the entrepreneur. In a headline-grabbing soundbite from July 2002—hotly denied by both administrations—Bush II even confided to Tony Blair that the problem with the French was that they had no word for entrepreneur. True or not, it *rang* true. According to the widely-held belief, America offers business opportunities that the statist interventionist Europe can only dream of.

Not so. The United States has one of the *smallest* small-business sectors of all developed countries. Its self-employment rate is, in fact, the second smallest after that other global economic powerhouse: Luxemburg. The percentage of self-employed Americans is barely one-fifth that of Italy and Greece (which lead the western world in this category). The U.S. sits at the third *lowest* place when it comes to the percentage of manufacturing by small businesses, third *lowest* in the number of small R&D firms, and second *lowest* in small companies that supply computer–related services.[2]

Asking why these and other sociopolitical fairy tales continue to dominate political discourse and public life in America, I focus on the six decades ranging from 1948 to 2008. Significantly, these historical bookends are set as much by life as art. The year 1948 saw the publication of the most divisive utopia of the century, pilloried for its scientific and, for many, fascist program of behavioural engineering. 2008 marks the last year of the divisive presidency of Bush II which lies, thinly veiled, behind the last novel and the last program of fascist engineering in my study.

Between them stretch six decades of American history, politics, and social institutions that promised to lead us to the promised land and led us by the nose in circles instead. Perish the thought of a land of milk and honey. The United States today is afflicted with political alienation, militarized violence, institutionalized poverty, and social agony. Worst of all, perhaps, it is afflicted with chronic *and* acute ahistoricism. America insists on ignoring the context of its present dilemmas. It insists on forgetting what preceded the headlines of today and on denying continuity with history. It insists, in short, on its exceptionalism.

"... Perish the thought of a land of milk and honey. The United States today is afflicted with political alienation, militarized violence, institutionalized poverty, and social agony ..."

Figure i.1   Clockwise: Demanding direct democracy (2006) / Militarized violence (2007 Iraq) / One of the unsung effects of poverty soaring / Riot police pepper-spraying WTO protesters (1999).

American Eutopia and Social Engineering sets out to correct this amnesia. It misses no opportunity to flesh out both the historical premises and the political promises behind the social policies of the period. These interdisciplinary concerns provide, in turn, the framework for the analyses of works of American literature inspired—perhaps a more accurate term would be incited—by their times and mores. This intimate conversation between American literature, American politics, and American experience forms the analytic backbone behind my approach.

United by their concern about social engineering an American eutopia, the five novels at the centre of my study stand apart from one another in almost every other way. Even their authors could hardly resemble each other less. In the order of appearance, they are: the greatest twentieth-century American psychologist, a counterculture revolutionary and leader of the Merry Pranksters, a West and East Coast professor of creative writing, a Southern Christian doctor of medicine, and one of only three living litterateurs to have his works published by the Library of America.

I thus kick off with B.F. Skinner and *Walden Two* (1948), easily the most scandalous utopia of the century, if not of all times. Next comes Ken Kesey's *One Flew Over the Cuckoo's Nest* (1962), an anatomy of political disfranchisement American-style. It is followed by Bernard Malamud's *God's Grace* (1982), a neo-Darwinian beast fable about morality in the thermonuclear age. After that comes Walker Percy and *The Thanatos Syndrome* (1986), a diagnostic novel about engineering violence out of America's streets and minds. Finally, Philip Roth and *The Plot Against America* (2004), an alternative history of homegrown 'soft' fascism.

All five are novel-length thought-experiments on the theme of engineering a better society and the consequences thereof. All five assume—albeit to different degrees and purposes—that the formula for progress vectors individual well-being and collective regulation aimed at reducing social conflict. In concert with them, I also assume that to make America a better place we need, at a minimum, a couple of things. The first is a genuine people's democracy, not the poor man's excuse for one we have now. The second is social institutions that enhance personal well-being within a framework of collective cooperation.

Mine is not, however, an exegetical exercise. I use literature as a vantage point from which to critique a number of faulty premises and specious reasoning, especially in would-be reformers who close their eyes to the social and biological facts of life. In contrast, I take the adapted human nature to be the *sine qua non* of any viable social reform insofar as homeostatic response to evolutionary pressures impacts the well-being of all individuals and all collectives. In the same spirit, I take exception to several facets of American democracy by taking critical stock of the country's voting system and its politics of spin.

On the way, I re-evaluate a constellation of precepts in contemporary psychology (Chapter 1), open an original avenue of research into the adaptive foundation of altruism (Chapter 3), lay down the foundations for the socio-empirical analysis of de-aggression (Chapter 4), as well as build a case for a rethink of America's voting procedures (Chapter 2) and political campaigns (Chapter 5). By integrating this research with literature-based interpretations, I make theory and policy feed off each other with a view to relating both to our current sociopolitical concerns.

SOME ASSEMBLY REQUIRED

> The way to knowledge through fiction is via the neo-Darwinian paradigm.
>
> Peter Swirski, *Of Literature and Knowledge*

Born in the aftermath of the French Revolution, Auguste Comte was profoundly influenced by the anarchy and social disorder that became synonymous with the *nouveau regime* and its reign of terror. Eventually, this experience translated into his foundational vision of sociology as a science capable of engineering order and wellbeing. More than a century and a half after his death, social engineering can still be usefully approached in his terms. For my purposes, it is nothing else than any systematic process, policy, program, or project designed to decrease disorder and suffering in society.

The paradigmatic example are IQ tests. The first, designed in 1905, was a brainchild of two French psychologists, Alfred Binet and Théophile Simon. The former was particularly influenced by Francis Galton's writing on hereditary genius and individual differences in populations. If a psychological test could be devised to identify children underperforming in academic instruction, reasoned Binet, they could be then helped by extracurricular tutorials. IQ tests are also paradigmatic in another sense. They reflect the best and the worst about social engineering, from the nobility of the original design to the history of their misuse and abuse.[3]

As for utopia versus eutopia, a small difference in orthography hides a big difference in semantics. Utopia, which Thomas More coined from the Greek for no-place (*ou-topos*), denotes an imaginary realm with the connotations of being also Edenic in nature. Of course, being essentially presocial, with only a couple of humans and the sentient serpent, the Garden of Eden from the Old Testament is not a utopia either in literary or sociopolitical terms. Still, it stands in profound contrast to eutopia (*eu-topos*)—a good rather than perfect place.

Where utopia is a literary make-believe about an ideal society, eutopia is a historical and maybe only marginally better place. Where utopia is all optimism and perfectionism, eutopia is pragmatism and gradualism. Utopia, if you like, is a primetime TV commercial in which immaculately groomed housewives flash perfect ivories as they burble over domestic robots doing the laundry. Eutopia is an advertisement for a refurbished washer with a warning on the instruction manual: some assembly required.

Eutopia is, in short, a real rather than a virtual place. To see what it looks like, look outside your window. Eutopia is attained with every social reform, even though, once attained, it may no longer seem so desirable. And yet, even as utopia is by definition out of reach, receding like the horizon with each step taken toward it, few things are as beguiling as a vision of a perfect republic. No wonder that, over two and a half millennia since Plato's Atlantis, like a lodestar, utopia has remained a fixed bearing on our socio-philosophical compass, impelling practical dreamers to map its virtues.

In his classic dissertation, *From Utopia to Nightmare* (1962), Chad Walsh tagged all utopias as little more than Plato plus footnotes (and dystopias Plato turned sour). Be that as it may, there was something categorically different about the blueprint unveiled by Thomas More in 1516. In contradistinction to centuries of visions of the Christian City of God or folk legends of Cockaigne, it was both secular and reformist. More was interested less in metaphysical speculation than in the brute problem of engineering a society less riven by the inequality between the rich and the poor.

During the three and a half centuries thereafter, the Renaissance and then the Enlightenment followed his example. Andreae's *Christianopolis*, Bacon's *The New Atlantis*, Campanella's *The City of the Sun*, and Harrington's *Oceana* were only the best known milestones on the road to perfect social order—or at least to a philosophical outline for it. In the end, Walsh did have a point. All of them shared any number of things with Plato: eugenics, elite government, checks and balances, education, meritocracy, redistribution of property. For all their forward thinking, utopian visionaries always borrowed from the past.

In America, however, life began also to borrow from art. Without doubt, Edward Bellamy's *Looking Backwards* (1888) was the most important utopia of the nineteenth century. Like Skinner's novel sixty years later, it catalyzed not only ferocious philosophical debates but an entire social movement. Scores of Bellamy societies sprang up all over Europe and America, composing charters, founding colonies, and experimenting with his blueprint for a good life. Determined to forge a social eutopia from the pages of a literary utopia, they flopped in no time, foreshadowing the fate of Waldenite communes in the twentieth century.

This is not to say that Bellamy's vision worked for everyone. In *Caesar's Column* (1890), Ignatius Donnelly tried his own hand at fiction, appalled like de Tocqueville before him at the steady subversion of America's political ideals. His Walden-like decentralized agrarian society offered a direct antithesis to Bellamy's conurban corporate utopia. Stunningly for three-time United States congressman and state senator, the better state of affairs was brought about by an international anarchist-terrorist organization the goal of which was the overthrow of plutocracy in America and abroad.[4]

As these two contrasting examples make clear, in cognitive terms utopias are thought experiments at their limits. Instead of multiplying scenario forecasts, which can be costly and time-consuming, it often pays to extrapolate the extreme cases in order to gauge the consequences of social policies. Technology, offers Walker Percy, may create the means of engineering aggression out of human nature. Would such a somatic

"... Over two and a half millennia since Plato, like a Lode Star, utopia has remained a fixed bearing on our socio-philosophical compass, impelling practical dreamers to map its virtues / There was something categorically different about the utopian blueprint devised by Thomas More in 1516 / Edward Bellamy's *Looking Backwards* (1888) was the most important utopia of the nineteenth century. Like Skinner's novel sixty years later, it catalyzed not only ferocious philosophical debates but an entire social movement..."

Figure i.2 Surviving papyrus fragment of Plato's *Republic* / Title woodcut of the island of Utopia for the first edition of More's *Utopia* (1516) / Equality colony (circa 1900), inspired by and named after the sequel to Bellamy's *Looking Backwards*.

makeover be invariably beneficial? Instead of tracking all intermediate states, focus on the best-case scenario. If a model of society engineered to refrain from war and killing still looks like a dystopia, you have your answer.[5]

Far from being mere narrative conventions, utopias, in my view, are cognitive shortcuts for thought-experimenting with boundary conditions of social policies. Utopias, if you like, are social reformers' drawing boards and litmus papers combined. In the words of one contemporary philosopher, they,

> investigate the ideals, undertakings, and institutions of contemporary society, encourage a critical perspective on them, inspire a thoughtful evaluation of the present and alternative individual and social ideals and activities, and consider if and where change is feasible and desirable.[6]

This is an apt characterization of utopias and, indeed, of sundry narrative thought experiments—including the thought-provoking ones that drive *American Utopia and Social Engineering*. But it is also incomplete.

Like temperature or pressure in classical physics (they are equivalent), society is a statistical aggregate. It is made of a myriad of individuals constantly interacting with one another in a myriad of ways. As such, society has statistically stable properties. Within a margin of error, you can predict how many people will die every day, how many will be born, how many will go mad, how many will be tortured. The difference is that physical particles exhibit no volition, no hopes, no happiness. But human beings do, and happy societies are aggregates of happy people.

The inference is clear. To engineer a good society we need to understand its composite elements: human beings. And to understand human beings we need to understand their nature—or, to be more precise, their *evolved* nature. It is here that literary and philosophical discussions of utopia begin to show cracks in their foundations. A recent collection, *The Philosophy of Utopia* (2001), is a good case in point. Neo-Darwinism, at once the bedrock and the avant-garde of research into human nature, gets virtually zero play from scholars who would lay down the fundamentals of a good society.

This is a conspicuous oversight. Already the nineteenth century was seized with the importance of evolution, notably through the scientific romances of H.G. Wells who, from *The Time Machine* and *The Island of Doctor Moreau* to *The War of the Worlds*, struggled with the ramifications of post-Darwinian biology for the human species. As utopian philosophy, so literary scholarship. With evolution at the heart of novels such as *God's Grace*, the few critics that mention it by name manage to sound like they wish they hadn't. None attempts to analyze its leading themes—morality and social engineering—in neo-Darwinian terms.[7]

Given that evolution underlies my own approach to the understanding of human behaviour, a quick recapitulation may be in order. Darwin was not the first to propose evolution as a means for accounting for the diversity and propagation of species. But he was the first to delineate the mechanism by means of which it works: natural selection. Even as he did so, he had no idea of the specific genetic mechanisms behind this process. That came from the research by Gregor Mendel, which in the twentieth century gave rise first to genetics, and then to molecular biology.[8]

Fuse Darwin and Mendel and you arrive at the so-called modern synthesis, the conceptual union of evolution-by-means-of-natural-selection and transmission of DNA-coded information. Cast in the form of a theorem, i.e., in the form of concurrent premises from which the conclusion *necessarily* follows, Darwin discovered that, as long as there are:

1. variations within populations—whether genetic, structural, functional, cultural, or any other,

and

2. inheritance mechanisms that causally link parent and offspring generations, and thus correlate their survival rates,

then

3. evolutionary processes *will* emerge and the populations in question *will*, whether it wants to or not, evolve.

A quick word about adaptations: adaptations are characteristics selected for by evolution because they were satisficing solutions to recurrent problems. In the language of evolutionary psychology, an adaptation is a "reliably developing structure in the organism, which, because it meshes with the recurrent structure of the world, causes the solution to an adaptive problem".[9] Not to look too far, eyes are an adaptation. Avoidance of inbreeding is an adaptation. So is preference for calorie-rich food. So is the theory of mind and sociability. So is, at the end of the day, culture.

Naturally, none of this is so straightforward. To take the first example off the shelf, natural selection would appear to dictate that human beings invest in the survival of their kin proportionately to the strength of the genetic link between them. This in turn ties to the view that the most important element of the human motivational system is maximizing 'fitness', i.e., genetic representation in future generations.[10] Problem is, taken at face value, neither view explains self-sacrifice, the undeniable fact that we do things for strangers that make no sense within a strictly utilitarian calculus.

This does not mean that there is something wrong with the neo-Darwinian account. Nor does it mean that it is blind to such 'anomalies', as one literary-evolutionary critic makes clear:

> No culture can deviate from human universals (by definition), but many individual people can and do deviate from species-typical norms of behavior. They murder their children, commit incest, fail to develop language, or otherwise behave in anomalous or dysfunctional ways.[11]

All it means is that, slowly but surely, ongoing research erodes the assumptions that guided our earlier picture of the natural world. Research into altruism, for example, is by now the mainstream of evolutionary studies, turning upside down the iconic image of the selfish gene.

It also turns upside down the data collected by the early twentieth-century anthropologists, with Margaret Mead in the lead. Celebrating cultural diversity, they slanted their descriptions and theories to evoke island paradises inhabited by peaceful peoples, free of jealousy and materialism rampant in the United States. Reprinted and sentimentalized, such accounts fostered the impression—amplified by the social conditions of the Great Depression—that American capitalist culture was responsible for these behaviours. If only we could be more like the island-ers, social utopia would follow.[12]

Evolutionary science teaches us why this is not true. It also teaches us that, with a better grasp of the interplay between human evolved nature with ecological and cultural conditions, we may be able to modify those aspects of social life that we would really be better off modifying. This is precisely where our five novels—five narrative thought experiments and five blueprints for eutopia—come handy. Forging their visions of a better society, they direct the spotlight to those facets of social and political life in America that, in their opinion, should be prime targets for modification.

Skinner grapples with human nature and with the nature of psychological mechanisms that can be employed to effect desir-able changes in social behaviour. Kesey contemplates changing social attitudes by changing the rules according to which society is governed. Malamud dissects the evolutionary baggage that plays havoc with the moral fitness of social reformers and reformees. Percy takes on the beast that slouches towards Armageddon: aggression. Roth converts the United States into a counterfactual laboratory in which he shows that our brave new present is a thing of the future past.

The significance of these literary thought experiments is matched only by their diversity. They range from the nature of communal existence to the nature of political power sharing, the nature of altruism, the nature of violence, and finally the nature of emotions in politics and beyond. Reflecting this diver-sity, I approach these novels in three distinct but related ways: *interpretively*, as works of literary art; *historically*, as works of American literature that reflect the conditions of their creation; and *cognitively*, as thought experiments on American utopia and social engineering.

As I showed in *Between Literature and Science* (2000) and *Of Literature and Knowledge* (2007), literature has a tremen-dous amount to contribute to the social sciences as a mind labo-ratory, as a corrective to overly rationalistic models of human psyche and behaviour, and as a social trend-spotter. With the help of the five novels and the social models outlined herein, I thus interrogate key aspects of sociobiology and behavioural psychology, voting and referenda procedures, morality and altruism, multilevel selection and proverbial wisdom, violence and chip-implant technology, and the adaptive role of emotions in our private and public lives.

On the way, I critique a range of assumptions that lie behind the social policies in America of the day. Combining the modes of inquiry practiced by literature and science, I take cue from Skinner, Kesey, Malamud, Percy, and Roth who, far from professing art for art's sake, could be mistaken at times for social philosophers and anthropologists. As storytellers, their purpose is to relate the last six decades of American experience to the nation's sociopolitical ideals. As a story scholar, my purpose is to relate their scenarios to the sociopolitical policies put in place to make America a better place.

All five novelists make heavy interdisciplinary demands on literary critics to which I am more than willing to accede. This is because, in my opinion, their literary and sociopolitical concerns go to the heart of what interdisciplinarity is all about. In other words, I could not agree more with Charles Lumsden when he speculates that the clues to the next advancement of knowledge will be "scattered subtly along the boundaries demarcating the traditional disciplines, since these are the fault lines where human imagination is at its weakest and the unity of existence splits into warring points of view" (xlviii).

And this is what I have to say about the book. It is time to let the book speak for itself.

1 How I Stopped Worrying and Loved Behavioural Engineering

or

Communal Life, Adaptations, and B.F. Skinner's *Walden Two*

AS GOOD AS IT GETS

Education is what survives when what has been learned has been forgotten.

B.F. Skinner, in *New Scientist*

Paul Johnson, historian and close adviser to Margaret Thatcher, argued in *Modern Times* (1983) that the twentieth century was the golden era of social engineering. As such, it is little wonder that Burrhus Frederic Skinner should have attained the kind of celebrity reserved for superheroes—or supervillains. Without doubt he was the century's most influential advocate, not to say ideologue, of behavioural engineering. When in 1971 he made the cover of *Time*, lionized as the country's greatest living psychologist, it was only a culmination of his quest to take his message out of the Skinner Box and into America's boardrooms and classrooms.

In 1989, when *The Simpsons* made their cartoon debut, Skinner became a household name even in popular culture, joining the supporting cast of America's favourite dysfunctional family (until *The Sopranos*). Like his namesake, Principal Skinner was an odd duck of a man but a caring and passionate educator. Learning was, indeed, Skinner's lifelong preoccupation, whether in the laboratory or in the classroom. His approach to learning, however, was as operant changes in response to environmental stimuli, and it was as a behavioural engineer that he left his mark on the century's thought and *zeitgeist*.

Yet, even at the peak of fame, Skinner found himself maligned not only by fellow psychologists but by scientists and humanists of all stripes. Indeed, a good testimony to his stature is the stature of his detractors: Spiro Agnew, Carl Rogers, Noam Chomsky, Margaret Mead, Joseph Wood Crutch, Stephen Jay Gould, et al. Skinner, they said, regarded people as equivalent to pigeons and rats. He kept his baby daughter in a cage, disfiguring her for life. He favoured fascist conditioning regimes, right down to physical punishment and electroshocks. He turned his back on science, turning behaviourism into an ossified pseudoscientific sect.

Neither did these allegations dissipate in the twenty-first century. William O'Donohue and Kyle E. Ferguson make that much apparent in the introduction to their *The Psychology of B.F. Skinner* (2001): "Our bet is that many of you have heard that Skinner's philosophy of science has been shown to be false, that his research has been shown to be wrong or has been superseded by more recent research, and that the practical extrapolations from his work are ineffective or cruel" (4). Significantly, the authors have little difficulty demonstrating most of these charges to be false. Myths can, however, be more potent than truth.

In the foreword to the book, Skinner's elder daughter reports on receiving a fresh query from a tabloid-minded researcher who just could not let go of the image of a behaviourist Minotaur who turned his house into a Skinner Box, before confining his younger daughter to it for twenty-one years, until she grew into a monster herself. For the record, Skinner did not cage Deborah, but designed a controlled environment (air-crib) for the first two years of her life. Today she is a well-adjusted adult who on occasion teasingly wishes she had had more operant conditioning in her childhood.[1]

The reason why the accusations persist may be because some of them are true—though not of Skinner but of the other early twentieth-century psychologist, John B. Watson. Watson's vision of behaviourist future can be easily mistaken for a dystopia. In the interest of efficacy, he argued, modern industrial societies ought to outlaw religion—which only condones weakness and failure—retrain poets and other artists into productive citizens, and allow physicians to condition children to eliminate unsocial behaviour.

At times, Watson's *Psychological Care of Infant and Child* shades off from behaviourist conditioning into a nightmare:

There is a sensible way of treating children. . . . Never hug and kiss them, never let them sit in your lap. If you must, kiss them once on the forehead when they say good night. Shake hands with them in the morning. . . . If your heart is too tender, and you must watch the child, make yourself a peephole so that you can see it without being seen, or use a periscope. But above all when anything does happen don't let your child see your own trepidation, handle the situation as a trained nurse or doctor would and, finally, learn not to talk in endearing and coddling terms.[2]

Incidentally, talking to infants in endearing or coddling terms is hardwired adaptive behaviour, a point wholly missed by Watson. More to the point, his methods of child-rearing were as reprehensible as anything attributed to Skinner (who was a caring, if somewhat distant, father). Later in life, Watson actually publicly repudiated much of his professional advice, although tragically too late to help a generation of children—including his own. This much is manifest from the autobiographical memoir published by his granddaughter, actress Mariette Hartley, who in 1991 went public about a lifelong struggle to survive her dysfunctional family.

Another fiction that gained much credence is that Skinnerian conditioning leans heavily on punishment. For many, *Walden Two* evokes images straight from *One Flew Over the Cuckoo's Nest*: brutal guards, electroshocks, even lobotomy. The truth once again belies the myth. Although Watson's brand of behaviourism was, indeed, not wholly averse to punishment, Skinner has always advocated positive reinforcement only. He never wavered from the tenet that negative reinforcement and punishment (they are not the same) had no place in the behavioural engineer's toolbox.

Later in life, Skinner became slandered for falling afoul of cognitive psychology. In truth, his opposition to 'mentalism' stemmed from the conviction that its basic categories—intentions, beliefs, desires—were far too coarse-grained to become building blocks of the science of behaviour. Skinner never doubted the reality of mental events or the fact that people act on intentions and beliefs, which endows these with causal powers. But as explanations of the psyche, he protested, categories such as beliefs, desires and aptitudes were about as useful as Aristotle's 'explanations' of why bodies come to rest (they have an aptitude for doing so).[3]

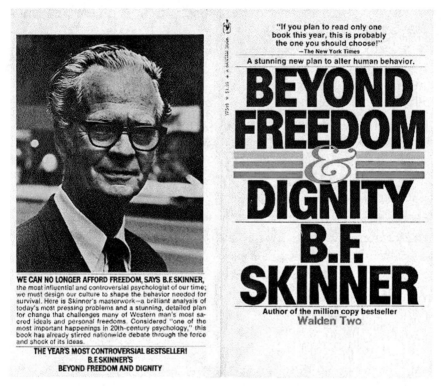

"If you plan to read only one book this year, this is probably the one you should choose!"
—The New York Times

A stunning new plan to alter human behavior.

BEYOND FREEDOM & DIGNITY

B.F. SKINNER

Author of the million copy bestseller
Walden Two

WE CAN NO LONGER AFFORD FREEDOM, SAYS B.F. SKINNER, the most influential and controversial psychologist of our time; we must design our culture to shape the behavior needed for survival. Here is Skinner's masterwork—a brilliant analysis of today's most pressing problems and a stunning, detailed plan for change that challenges many of Western man's most sacred ideals and personal freedoms. Considered "one of the most important happenings in 20th-century psychology," this book has already stirred nationwide debate through the force and shock of its ideas.

THE YEAR'S MOST CONTROVERSIAL BESTSELLER!
B.F. SKINNER'S
BEYOND FREEDOM AND DIGNITY

". . . He even declared in *Beyond Freedom and Dignity* that 'all reinforcers eventually derive their power from evolutionary selection'. Conceding that human nature is a child of its ancestral prehistory, he came close to conceding that biological imperatives may trump operant conditioning . . ."

Figure 1.1   First edition of Skinner's *Beyond Freedom and Dignity*, his most controversial book after *Walden Two*.

Skinner did regard the human psyche as John Locke did: a *tabula rasa* on which virtually anything could be imprinted by means of respondent conditioning. But even here the picture is not as one-sided as his debunkers painted it. His later writings reveal a degree of appreciation that behavioural plasticity is enabled by a bed of phylogenetic (species-typical) adaptations. He even declared in *Beyond Freedom and Dignity* that "all reinforcers eventually derive their power from evolutionary selection".[4] Conceding that human nature is a child of its ancestral prehistory, he came tantalizingly close to conceding that biological imperatives may trump operant conditioning.

This is, however, as good as it gets. Outside such sporadic bows towards evolution, Skinner never relinquished his faith in the almost limitless plasticity of the human psyche. In *Walden Two* he enunciated it loud and clear: "men are made good or bad and wise or foolish by the environment in which they grow".[5]

Alas, the consequences for his program could hardly be more disastrous. It is not, after all, the vision of the good life that distinguishes *Walden Two* from other eutopias but the science behind it. As a narrative thought experiment, the novel stands or falls with the behaviourist postulates that spawned it. Unfortunately, Skinner's conviction that people's genetic architecture can be overwritten and overridden at will is precisely where his would-be scientific eutopia devolves into a fairytale utopia—or worse.

I cannot overstate, however, that the upshot of my analysis is *not* limited to any one novel, any one variety of behaviourist tenets, or any historical experiment in communal living.[6] This is to say that the evidence I marshal below applies not merely to *Walden Two*, but to *any* form of social engineering, no matter if expressed as a fictional narrative, a psychosocial thought experiment, or a specific social constitution.

Evolution nests too deeply within the human psyche to be ignored when it comes to designing a better society—or just a better blueprint for a better society. Understanding the role that natural and sexual selection play in sculpting human nature is crucial to understand the behaviour of *any* social group. The analysis of the behaviourist eutopia composed by one of America's greatest psychologists is just a step along the way. But this small step is also a giant leap, inasmuch as only by acknowledging our evolved nature can we hope to engineer social habitats that will nurture prosocial behaviours.

A VERY AMERICAN UTOPIA

> I had failed as a writer, because I had nothing important to say ... I was to remain interested in human behavior but the literary method had failed me; I would turn to the scientific.
>
> B.F. Skinner, "Sketch for an Autobiography" (unpublished)

In the sweltering summer of 1945, as carpets of bodies decomposed on the killing fields from Berlin to Hiroshima, a middle-aged professor of psychology sat down to fulfil his youthful dream of writing a novel. Stooping, bespectacled and socially awkward, he was everyone's idea of a scientist geek. But after hours he was not only a consummate musician but also a connoisseur of literature, fond of reading Diderot, Stendhal, and Proust in the original. In his spare time he even dabbled in literary criticism, composing essays on Ezra Pound and Gertrude Stein, the latter for the prestigious *Atlantic Monthly*.

As a young man, before he ever completed his first psychology paper, he had actually decided to be a writer, bolstered by accolades from none other than Robert Frost. "I ought to say you have the touch of art", complimented the freshly minted Pulitzer winner the future behaviourist, adding: "You are worth more than anyone else I have seen in prose this year".[7] Now, as the summer sun beat down, Skinner banged out *Walden Two* in seven weeks of white-heat effort. Finished, he read the book to his wife—who hated it and its entire social-engineering program— and decided against revising it beyond the barest minimum.

Mistake. Over the next three years rejections uniformly censured the static plot, cardboard characters, and ham-fisted style. Fellow professionals raised a raft of questions about the appeal of Skinner's ideals and about the very desirability of behavioural engineering. One such dogged critic, philosopher Alburey Castell, even became incarnated in *Walden Two* as a verbal punching bag for the novel's chief behaviourist. In the end, Skinner's academic reputation won the day. Macmillan made him an offer he couldn't refuse: they would publish the novel but only if he also wrote them a textbook of psychology.[8]

They rest, as they say, is history. But even though *Walden Two* would go on to become the most influential and the most contentious utopia of the century, few could have guessed it from its humble beginnings. For more than a decade it sold only a few hundred copies a year, waiting for the rebellious sixties to pluck it out of obscurity. This they did with a vengeance, so much so that by the seventies sales exceeded a hundred thousand a year. By now, of course, *Walden Two* is a byword: two and a half million copies in all the major and many minor languages of the world—and more condemnations than any utopian fiction ever.

Many readers, in fact, took it to be an outright dystopia. The editors of the 1952 anthology, *The Quest for Utopia*, even denied it an entry, clamouring that it violated the utopian spirit. By then, of course, reviewers have had a field day with Skinner's recipe for a good life. *The Journal of Philosophy* led the assault, flaying it as horrible and predicting that it would only produce "contented non-political robots".[9] Ratcheting the rhetoric, *The Philosophical Review* put Skinner on a par with the Nazis. His views on American democracy and capitalism, it concluded, were "hardly distinguishable from the attacks of the National Socialists".

If Skinner's new republic did little for the philosophers, the culturati were even less amused. "Sadistic, fascistic", howled the normally restrained *New York Times Book Review*.[10] A miniature, "vicious in principle, of *Brave New World*", echoed *Fortune*. More than twenty years later, Ayn Rand's broadside at Skinner's *Beyond Freedom and Dignity*—commonly seen as a nonfiction version of *Walden Two*—was even more hysterical. "Boris Karloff's embodiment of Frankenstein's monster", she spluttered, typifying the countless political, scientific, and cultural heavyweights who rallied against behaviourism and its professor-in-chief.

If such vehemence seems almost inappropriate vis-à-vis a work of fiction, especially in such a never-never genre as utopia, the timing was unique. *Walden Two* appeared only four years after social engineering was publicly extolled in the United States by Gunnar Myrdal in his widely influential study of black-white relations, *An American Dilemma*. His was the first systematic attempt to persuade political leaders that induced social change could become a new paradigm for public regulation. As in Skinner's novel, laissez faire was to yield to statism, with the underpinning for the American welfare state drawn from the sciences of sociology and psychology.

What was it about *Walden Two* that sent everyone screaming murder? The plot, such as it is, opens in the office of Professor Burris, senior psychologist and one-time fellow graduate student of a brilliant maverick, T.E. Frazier. In walk two demobbed GIs who, stirred by rumours of Frazier's experimental community, ask Burris to help them get to it. In no time a party of six—Burris, the two young men and their girlfriends, and a querulous philosopher Professor Castle—embark on a short bus ride to Walden Two. With Frazier as their guide, they stroll around the commune for a few days, getting an earful of his behaviourist tirades. The end.

Whatever was threatening about Skinner's agenda could not have anything to do with the generic plot in which a visitor explores a utopian commune with a local cicerone. Nor could it be the structure, stitched as it is out of classical unities of time/place/action, and discrete dialogue-driven scenes. Nor could it be the cultivation of human potential which owes to American Transcendentalism and the nineteenth-century European tradition of *Bildung*. Instead, even as it embraced classic utopian ends, such as egalitarianism and welfare, *Walden Two* was a utopia of means—a do-it-yourself book of behavioural science.

In American letters, this didactic strain harks back at least to Benjamin Franklin, like Skinner a scientist, inventor, public figure, reformer, and prolific writer. And yet, with all the horrors visited on humanity in the name of engineering a better world, the twentieth century was not a good time for utopias. Thinkers like Karl Popper, Leszek Kolakowski, Frederick Hayek, Isaiah Berlin, and Michael Oakeshott condemned them as one-way tickets to totalitarian orthodoxy. Utopias, harangued one historian, are mere "justifications for terrible wrongs. The last thing we really need is more utopian visions."[11]

Skinner could have hardly dissented more. In calculated defiance of the faraway utopias of yore, he set his community squarely in mid-twentieth-century United States, just thirty miles from the largest city in an unspecified Midwestern state. In his 1972 address to the Thoreau Society he even made a special point of this 'hereness and nowness' of his vision:

> You don't need to go to a Shangri-la behind high mountains, or to a new Atlantis on some hitherto undiscovered island, or move about in time to a distant past or future. You can have the kind of life you want in the present setting. (2)

His eutopia is, in short, a place in the heart of America's heartland, a very American better place. No matter that, in *Beyond*

Freedom and Dignity, Skinner debunked what most Americans took to be the essence of being an American. His community is Smalltown writ large, mythologizing a country born in the country where regular folks practice liberty, equality, and pursuit of happiness. Given its classic expression in the writings of Thomas Jefferson, this Virginian landowner's vision of agrarian simplicity permeates *Walden Two*, abetted by the Thoreauvian distrust of large-scale social institutions.

Never mind that, even as he inveighed against the corrosive effects of city life, the third president amassed exorbitant debts carting tons of European luxuries to Monticello. Never mind that he sold his vision of gentrified yeoman's America to Alexander Hamilton for the price of removing the capital to the swamplands on the Potomac. Hamilton's blueprint for an industrial and financial powerhouse has come to define the United States and its holy trinity of laissez-faire, free trade, and world hegemony. But, in a conceptual schism, Skinner resurrects the Jeffersonian ideals as an alternative to Hamilton's vision of urban prosperity.

Like the Amish or the Hutterites, Skinner's community is said to prosper in happy mediocrity, practicing the have-not-want-not ethic of self-sufficient sustainability. Skinner almost certainly had the Hutterites in mind when writing *Walden Two*.[12] The work ethic, the collective ethos whereby members serve the group organism, the strong leadership (exemplified by the sect's mid-seventeenth-century founder, Ehrenpreis), the self-sufficiency, the high birthrate—all are mirrored in Skinner's fiction, right down to the decree to divide down the middle and settle new lands when the numbers swell past a certain point.

For what is the behaviourist prescription for communal welfare? It is aggressively anti-city, anti-money, and anti-heavy industry—so much so that if fixes maximum population at one thousand. Not that you would notice, anyway. There is no reason, snorts Frazier, to bring people together. "Crowds are unpleasant and unhealthful. They are unnecessary to the more valuable forms of personal and social relations, and they are dangerous" (37). For all the world he sounds like Jefferson who, in an 1803 letter to David Williams, excoriated the cities of Europe and America as "sinks of voluntary misery".[13]

Another quintessentially American trait—much like in Bellamy, to whom Frazier makes a direct reference—is Skinner's studious avoidance of the term 'socialism'. Of course, his classless, moneyless collective, who work for the common welfare guided by planners armed with a central plan, is socialist in everything but name. The reasons for this ellipsis are not hard to reconstruct. Prominent among them is the post-World War I suppression of the Socialist Party as a political force, and the post-World War II communist phobia stoked by the military-industrial-congressional complex and its civilian branches, such as RAND.[14]

Skinner himself acknowledged what a number of reviewers have pointed out, namely that Frazier is an incarnation of many of his own views.[15] To be precise, the author partitions himself *à la* Thomas Moore in *Utopia*, wherein Moore writes himself into the story as a sympathetic listener, while voicing his opinions through the mouth of Hythloday, the bearer of news from nowhere. Skinner, whose first name was Burrhus, names his narrator Burris, happily conceding in *A Matter of Consequences* that "Burris and Frazier are parts of me" (180).

Alas, his fictional mouthpiece does not bring him too much credit. "We don't propagandize in favor of our way of life", proclaims Frazier, "except to present what we think is a fair comparison of other types of society".[16] In other words, we don't propagandize in favour of our way of life, except when we do. Or, in the same vein, he rants: "We don't poke fun at the rest of mankind or laugh at their stupid economic or social practices". In other words, we don't poke fun at the stupidity of mankind, except we do.

It would have been bad enough if this was all there was to Skinner-as-Frazier—but it isn't. The arch-behaviourist finds nothing amiss in contending: "we don't pay much attention to the apparent success of a principle in the course of history".[17] Later on, he is even more peremptory: "History tells us nothing". It is nothing short of bizarre to hear these words from the mouth of a scientist who at every opportunity extols the experimental method, for without retrospective analysis there would be no science, period. To the extent that they are useful, experiments are historical events.

Naturally, between Henry Ford's "History is more or less bunk" and Francis Fukuyama's *The End of History and the*

Last Man, the twentieth-century was chockfull of self-serving attempts to consign history to the dustbin. Skinner himself joins their chorus: "history never even comes close to repeating itself. Even if we had reliable information about the past, we couldn't find a case similar enough to justify inferences about the present or immediate future" (224).

In this, as in so many other places in the novel, Skinner plays with loaded dice. Analogy or even homology does not entail sameness. Metaphors, for one, highlight conceptual similarities without obliterating differences. His utopian dice are no less loaded in the communal kitchen. Forget individual tastes, allergies, gastro-viral ailments, or food cravings. Every Waldenite has a cast-iron stomach, ideally suited to dietary orthodoxy. More loaded dice in the lumber yard. Where real communards found farming to be backbreaking toil, assigned to wood chopping the elderly academics find it pleasantly invigorating and vastly superior to grading papers.[18]

By fiat, everyone at the farm is well adjusted and cured of all manner of behavioural instincts, emotional drives and evolutionary adaptations. Sex, for an example, is strictly a mommy-and-daddy-love-each-other-very-much affair. There is no philandering, sexual deviance, or incompatibility. Wed as teenagers, advises Skinner, and all behaviours grafted by evolution onto sexual selection and parental investment will go the way of the dodo. No wonder that one reviewer panned his behaviourist Eden as a "kindergarten for adults in a well-run summer hotel".[19]

Like other revolutionary fictions, *Walden Two* inspired a wave of social transformations. Beginning in the late 1960s, no less than three dozen experimental communities sprang into existence in order to make Skinner's social-engineering blueprint come true—or at least to put it to the test. In their yearning for a better way of life, however, many mistook a thought experiment for a *fait accompli*. Kat Kinkade, co-founder and co-leader of the Waldenite Twin Oaks community, is in many ways a paragon of a clear-headed behaviourist. Yet, stunningly, she admits:

> In *Walden Two* Frazier tells his visitors that techniques of behaviour-management for human society are developed

and ready for use. It was years before I recognized this as part of the fiction. I thought it was literally true . . .[20]

To be fair, Skinner himself occasionally muddled the distinction between the laboratory and fiction by referring to *Walden Two* as a pilot experiment.[21] One of his exegetes even hailed the novel as the "first large-scale application to human behavior of the scientific principles he had drawn from his experimental work" (18). Application? Even if Skinner used the word 'experiment' on every page, it would not transform utopian make-believe into applied science. Even so, *Walden Two* clearly convinced generations of readers that it was as real as death and taxes, and the efforts by some to turn it into reality are of immense importance.

Lenin's 'perestroika', Stalin's collectivization, Mao's great leap forward, Pol Pot's cultural revolution are just the most notorious chapters in the book of horrors written by modern states in the name of engineering better societies. The issues raised in *Walden Two* continue to make headlines whenever democratically elected dictators try their hand at nation-building. For witnesses of the debacle of democratizing Iraq—and the concurrent conditioning of Americans at home with terrorist alerts, nationwide surveillance, and erosion of civil rights—behavioural engineering is never about the past.[22]

The twentieth century witnessed no shortage of Orwellian swine trying to remake societies in their own image. "Only by radically remolding the teaching, organization and training of the youth shall we be able to ensure that the efforts of the younger generation will result in the creation of a society that will be unlike the old society" (23), harangued Lenin at the zenith of his power. As if in reply, in the year of Skinner's death, a Nobel-winning economist reflected on the legacy of social engineering in words that could be mistaken for a critique of *Walden Two*.

In our century we have watched two great nations, the People's Republic of China and the Soviet Union, strive to create a 'new man,' only to end up acknowledging that the 'old man'. . . self-interested and concerned with his or her economic welfare, or the welfare of the family, clan, ethnic group, or province, was still alive and well.[23]

As a literary utopia, as a behaviourist blueprint for a 'new man', and as a sociopolitical blueprint for a kinder and gentler America, *Walden Two* is premised on radical associationism, whereby any behaviour at all is said to be learnable with equal ease. For Skinner, much as for the majority of today's social scientists, human action is a product of the social environment and nothing else besides. Aggression, to take his own example, is merely a by-product of the social preference for aversive control. Remove coercion and the power to punish, replace them with rational suasion and positive reinforcement, and human beings will never aggress again.

This is a dangerous illusion. Aggression is an instinctive manifestation of human behavioural economy, an expression of our adaptations for survival, status seeking, territoriality, and the need to attract mates.[24] More generally, evolution, so resoundingly dismissed in *Walden Two*, is indispensable to understanding why the behaviourist recipe for a better society utterly failed to produce the happiness it promised. Significantly, in the later years Skinner never returned to the specifics of *Walden Two*. This alone was a loud admission that what he had overlooked is exactly what he should not have.

So was his persistent refusal to have any truck with the flower children—never matter that, thanks to their fervent response, the sales of *Walden Two* shot through the roof. Perhaps most tellingly, he even refused to get acquainted with their behavioural techniques and experiential findings, as in the case of the Dandelion group which had tried for years to invite him for a visit. Adding insult to injury, an a 1984 article "News From Nowhere", Skinner openly derided their utopian revolution, even as Waldenite communities kept pleading for his advice.

YOU TELL ME THAT IT'S EVOLUTION (WELL, YOU KNOW, WE ALL WANT TO CHANGE THE WORLD)

> Blood is thicker than water. And blood will tell. Can you deny that? Where does your behavioral engineering come in there? The family has a *biological* basis.
>
> B.F. Skinner, *Walden Two*

Writing about *Walden Two*, one utopian scholar remarked that "one can actively influence the evolutionary process by using behavioral engineering".[25] It is true that group selection can propagate prosocial attitudes. Culture has evolved (i.e., become an adaptation) in part because social engineering can make a difference over time. On the other hand, to the extent that the statement smacks of Lamarckian inheritance of acquired (phenotypal) traits, it is simply wrong. If you teach your children to recycle plastics and paper, your grandchildren will not inherit this trait and will have to be taught the virtues of recycling all over again.

Few people today subscribe to Lamarck's theories which, resuscitated by Lysenko and Maltsev, in the single decade of the 1950s precipitated the death by famine of twenty to forty million people in China. But even though it carried the day, neo-Darwinism remains largely misunderstood—or just not well understood—even as it is indispensable to get to the bottom of the behavioural problems that plagued the experimental communes modelled on *Walden Two*. Why? Because to the extent that behavioural conditioning clashes with evolved adaptive behaviours it cannot be effective in the sense Skinner envisioned.[26]

Put bluntly, human adaptive mechanisms limit the efficacy of any project to ameliorate human nature and society. One of the most salient points on which Skinner finds himself at loggerheads with evolution is reproductive investment in one's offspring. At Walden Two, instead of being left with parents selected by the biological lottery, children are reared by professionals in a controlled environment designed to minimize frustrating social experiences. Given that parents no longer need offspring for economic security and that the community is said to function as a large family, Skinner concludes: "Blood ties would then be a minor issue" (xi).

Would they? Bearing in mind that we are talking about behaviours present in all humans—having been central to solving ancestral survival problems—let us look at this thesis in more detail, starting with Skinner's own household. Although the behaviourist did not regard the blood ties between parents and offspring to be difficult or harmful to sever, he never surrendered his own children to group care. His wife's hostility to the idea is even more revealing. Upon the release of Kinkade's first book about Twin Oaks, Eve Skinner confided to her: "I don't like behaviorism, I never did, and I didn't like *Walden Two*".[27]

Toward the end of the novel, psychology professor Burris—and alongside him psychology professor Burrhus Skinner—actually concedes that the family has a biological basis. Yet, he continues,

> aside from the role of physical resemblance, I could not see that hereditary connections could have any real bearing upon the relations between men. A 'sense of family' was clearly dependent upon culture, for it varied in all degrees among cultures (291).

In degrees, maybe, but not in kind. The theory of kin selection is emphatic on this point. Matter of fact, if there is one incontrovertible tenet in neo-Darwinism, it is that hereditary connections strongly correlate with the relations between people.

Much of the paradigm hinges on *inclusive* fitness, which is all about blood ties. In classical fitness, all that counted was individual behaviour that maximized reproductive success. In inclusive fitness, another factor comes into play: genetic relatedness. Made famous by Dawkins as the 'gene's eye' point of view, it hinges on the fact that—as he put it in *The Selfish Gene*—parents and children share 50 percent of genes; full siblings 50 percent (identical twins 100 percent); grandparents and children (also half siblings, and uncles and nieces) 25 percent; first cousins 12.5 percent; and so on.[28]

Taken literally this is, of course, arrant nonsense. We share no less than 60 percent of our genome with fruit flies, which would entail that we should ensure the propagation of *drosophila* at the expense of our own siblings (with whom we are said to share only 50 percent). The fact is that all people on earth share no less than 99 percent of genetic material with one another. Most genes are the same for all individuals of the species because they code for essential functions of the organism. Clearly, Dawkins's shared genes are only a shorthand for degrees of relatedness among kin—half, quarter, one-eighth, and so on.

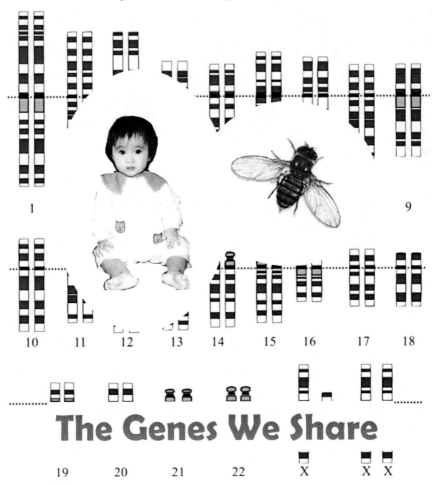

"... Taken literally this is, of course, arrant nonsense. We share no less than 60 percent of our genome with fruit flies, which would entail that we should ensure the propagation of drosophila at the expense of our own siblings (with whom we are said to share only 50 percent)..."

Figure 1.2   Which to cuddle and which to kill: the baby or the insect?

Genetic success means not just the propagation of one's own genes, but also those of blood relatives, adjusted for the degree of kinship and investment of resources. Not surprisingly, when it comes to kin selection, family members with the strongest hereditary links typically top this genetic 'to help' list. This is not to say that genetic relatedness explains all forms of altruism or social cooperation, any more than it explains the violent feuds that sometimes bedevil family groups. From neglectful mothers to abusive fathers, there is much evidence pointing away from genetic determinism. But the evidence for a biological foundation of family ties is incontrovertible.

Psychological propensities such as parental investment evolved to regulate behaviours with a view to hiking the odds of successful reproduction. One aspect of this adaptive behaviour is worth highlighting in the context of J.B. Watson's injunction to abstain from baby-talk. Firstly, bonding with offspring, exhibited in this case through verbal behaviour, must be instinctive and universal to warrant his blanket call on parents everywhere to avoid it. Secondly, given that baby-talk—technically, infant-directed speech or IDS—is instinctive and universal, any such order can be only partially or superficially successful.

Cutting parents off from their children is always possible (look no further than *Sophie's Choice*), but at the price of psychic damage and howls of protest from our ancestral heritage. Parental investment is wired into our species and, as research in evolutionary psychology confirms, it is not for the taking—or leaving. Although males are somewhat less demonstrative than females, and the Japanese less than the Westerners, Motherese (IDS) manifests itself irrespective of sex, culture, or even parenthood. Moreover, contact with infants brings it out not only in adults but in children as young as four, further testifying to its instinctive character.[29]

Its linguistic features are easy to identify from watching people coo to a baby. Exaggerated pitch contours, sing-song musicality, vowel elongation, slower tempo, enunciation (hyperarticulation), simplified syntax, and repetition manifest themselves across all cultures.[30] Ironically, given Skinner-as-Frazier's disdain for history, the history of the twentieth century provides another source of evidence about the biological basis of the family. To take the most obvious example, social engineering in the USSR, which was to replace the family as the locus of social affiliation with love for the Soviet state, proved an abysmal failure.

Admittedly, such indoctrination was partially successful, especially when grafted onto the tsarist ideology of Mother Russia. Denunciations of parents by children—among whom the case of Pavlik Morozov may be the most egregious—though never as common as propaganda made them out to be, show that on occasion blood ties can indeed be suppressed (although not without feelings of guilt, regret, and trauma). Liberalized divorce and abortion laws, in conjunction with the exodus of housewives into the workforce, had by themselves altered the traditional Russian family. But historically, the absorption of the family into the state proved to be only skin deep.[31]

The primacy of the parent-child bond is once again reaffirmed by decades-long communal experience in Israel. In their classic study of three generations of women *kibbutzim*, Lionel Tiger and Joseph Shepher report how, notwithstanding zealous ideological commitment to communal rearing, the adaptive behaviours returned through the back door. Kibbutz mothers first revolted by insisting that children live with them; then took political control by outvoting the behavioural codes that mandated communal rearing. The experiment in erasing the primeval relationship between parent and child crumbled into dust.

The same pattern is mirrored in every culture and every social experiment, including Twin Oaks. No matter how committed to behaviourist ideals, members left rather than abandon their young to communal care. "When I left Twin Oaks, it was because of Maya", recalled one mother. "I just wanted to be able to teach my kids more what I believed, and wanted to stop pretending that it wasn't important to me".[32] Another parent recalls that prior to the birth of his daughter he wholly endorsed communal parenting. After all, shrugged the father-to-be, all there was there was just a mix of genes. "I can't believe any of it anymore. I didn't know what the hell I was talking about".

Next to parenthood, the most fundamental and irrepressible behaviour in the service of the genome is sex. What would evolutionary science predict in this regard? Despite the free-love ethic among the communards, many of whom were flower children, pair-bonding should resurface when the novelty of sexual liberty wore off. This is precisely what happened at Twin Oaks where pairings, whether boyfriend-girlfriend or even formal marriages, re-emerged in the absence of any conventional norms of pair bonding. As Hilke Kuhlman reports, "a lot of them got married, and are still married and have children" (113).

To Frazier's rants that the family is the frailest of modern institutions, the proper answer is that it is neither modern nor frail. Family ties are the bricks and mortar of social groups, regulating the intensity of our attachments and our willingness to extend ourselves and our resources to people around us. Although in times of affluence behaviours tend to be more altruistic, times of need invariably bring out the underlying order: family first, then friends, then the tribe. Tellingly, deploring the challenges of governing Twin Oaks, Kinkade deplored "people wanting decisions to go a certain way because how it affects them or their families or their friends."[33]

Although willing to share living space, people are also innately territorial. One Waldenite planner insisted that his leaving Twin Oaks had nothing to do with communal policy, it's just that his needs could not be accommodated within it. "I wanted private space. I had my own bedroom, but I just wanted more physical space around me that I didn't have to share."[34] No less innately, people grope for power regardless of what the utopian catechism preaches about egalitarianism. Ian Murrey, cofounder of the Canadian Waldenite group, Headlands, summed up four years of power struggles before its demise with: call the planners Board of Directors "and be done with the bullshit".

In *Hierarchy in the Forest* (1999) Christopher Boehm proposed that social hierarchies became entrenched only during the agricultural revolution, when food surpluses engendered a problem of unequal redistribution. Hunter-gatherer groups indeed tend to be fairly egalitarian, enforcing the ethos through mockery of those who brag or claim too much. Boehm maintains that, even as we like to dominate others, we have an even

"... One Waldenite planner insisted that his leaving Twin Oaks had nothing to do with communal policy. It is just that his needs could not be accommodated within it. 'I wanted private space. I had my own bedroom, but I just wanted more physical space around me that I didn't have to share.'. . ."

Figure 1.3   Community clothesline outside Harmony, the first building constructed by Twin Oakers (the two rows closest to the building are for communal clothing).

stronger motivation to avoid being dominated (reverse-dominance theory). In the absence of resource accumulation, goes the elegant argument, the latter motivation dominates hunter-gatherer societies.[35]

The entire situation, however, can be stood on its head. The reason hunter-gatherers need to be constantly vigilant about resource monopolists and enforce the egalitarian ethic is because of the ubiquity of self-elevation. Studies of our closest genetic cousins show that the ability to appraise the social balance of power and to use it to one's advantage is inbred into every chimp, orang, gorilla, and even the darling of utopian feminists, bonobo.

Given our joint pedigree—chimps and humans share 98.75 percent of their genome—entrenched hierarchy may far precede the advent of agricultural surpluses, albeit mitigated by our capacity to include others in the social equation.

Virtually all Waldenite communities, as well as the more established and long-lived Anabaptist communities, such as the Amish, have elaborate systems—including selective lottery—to countervail the inevitable effects of hierarchy and dominance. These compensatory or inhibitory social mechanisms strike me as homologous to the reasons why early hunter-gatherer groups needed to enforce egalitarianism—precisely because it was under a constant threat. In short, of the two competing forces at work: pro-individual and prosocial, the former is by definition the more dominant, even if only because the latter evolved as a response to it.

Evolution strikes back in other ways. Consider social cheaters. Bronislaw Malinowski's functional studies of Trobriand islanders paint an iconic picture of the transcultural universality of free-rider behaviour: "whenever the native can evade his obligations without the loss of prestige, or without the prospective loss of gain, he does so, exactly as a civilised business man would do" (30). Data from the USSR and its satellites prove that parasitic behaviour is ineradicable even in ideologically most fervid environments. Evolutionary theory predicts, in fact, that free-riders will arise in all groups, no matter how highly motivated by ideology.

Rationally, it makes perfect sense for individuals to mooch off the system. They get all the benefits while exploiting the willingness of others to abide by the rules. Frazier may spout off utopian bromides: "The really intelligent man doesn't want to feel that his work is being done by anyone else" (50). Yet, contrary to this idealism, not all intelligent people desire to do menial service work like cleaning, waiting on tables or collecting garbage. Frazier overlooks the fact that most would rather leave the unpleasant jobs to someone else, while enjoying the benefits. Free riders are anything but dumb—they are unsocial and exploitative, but cunning.[36]

But the best benchmark for evaluating Skinner's tenets is, once again, the experimental data. Here, the experience of the Twin Oakers is unequivocal. One of the key abuses of the labour-credit system, whereby people were to report their preference for various types of work, was "conscious and repeated manipulation". Many would "find fault with the work performance of their fellow workers", while assiduous toilers would "feel underappreciated".[37] In fact, complaints about unscrupulous individuals who far from gave their best were the norm, mirroring the state-wide communist experiments in post-WW2 eastern Europe and Africa.

The verdict from history and from the laboratory is loud and unanimous. Try to engineer social behaviour without factoring in the evolutionary bedrock of human motivations and you're bound to fail. Even Kinkade, one of the staunchest adherents to the Skinnerian system, has come to appreciate this: "Cooperation and group reinforcement alone just won't do" to eliminate cheating.[38] In fact, she goes as far as to condemn the utopia of the labour credit system—indeed, any honour system—in an explicit reference to *Walden Two*:

> Castle challenged Frazier on this very point. Castle said, 'You've taken the mainspring out of the watch.' And Frazier replied, 'That is an experimental question, Mr. Castle, and you have the wrong answer.' Or something of that sort. I was absolutely delighted with this when I first read it. But at this point I'm prepared to say: 'It's an experimental question, Mr. Castle, and you're right'.

According to Skinner, humans can be engineered out of another form of adaptive behaviour: gossiping. At the farm no one shows any interest in anyone's ranking on the communal power-and-status stock-exchange or, for that matter, in the gamut of personal affairs among the members. "It's part of the Walden Two Code to avoid gossip about personal ties" (130), boasts Frazier. In reality, as Brian Boyd documents in *On the Origin of Stories*, people are by nature incorrigible gossips. Contrary to his own party line, even Skinner concurs. Overhearing a chatty group of locals, the narrator notes: "Their conversation was a sort of non-malignant gossip" (198).

I would be willing to bet anything you like that you have never run into a gossip-free community. People have an innate hunger for strategic social information, for we reap benefits when we can understand the inner workings of our groups. Who is allied with whom? Who is sleeping with whom? Who is up and coming? Whose friendship is it prudent to embrace or decline? Call it sharing, comparing notes, touching base, keeping up to speed, or staying in the loop, but gossip is a social glue and a social weapon, and thus a major form of adaptive behaviour for such a highly social primate as *homo*.[39]

Another point on which behaviourist engineering clashes with evolution is envy and jealousy. Mrs. Nash, a Waldenite nurse, is about twenty years of age. Since the farm is only about eight years old, this means that, straddling the Jazz Age and the Great Depression, the first twelve years of her life were spent in the United States at large. Yet having joined the community, Mrs. Nash apparently no longer knows what jealousy and envy are. Incredibly, she does not even recognize the terms. And when Frazier treats her like a meathead, she does not protest either—because she just does not have a clue.

> In a moment five or six children came running into the play-rooms and were soon using the lavatory and dressing themselves. Mrs. Nash explained that they were being taken on a picnic.
> "What about the children who don't go?" said Castle.
> Mrs. Nash was puzzled.
> "Jealousy. Envy," Castle elaborated. "Don't the children who stay home ever feel unhappy about it?"
> "I don't understand," said Mrs. Nash.
> "And I hope you won't try," said Frazier, with a smile. (91)

Readers who react with anger to this patronizing classism may not realize that Skinner imports it wholesale from *Walden*. Thoreau's sketch of Alek Therien, a *sympathique* but head-simple woodchopper, brims with the same overtones for, even as he admires his humbleness and diligence, Thoreau calls him infantile and not fully human. More to the point, the scene exposes a critical design problem in Skinner's eutopia. People could never forget what jealousy and envy are because both are adaptive behaviours wired into human nature. Like it or not, jealousy and envy crouch inside our genes, waiting to be triggered by social context.

Insofar as the Waldenites visit nearby towns, watch movies, listen to radio, and otherwise partake in the life of the country, they could hardly make sense of the behaviours of other people without understanding such fundamental emotions as envy or jealousy. Theory of mind (ToM), one of the foundational elements of evolutionary psychology, makes that much clear. ToM refers to our amazing and amazingly successful ability to read other people's minds—more precisely to read their minds off behavioural and linguistic cues often provided for that purpose. Ultimately, it refers to our ability to recognize other people as intentional agents.

Such mind reading is an innate, universal and indispensable component of folk psychology by means of which we attribute mental states (beliefs, desires) to other beings, and have mental states attributed to us. ToM is, in short, a process of hypothesis formation about one another's minds to make sense of one another's behaviour. It is about recognizing intentions and goals—whether in real life, in a story, or on the screen—within a framework of human behaviour. The Waldenites could not interact successfully with the outside world if their social equipment was so deformed. They would be emotional and social cripples.[40]

Jealousy, writes Skinner, "has served its purpose in the evolution of man; we've no further use for it" (93). Yet the adaptive effects of jealousy were known even in his time. In the very year *Walden Two* came out, psychologist Boris Sokoloff recapped the research on the matter: "jealousy is not only inbred in human nature, but it is the most basic, all-pervasive emotion which touches man in all aspects of all human relationships" (18). Indeed, together with romantic love, it forms the emotional cement that keeps pairs bonded. It keeps the male attentive even during pregnancy or after birth. It makes the female alert to her partner's roving eye.

Have these adaptations outlived their purpose? Hardly, documents David Buss in *The Dangerous Passion: Why Jealousy Is as Necessary as Love and Sex.* Jealousy is "a supremely important passion that helped our ancestors, and most likely continues to help us today, to cope with a host of real reproductive threats" (5). It fires up the emotional boiler that drives us to confront rivals who make designs on our partner. It motivates us to unflagging surveillance in the face of a threat of the partner straying. And it communicates emotional commitment both to potential competitors and to the partner, gluing the relationship from the inside.

This is not to say that jealousy cannot be maladaptive. Its consequences can certainly be tragically and even fatally violent.[41] But, most of the time, it is a satisficing solution to a raft of sexual, reproductive, and social problems our foreparents faced over the eons. This is exactly why the wisdom of the eons past codifies it in proverbs ranging from Europe (*No jealousy, no love*) to Asia (*Jealousy is the life of love*).

Envy, on the other hand, is an adaptive behaviour linked to status seeking, group ranking, and social domination. It is a coping strategy evolved to motivate us to do better in situations involving hierarchy and dominance—that is, in virtually all of them. Humans are inveterate status seekers, because keeping up with the Joneses is inherited with our mothers' milk.

Consider the commonest expression of envy: material status. Rationally, once you have a warm cave, a few skins to plump the bed, and a roast on the fire, you should not care what happens next door. Frazier expostulates: "we don't go for personal rivalry; individuals are seldom compared" (117). But we do, and they are, because doing so is in our socially adaptive genes which measure domination and success not in absolute, but in relative terms—males and females alike.[42]

In another misunderstanding, Skinner maintains: "the very nature of the struggle to survive cannot give birth to a non-competitive intelligence" (280). Not so. Reciprocal altruism is rooted in the survival-of-the-inclusively-fittest calculus by which evolution operates on populations. As Matt Ridley notes in *The Origins of Virtue* on the basis of data that once again predates Skinner's utopia, even though we are predisposed to competition, territoriality and status-seeking, we are also remarkably groupish and inclined to band together and trade with benefits to all. Matter of fact, the price for belonging to a tribe where we get along is antagonism towards other tribes, in a pattern of bloodshed borne out by history.[43]

It would be easy to go on, but the point is by now clear. Adaptive human behaviours must not be excluded from any social design. As such, the foregoing analysis is not so much a critique of a particular behaviourist blueprint as a baseline for evaluating *any and all* forms of social engineering. In *Walden Two* some of the counterevidence is so plain, it beggars belief to see a great scientist fail to pay heed. Some is more subtle. But in all cases the message is the same. Evolutionary currents course through our veins, and social planners who disregard the degree to which we are children of our genetic ancestors are in for a rude awakening.

THE NUTS AND BOLTS OF SOCIAL ENGINEERING

> I said they should experiment; they should explore new ways of living as people had done in the communities of the nineteenth century.
>
> B.F. Skinner, *The Shaping of a Behaviorist*

The story of *Walden Two* does not end in 1948, but continues into the twenty-first century. Utopias are still being written, social engineering is everywhere in sight, and experimental communes still eke out their existence. True, almost all of the settlements spawned by *Walden Two* have long since imploded, but Twin Oaks and Los Horcones are still going propositions. And there are fundamental lessons to be learned from the experience of those who followed literary fiction into reality only to discover that it was very different from what the piper's song had led them to believe.

Alternative societies have been subjects of many studies. Their history—sometimes tragic, often fascinating, always instructive—is also surprisingly rich, with more than two hundred of sociopolitical heterodoxies founded in nineteenth-century

America alone. Remarkably, the trajectories of all these would-be utopias turn out to be similar. It's not even the fact that almost all fell apart in a relatively short time. Even more to the point, all were plagued by, and eventually succumbed to, a similar range of problems. In Keith L. Miller and Richard Feallock's unflinching synthesis,

> reading descriptions of past attempts at experimental living, one is struck by the frequency with which behavioral problems are mentioned. Many people did not do their share of work, others weren't thrifty enough, tools and equipment were ruined, people were argumentative and cruel, and so on.[44]

Given the enormous differences in size, ideology, race, historical era, and geographical location among these and other communes, we are clearly dealing with factors that transcend this diversity. Remarkably, institutional studies of mental patients also mirror the experience of the experimental groups. This is startling, to say the least. Given the vast motivational differences between normal and mentally ill individuals, their behaviours ought to be worlds apart. Yet, as Teodoro Ayllon and Nathan H. Azrin report, their 'token economy' group of psychiatric patients displayed many of the patterns of normal groups.

Despite the best motivational techniques, the same behaviours emerged in social-engineering experiments in other closed settings, such as classrooms or camps. Even more remarkably in all cases efforts to condition these behaviours out of existence came to nought. The most plausible explanation for these behavioural universals is, of course, that they are rooted in evolutionary adaptations. Look again at the synthesis of utopian ills. People not doing their share of work? Free riders. People failing to practice parsimony and thrift? Status seeking. Being argumentative and cruel? Envy and aggression.

To paraphrase John Lennon, if you say you want a social revolution, you must first come to terms with evolution. The evidence is unrelenting. Behaviourist ideals to the contrary, nepotism reared its head in Lake Village where, outside the leader's family, no one was permitted to purchase land. Communal child-rearing at Twin Oaks came to a shuddering stop, with parents en masse opting out of the group care and reasserting their biological prerogative of raising children as they saw fit. The egalitarian ethic suffered as soon as there was any furniture for the taking, with everyone fighting for it.

Despairing whether equality could ever be achieved, Kinkade concludes: "envy seems to be built into the human, and I can see evolutionarily why that might be true".[45] Indeed, for any social theorist or pragmatist, the experience of Twin Oaks, Lake Village, Los Horcones, and other Waldenite groups provides a welter of invaluable research data. Collectively, it furnishes a record of irrepressible sociobiological impulses latent in all communards and all communities. Overlooked by planners fixated on Skinner's fiction, in time these impulses triggered major overhauls of theoretical precepts and practical policies and, in most cases, the community's demise.

"... True, almost all of the settlements spawned by *Walden Two* have long since imploded, but Twin Oaks and Los Horcones are still going propositions ..."

Figure 1.4   Skinner at Walden Pond in Massachusetts flanked by Mireya Bustamante, Juan Robinson, and Linda Armendariz, founders of Comunidad Los Horcones.

A quintessential incident involved Lake Village where acrimonious debate over whether to allow snowmobiles on the property led to the abandonment of all pretense of enforcing the Skinnerian line. It exposed profound disagreements over private property, environmental protection, and the system of government (in the case of Lake Village, control by one individual). Worst of all, rival behaviourist factions agitated for their agendas in utter disregard of scientific evidence or even canons of rational debate. One member who, as a result, quit the commune summed up the prevailing disillusionment: "people with money and control would prevail over any objections on my part, regardless of data presented by anyone for either side".[46]

So much for the utopia of enlightened planners and trusting followers. In fact, the incident typified behaviours that proved the undoing of all communities. Members were loath to leave decision making to others, regardless of their actual or alleged behaviourist credentials. Where Skinner envisaged rational consensus and unity of purpose, power struggles and discontent were the norm, even in cases where the malcontents admitted they would have made the same choices. Having learned her lesson, Kinkade cautions all political utopians: "like sewage, power is right there under the surface, and unless it is properly controlled, channelled, and turned to good and fertile purposes, it will pollute."[47]

Not surprisingly, the government of Walden Two is one of Skinner's most contentious proposals. Flaunting the political gospel of our times, the farm does not practice democracy and, unlike the Big Nurse in *One Flew Over the Cuckoo's Nest*, does not even pretend to do so. Even though American political orthodoxy stipulates that democracy is always good, America itself is the best argument to the contrary. In the last half-century alone, in the name of democracy the United States violated the Constitution, invaded other democracies, committed genocide and torture, and maintained over 7,000 military bases in 130 countries around the planet.

But if Skinner can be forgiven for looking askance at the American way, what is his alternative? "I'm not arguing for no government at all," offers Frazier, "but only for none of the existing forms". He concludes: "We want a government based on the science of behavior" (182). By default, then, the farm is governed by behaviourists since only they are said to have the requisite expertise. This presents an obvious problem. It is by virtue of operant conditioning at the commune that individuals become groupish and selfless. By that token, no one ought to trust Frazier's scientists inasmuch as they are not a product of Walden Two.[48]

Skinner covers up this nonsequitur with blandishments that sound as naïve today as in the 1940s when Dr. Mengele's scientific 'experiments' were dragged, kicking and screaming, into the light. The researcher's motives are never immoral or impure, he avows. "What scientist worth the name is engaged, as a scientist, in the satisfaction of his basic needs?" (13). But if that is his criterion, few mortals would be worthy of the name. Scientists are as prone to status-seeking, envy, and malice as anyone else as exemplified by historical accounts of personal animosity, hostile reviews, falsified data, and outright thefts of results.[49]

Skinner's government stipulates six planners: three women and three men. Why? Either the politically correct balance of sexes trumps their performance, or the six are the best for the job and their sex matters not one iota. In short, you may endorse the principles of meritocracy or affirmative action, but not both. Besides, why stop at sex. Why not a rainbow of planners: black, Latino, Arabic? Why not a palette of ages, careers, or even IQs (shouldn't loonies be represented too)?

Presumably because good planners work on behalf of all. But then, why the artifice of three men and women or, for that matter, the statutory ten-year limit? Could it be because power corrupts? But, once again, Skinner is not interested in devolving power to the people. New planners are selected by the old, perpetuating a sclerocracy straight from *Yes, Minister* where Sir Arnold grooms Sir Humphrey to be his successor.

Of course, the planners are said to have communal interests in mind, not the quest for power. But insofar as they are not graduates of Walden Two, and as such not conditioned to be nice and selfless, why exactly should they be trusted? Frazier, the Skinnerian commissar, is their iconic example. Taken at his word, he is utterly unfit for government. "I'm conceited, aggressive, tactless, selfish," he concedes. "My motives are ulterior and devious, my emotions warped" (233).

To ward off accusations of elitism, in *A Matter of Consequences* Skinner actually denied that Walden Two is run by behavioural engineers. At other times he conceded the difficulty of engineering the requisite checks and balances. Yet when it came to staving off trouble in his own paradise, his answers are thin and evasive in the extreme.[50] Astonishingly, this prelapsarian vision became an article of faith for real-life communards who "did not think it necessary to have more safeguards against the accumulation of power. They firmly believed it was neither possible nor desirable to hold power in an income-sharing community of free people because there was nothing to be gained from it".

This again shows a lack of appreciation for evolved human nature. In the eschatology of motives, money is seldom a goal in itself—or else the Rockefellers would never spare a dime for nonprofit foundations or public endowments.

In *The Theory of Leisure Classes* Thorstein Veblen identified acquisition of wealth as behaviour aimed at status enhancement and domination, sometimes at a very high cost. A fat account is only a stepping stone to power for, whereas money is a relatively recent invention to facilitate trade and credit, status and domination are deep-seeded adaptations to help us climb the social ladder. Under these conditions the drive for power will manifest itself even where profit does not come into play.

If income-sharing turned people into cooperative egalitarians, Waldenite communities would never have suffered the toxic power struggles they did. As a Twin Oaks planner, insisted Kinkade, she ought to have remained a planner, being better at it than others. "It wasn't supposed to be any bigger deal to be a planner than it was to be a mechanic".[51] Spoken like a planner. Endorsing government *for* the people but not *by* the people, she also took exception to one of the foundational American myths. Her remarks on the hierarchy of planners and ordinary members are worth citing in full:

> The only thing we did not predict and could not control was the feeling that the average citizen had about somebody else

doing the government. They just hated it. And even though you say to them, 'What decisions would you have wanted to be different?' They would say, 'I don't know what decisions I would have wanted to be different, the decisions were fine. I just wanted to be a part of it.' So at this point I conjecture that Skinner was wrong: the average citizen will not in fact be satisfied with such an arrangement.[52]

Like in Percy's *The Thanatos Syndrome*, the conformist bliss of Walden Two, where unorthodoxy is described as unthinkable, is achieved entirely through noncoercive means. There is no need for punitive control because, presumably, it has been stamped out through operant conditioning. Yet even Frazier admits that things could go awry. The power elite could harness the behaviourist methods to indoctrinate people to their own ends. "I don't deny that it would be possible", he allows. "Something like that has always been done by well-organized governments—to facilitate the recruiting of armies, for example. But not here" (46).

It can't happen here because, after the behaviourist makeover, people are apparently more benign than sheep. In an early scene, the visitors observe a flock of sheep conditioned not to stray outside the pasture staked out by a length of string. Yet, in a startling admission, Frazier lets on that the conditioned sheep do stray and that no small part of their obedience owes to the claws and fangs of the sheepdog. So, if even sheep need law enforcement but not people, what kind of sheeple is Frazier talking about? And why exactly are the planners immune to the sweet stench of corruption?

One of the strongest reasons to doubt Frazier's assertions about universal goodwill and love is the fact that—in a vivid corroboration of neo-Darwinian theory and fact—it is limited to in-group members. In dealing with the outside world, the instincts to dominate and subjugate flourish. Nothing brings it out like his robber-baron tactics with regard to adjacent communities:

If we buy up half the farms which do business in a particular town, we control the town. The feed dealers, hardware stores, and farm machinery salesmen depend on us. We can put them out of business or control them through our trade. The real estate values in the town can be manipulated at will, and the town itself gradually wiped out.[53]

Skinner would be discomfited to learn that evolutionary science predicts exactly what his knowledge of human nature led him to write. Natural selection is still at work even when love-thy-neighbour utopia establishes within-group cooperation. It simply takes the form of slash-and-burn capitalism among competing groups.

Finally, economic viability. Like Thoreau at Walden Pond, the austerity practiced by Skinner's Waldenites is fostered as much by their eco-friendly ethos as by necessity. Thoreau was, of course, his own carpenter, mason, farmer, angler and cook. Educated, disciplined, robust, unencumbered by family and children, he was also singularly *un*representative of the humanity he would reform. Moreover, as his punctilious journal entries reveal, his return to nature was enabled by the industrial boom outside Walden pond. Without ready-made windows with glass, plaster, horsehair, and a latch, he couldn't have even fashioned a functional abode.

Similarly, alongside unemployment and other benefits, the Twin Oakers mooch free health care provided by the state of Virginia to the poor. They exploit unemployment insurance laws which allow communards to work for three months and then draw the dole. As some admit, "for the whole life of the commune, we did well on that very corrupting—and it is a corrupting thing—'outside work for three months, come back and still draw a lesser paycheck' system".[54] Nor do they mount a police force, train brain surgeons, build cement plants, or maintain roads and railways. They exist, in short, by parasitizing society at large.

Preaching E.F. Schumacher's 'small is beautiful', Skinner prided himself on devising a way of life that is "not only minimally consuming, it is minimally polluting".[55] Admirable econsciousness aside, however, his economic calculus is pure fiction. To take only one example, the community is said to own automobiles and trucks. So, who maintains gas stations? Who builds refineries? Who hires the engineering teams and the shipyards needed to design and build megatankers to ship it around the globe? Who drills for oil? Who, for that matter, conducts the geological surveys and research into oil-bearing strata?

Boasting that Waldenites consume on average less than most Americans, Frazier commits the environmentalist fallacy of ignoring the broader picture. We should all buy organic, we are urged nowadays, because it's better for the planet. But to reach the local grocer, organic produce is often shipped around the world, requiring fuel, cargo vessels, complex logistics. In the end, the carbon footprint of the organic tomato may be the size of Bigfoot's. Frazier's utopian calculus looks attractive because it is deceptive. As with Twin Oaks, there are millions of hidden costs which don't show in the ledger because they are borne by the outside world.

The dependence on the outside is equally evident in the discrepancy with Skinner's promise of a four-hour working day. Fulltime work at Twin Oaks offers barely decent existence, far from the opulence most people would associate with a utopia.[56] In principle, it might be possible to reduce working hours following the Japanese model of saturating the commune with computerized and automated robots. But where would this investment in metallurgy and software development—not to mention R&D and scientific and industrial infrastructure—come from in Skinner's society of one thousand farmers (or the Virginian one of fifty)?

The most eloquent testimony to the unsustainability of Waldenite lifestyle comes from personnel turnover. Perish the thought of stable self-sufficiency. At Twin Oaks people leave at a stunning rate of 70 percent during the first year, to an average of 25 percent a year. To overcome these crippling losses, the commune nonstop recruits idealistic, educated, healthy newcomers without whom it would vanish in no time.[57] Also, perish the thought of utopia for all. The group carefully screens new members—lest their lifestyle or temperament disrupt the equilibrium—and limits 'immigration' to preserve the quality of life.

As all this makes apparent, Waldenite communities will never rival the American Main Street. Call them parasitic or symbiotic but, inasmuch as their viability depends on society at large, they do not amount to a plausible alternative to social organization as we know it. This is true even of Los Horcones which—to the extent that it can be surmised from scarce data—recorded fewer problems of the kind that rocked Twin Oaks. Significantly, although the Mexican group prides itself on applying behaviourism to their lives, they never implemented a number of Skinner's proposals.

Neither Graham and Kinkade, who know Los Horcones from the inside out, believe that what made them work was behaviorism.[58] Many policies appear, in fact, to be in line with sociobiology rather than with behaviourist engineering. Los Horcones respect the biology of parental investment (there is no communal child-rearing) and the need for some private property and territoriality. They have a hierarchical power structure consisting of the leader, lieutenants, and the group at large (of about thirty). Perhaps most of all, the dominant faction in the group is an extended alpha family, linked by blood ties into a unit resembling a tribe.

THE SUN IS BUT A MORNING STAR

> I am quite sure that when I did work with rats and pigeons I was always imagining parallel cases in human behavior.
>
> B.F. Skinner, Letter to Yolande Tremblay, 1970

Skinner wanted to call his utopia *The Sun Is But a Morning Star*, in an allusion to the concluding line of Thoreau's *Walden*, which in many ways parallels his own exploration of the relation between literature and science, or between art and life. Of course, the parallels go far beyond the titles. Quite aside from the spell it cast on the millions who read it and the thousands who lived by it, like *Walden* the conceptual repercussions of *Walden Two* are as urgent today as ever. Indeed, to the extent that utopias transcend the times in which they were written to reflect the times in which they are read, they are never obsolete.

As if on cue, at the end of his retrospective essay "*Walden Two* Revisited" Skinner reiterated his message: "What is needed is not a new political leader or a new kind of government but further knowledge about human behavior" (xvi). Unfortunately for his vision, its principal novelty—the body of knowledge about human behaviour—turns out also to be its principal drawback. Even the erstwhile apostles have seen the light. After decades of failure to create Waldenite harmony at Lake Village, Roger Ulrich dismisses the gospel according to Skinner as literary bullshit.[59]

There are no two ways about it: insofar as it overlooks the register of our evolved adaptations, *Walden Two* is literary make-believe rather than a workbook for social engineers. In fairness, Skinner may have had some grounds for pleading ignorance of neo-Darwinism when he sat down to write his utopia, even though so much of the knowledge that gives it the lie has been around before mid-forties—to say nothing of the next four decades during which, in contrast to Watson, he has never owned up to his mistakes.

No extenuating circumstances, however, can be invoked today when the evolutionary sciences in the United States routinely fall victim of evangelism-driven intolerance and ignorance. A 1988 survey by researchers at the University of Texas revealed, for example, that one in three of American biology *teachers* believes that dinosaurs and humans walked the earth at the same time (or is not sure).[60] In 2000 Fordham Foundation reported that more than a third of American states fail to teach not just the basic facts about evolution, but even the central place of Darwin's theses in contemporary science.

A 2001 Gallup poll, confirmed by a 2004 CBC News/*New York Times* poll, found that while only one in ten Americans accepts evolution, one in two is a Creationist, and two out of three want to see Creationism in school curricula. As tracked by the Pew Research Centre, these numbers have little to do with George W. Bush's theological presidency—they have remained rock steady for thirty years. In the context, the reaction to the recent PBS documentary series *Evolution* speaks for itself. The maelstrom of protests from the Christian right kept the teaching materials that accompanied the series from most schools, while Bush officials began to monitor all PBS productions for the alleged liberal bias.

Evolution may be the ur-science of our times but most social scientists still believe that Darwinism changed little for the way the knowledge game is played in their own backyard.[61] In this they follow the father of sociology, Emile Durkheim, who held that the human drives such as sexual jealousy or parental love were cultural constructs, rather than adaptive elements of human evolution. Little has changed from *Walden Two* wherein Skinner swept human nature clean with an allusion to the alleged Jesuit boast: "Give me the specifications, and I'll give you the man!" (274).

The situation is even worse among humanists. For those who explicitly or implicitly embrace the tenets of poststructuralism and top-to-bottom acculturation—i.e., most—evolution remains a stepchild, ignored by daylight and beaten with a stick by night. If only for this reason, it is essential that we periodically reassess our grasp of evolutionary theory and fact. Humanists or scientists, we need to do so lest, like Skinner, we end up with an inadequate conception of human nature and, as a consequence, inadequate conceptual tools to engineer the human use of human beings.

2   You're Not in Canada until You Can Hear the Loons Crying

or

Voting, People's Power, and Ken Kesey's *One Flew over the Cuckoo's Nest*

THE KEY HITS THE LOCK

> You know them by the empty eyes, like the eyes are holes spiked in the shell and all you can see inside are the dilapidated organs, grinding through their organ duties out of loyalty? instinct? habit?
>
> Ken Kesey, letter to Ken Babbs

The key hits the lock. It is early morning and the patients are not up yet. Only the ward aides go about their business as usual. They lack high school diplomas but the Chief Nurse sees to it that they know their job inside out. Now they look up as she glides through the door, swept in by a gust of cold outside air. She dips them a nod and rubber heels to the Nurses' Station to get busy with the ward machinery. All ready, she takes up her spot at the observation window and cranks up the day lights. Sleepy-eyed Acutes leave the dorms and head for the shower rooms before picking up their breakfast trays, meds, and games in the Dayroom.

A major hospital is a major bureaucracy, subject to systemic inertia that works against innovation or even just a change in the routine. But, in certain circumstances, an entire ward can be taken out of the system without concurrent institution-wide approval. In a case like that, the department heads do not interfere with the enforcement of the procedures prescribed for the patients' benefit. The daily care for the rainbow of their behavioural maladjustments—psychoses, phobias, senile disorders, substance addictions, sexual difficulties, retardation, neuropathologies, chronic disculturation—is left to the ward supervisor, the Chief Nurse.

This ward is small as far as wards go. Forty odd same-sex patients, the youngest over thirty, the oldest past seventy. Some have never uttered an intelligible word and are regarded as mute. Most do housekeeping duties. All receive the alphabet soup of therapies. But this is where all semblance to Ken Kesey's *One Flew Over the Cuckoo's Nest* ends. There is no punishment, no electroshocks or even verbal threats, even though all patients have a history of being unruly and unresponsive. Three nurses serve at different times to ensure that nothing depends on any one personality. The aides are rotated as well, under close supervision by the doctors.[1]

All the same, one may be excused for being momentarily confused where fiction ends and reality begins. Not only are there significant parallels between the ward and the word, but even the timeline of Kesey's narrative thought experiment coincides with the timeline of the clinical experiment in behavioural engineering. Written in 1961, *One Flew Over the Cuckoo's Nest* was not published until 1962. Teodoro Ayllon and Nathan H. Azrin's pioneering experiment in motivational therapy at the Anna State Hospital, Illinois, was also initiated in 1961, with the core method not in place until the end of 1962.

No one could, of course, confuse the poetic with the psychiatric licence for long. Despite the accuracy of his diagnosis—and his real-life stint as a psychiatric aide at the Menlo Park Veteran Administration Hospital—Kesey's cure could never engineer the behavioural metamorphoses depicted in the novel. But then, it was never meant to. Casting his hero as an archetypal American cowboy, Kesey made no bones that McMurphy's therapeutic technique owes more to *Shane* than *General Hospital*. In the words of his creator, Mac is every gunslinger who "rides into town, shoots the bad guys, and gets killed in the course of the movie".[2]

In contrast, the Anna State psychiatrists staked their reputations on results-oriented behavioural psychotherapy. By design—if clearly not by method—their ward became a page torn out of Nurse Ratched's textbook on social engineering: a total motivating environment for inculcating skills sought by the experimenters. Initially spontaneous behaviours were reinforced by means of candy, cigarettes, or metal tokens exchangeable for services or commodities. Emphasis was placed on teaching behaviours that would continue to be reinforced after training. Most of all, in line with the Skinnerian tenets, there was zero punishment or coercion.

The transformation was stunning. Most patients greatly improved in their socialization skills and in some cases in their overall medical condition. But even as the experiment substantiated some theories, it overturned others. Perhaps the biggest eye-opener was that society's beliefs about reinforcers for mental patients are grossly inaccurate. Persuaded by the film version of *Cuckoo's Nest*—which in many ways violates the book—many of us presuppose that mental patients chafe under confinement.[3] In reality, most exhibit profound indifference to the Outside, with many actively shunning 'intrusions' such as visits from relatives or friends.

"... Persuaded by the film version of Cuckoo's Nest—which in many ways violates the book—many of us presuppose that mental patients chafe under confinement. In reality, most exhibit profound indifference to the Outside, with many actively shunning 'intrusions' such as visits from relatives or friends ..."

Figure 2.1   Aided by the chief, Mac escapes to the Outside—this scene from the film (which Kesey refused to see) is one of many that are not in the book.

Modern-day mental hospitals pride themselves on their open door policy. Because it does not result in a mass exodus of patients, trumpet public relations releases, our society and our medical practices must be truly enlightened. After all, even psychotics vote with their feet. But, quality of the facilities and treatment aside, patients may simply have little desire to leave. In fact, as became apparent at Anna State, few would leave the ward even when the attendants insisted on it. In short, it doesn't take the oppressive regime from *Cuckoo's Nest* to dehumanize patients as surely as a prison does. Almost any mental institution will do.

The evidence is unforgiving. The least treated and least studied patients in mental institutions are over sixty. They are uneducated, unemployed and—if only because of age—unemployable. Worst, they have no families to be reintegrated into. Never mind the reasons for which they were institutionalized in the first place. Even if their behavioural disorders could be brought under control, there would be no place for them Outside. Behavioural deterioration and chronic disculturation cut them off from the rest of us as effectively as prison bars do. Cured or not, they are inmates for life. The ward is their world.

Like Ken Elton Kesey, the Anna State psychiatrists do not hesitate to draw parallels between the America Inside and Outside. Much like in the case of the renegade scientists in *The Thanatos Syndrome*—though for categorically different reasons—this includes applying the techniques of behavioural engineering that work for institutionalized inmates to society at large. A procedure found to be effective in the controlled setting of a mental hospital,

> would probably find great applicability in many different disciplines concerned with human behaviour. A method of controlling the aggressive outbursts of a destructive patient would seem to have great relevance for the control of criminal behaviour outside of the hospital. Similarly, a procedure that could motivate a vegetative psychotic who has been hospitalized for twenty years might be appropriate for motivating a high school dropout to return to school (4).

This is true to the extent that our diagnoses of abnormality—and hence our tolerance of mental disorders—are anything but consistent. As long, for instance, as individuals can function in society, their erratic behaviour is often tolerated. A professor incoherently mumbling to himself; a matinee idol suffering from acute paranoia; a rock star notorious for uncontrollably destructive outbursts; a neurotic tycoon averse to contact with people; a president pathologically driven by an inferiority complex—all are as real as Kesey's Big Nurse, knotted into obsessive-compulsive fury when anything on her ward gets out of kilter.

In the words of one of Kesey's doctors, their aim is to create "a little world Inside that is a made to scale prototype of the big world Outside" (47).[4] Given the phenomenal success of the book—over eight million copies in eighty reprints, not to mention multiple allusions on *The Simpsons*—each generation clearly feels it can learn a great deal about America from its depiction of America's misfits. With *One Flew Over the Cuckoo's Nest* as our guidebook, then, let us examine aspects of social engineering ranging from institutional dementia to institutional politics, and from the United States of America to the Swiss Federation of Comrades to the Oath.

AND THE WARD BECAME FLESH

> *Cuckoo's Nest* is, to some extent, anti-American. It's about American terror . . . the inhuman part of American industrialism.
>
> Ken Kesey, "The Art of Fiction"

Although behaviourism is often regarded as intellectually passé, to say nothing of dominated by control freaks who work in isolation from mainstream psychology, the facts do not support that picture. Not only is Skinner's brand of behaviourism (there are many others) far from dead or even smelling funny, but during the last decades it has enjoyed quite a renaissance. The reasons are simple. Much as on the psychotic ward at Anna State, operant conditioning has proven its mettle in virtually all areas of special education, pediatrics, occupational therapy, physical rehab, treatment of substance abuse, and penal enforcement, to name a few.[5]

The same methods decried as totalitarian in the context of wholesale social engineering turn out to be remarkably adept when applied selectively and/or therapeudically to target groups. For decades now, Skinner's behaviour-modification techniques have been used to alleviate behavioural problems in delinquent youth, minimize on-the-job accidents, help mentally retarded or autistic individuals (especially children), and even better test the effects of pharmaceuticals. The clinching testimony to their efficacy comes from all branches of the U.S. military which routinely use operant conditioning to improve training and engineer combat-ready behaviour.[6]

Put simply, operant conditioning works—albeit in a radically different manner than outlined in Walden Two. The essence of its efficacy are found in Skinner's own admission that "all reinforcers eventually derive their power from evolutionary selection".[7] To put it bluntly, operant conditioning comes into its own when it does not attempt to encroach into the territory staked out aeons ago by the adaptive psychology of survival and reproduction, and it works even better when grafted onto the evolutionary drives that hum, whether we want it or not, in all of us.

Reinforcing impulses initially exhibited spontaneously by patients, therapeutic behaviour modification does not attempt a wholesale makeover of human nature. Instead it relies on identifying, isolating, and nurturing the 'seeds' implanted in many cases by evolution. In the context it is less of a surprise that, in a preface to the 1976 edition of *Walden Two*, Skinner proudly referred to the application of behavioural engineering to communities of ward patients or classroom students—and spared not a single word to the real communities struggling to make something of his fictional utopia.

Lest the word 'control' that crops up regularly in his writings awaken the ghost of Nurse Ratched, never does behaviourist therapy advocate aversive conditioning. Ayllon and Azrin may refer to their technique as behavioural engineering but their sole method, even with severely retarded and/or psychotic patients, is positive reinforcement. Just like the last man on Earth in *God's Grace*, Skinner is adamant that positive conditioning is more effective and long-lasting than punitive control, which exhibits destructive side effects and tends to disappear when the controls are lifted.

Under Bush II—with explicit sanction by the president himself, Attorney General Gonzales, Secretary of State Rice, Secretary of Defense Rumsfeld, not to mention sundry members of Congress—the United States widely availed itself of the so-called enhanced interrogation techniques. Perversely, much of the censure at the revelations of the CIA torturing captives on behest of the White House was that it yields low-grade 'intel', rather than that it is totalitarian and sick. With Skinner it was just the opposite. Critics objected that he preferred the carrot over the stick not because it was the right thing to do, but merely a more effective one.[8]

What would Skinner's or, for that matter, Barack Obama's directives be, one wonders, if aversive controls—such as those hypothesized by Anthony Burgess in *The Clockwork Orange*—were found to be more efficacious and long-lasting than positive reinforcement?[9] Or if, with a little help from science, they could be made so? Historically speaking, there is no reason to believe that it would make much difference, not at least to a certain breed of social engineers. Like Dr. Faustus of Wittenberg, avid for the chance to put their theories to practice, they have been peddling their souls to the weak-eyed devil of a rapacious and pitiless folly.

Some have been gainfully employed by the Nazis, others took their orders from Stalin, others plied their trade in the United States, others still prostituted themselves in the normally squeaky-clean Canada. Some of their practices were unprofessional, some were abusive, some verged on criminal. A few—like those at McGill University's Allen Memorial Hospital in the 1950s—*were* criminal. The proof came in the form of the then largest settlement of a class-action suit against the CIA, followed by the Canadian government's grudging payout to the victims of psychiatric torture.

A Montrealer, in the fall of 1992 I was busy working on my doctorate at McGill University. I still recall the collective gasp that greeted the November 18 headline on the front page of the *Gazette*: "Brainwashing Victims to get 100,000". There was no

"... A Montrealer, in the fall of 1992 I was busy working on my doctorate at McGill University. I still recall the collective gasp that greeted the November 18 headline on the front page of the *Gazette*: 'Brainwashing Victims to get 100,000' ..."

Figure 2.2   It *can* happen here.

end to whispered speculations in hallways and dorms. In private, friends employed as psychologists at the Allen Memorial were at pains to distance themselves from the psychiatrists, from the past, from the criminal experiments in depatterning, and from the psychotic drivel of psychic driving. Little wonder why.[10]

The story of a homegrown psychiatric concentration camp should make a convert out of every skeptic brainwashed into thinking that it can't happen here. It involved a McGill University professor who desecrated every professional ethic in existence. It involved U.S. military and espionage establishments laundering money for his research. It involved the Canadian government which continued to fund these insane experiments when the CIA money dried up. It involved clinical procedures designed to regress patients into a preverbal vegetative state, with the aim of re-engineering their erased identities at the experimenters' will.

In a scenario far more terrifying than anything in *Cuckoo's Nest*, Dr. Ewen Cameron took into his professional care patients suffering from mild psychiatric maladjustments: depression, anxiety, marital problems, fatigue. Like in Kesey's novel, all were volunteers. All signed consent forms entrusting their psychiatrist to undertake appropriate treatment, up to and including electroshocks and frontal lobotomy. In return, the good doctor sedated his human guinea pigs for weeks on end, isolated them in torture chambers of sensory deprivation, delivered scores of crushing jolts of electricity, and administered obscene amounts of psychedelic and hallucinogenic drugs (mostly LSD and PCP: acid and angel dust).

The natural response is to attribute such acts to aberration. Normal people are not monsters and could never countenance such inhumanity. But where is the borderline between a monster and everyman? Which is worse: that the Nazi democide in Europe or the American genocide in South-east Asia was perpetrated by monsters or by normal individuals? Rationality has never stopped anyone from committing heinous acts in the name of this or that doctrinal ideal. The Vietnam-era administrations of Lyndon Johnson and Robert McNamara, or Richard Nixon and Henry Kissinger, boasted the best and brightest minds of their generation.[11]

René Descartes was a great philosopher, a rationalist, an embodiment of the Enlightenment. Few know about his experiments on dogs which he vivisected alive while they died a thousand deaths, screaming in torture, defecating in agony. By dint of his philosophy, Descartes convinced himself that, all appearances to the contrary, these were merely physiological reflexes rather than signs of genuine suffering. By all accounts a devoted dog owner, his letters from 1632 to a fellow knowledge seeker gush about what happens when "you slice off the pointed end of the heart in a live dog, and insert a finger into one of the cavities."[12]

Bertrand Russell was one of the greatest logicians and humanists of the twentieth century. John von Neumann was the greatest mathematical physicist of our time and arguably of all time. Both epitomized the modern spirit of rationality and enlightenment. Both made incalculable contributions to mankind. Yet, in the heat of the Cold War, both advocated a preemptive nuclear strike on the Soviet Union. Fearing that the postwar balance of power could never be sustained, both countenanced the annihilation of millions of unsuspecting human beings so that others might live in peace.

How is one to regard such policies, behaviours, actions? Are they normal and sane, having been promulgated by the paragons of modern civilization? Or are they demented and criminally degenerate? Is it actually possible to distinguish human behaviour that is certifiably insane from one that is merely rationally mad, as demanded by the strategic calculus of Mutual Assured Destruction? If model citizens and avatars of reason can rationally advocate democide, does criminality or sanity retain any of its normal sense? And who is to arbitrate what is normal? Social scientists? Supreme Court justices?

In the nineteenth century, under the influence of Darwinism, some social scientists insisted that recidivist antisocial behaviour was 'in the blood', caused by degenerate evolutionary development. According to the famous anthropologist and criminologist, Cesare Lombroso, criminals were proto-humans who failed to evolve much above the level of apes. They were held to be prone to violence and otherwise lacking control over their animal instincts, while their cranial shapes and facial features were supposed to be indicative of this degradation. McMurphy who jokes to Dr. Spivey that he fights and fucks too much would be a textbook specimen of the species.[13]

Even as Lombroso recommended isolating such 'brutes' from society, he always viewed them with compassion as victims of their nature. Not so in today's United States. It is true, reports George Annas, Director of Law, Medicine and Ethics Program at Boston University Schools of Medicine and Public Health, that in today's penitentiaries "the flagrant use of lobotomy as punishment, so well captured by Ken Kesey in *One Flew Over the Cuckoo's Nest*" (30), may no longer be acceptable. But there is nothing to mitigate the use of electroshocks for the purpose of behavioural engineering, so long as it is ordered by a psychiatrist.[14]

Worse still, early in 1990 with little fanfare or demur from the libertarians, the Supreme Court turned parts of America into cuckoo's nests. Its ruling was in response to an appeal from a competent adult who protested that his constitutional rights were systematically violated. The competent adult in question was a jailbird diagnosed with mental problems—a real-life R.P. McMurphy. In a six-to-three decision, the nation's highest court permitted antipsychotic drugs to be forcibly administered to competent inmates in order to maintain order—*even if it might lead to death or permanent disability.*

In other words, the ruling gives prison management the right to engineer behaviours simply to make their lives easier, even when the effects of the drugs have nothing to do with ameliorating the inmate's condition and may in the long run kill him. Such a patient has no right to refuse any pharma-cocktail forced upon him by prison psychiatrists merely to render him less burdensome to supervise. Like Ewen Cameron's victims, he can be constitutionally drugged into a perpetual semi-catatonic state, controlled with mood-changers, spiked with uppers, crashed with downers, in a regime Nurse Ratched would be proud of.

All this comes more than half a century after the infamous 1927 *Buck vs Bell* ruling from the United States Supreme Court. The bench upheld a law that instituted compulsory sterilization of Americans diagnosed, like Carrie Buck, as mentally retarded. It did not matter that Carrie Buck was *not* retarded. The ruling, passed by the justices with the express intention to protect the state and improve its health, led to more than sixty thousand citizens being sterilized. In each case the procedure was performed without their consent or the consent of a family member.

It was a generation later that a featherweight book with a heavyweight punch finally rocked postwar complacency. *The Shame of the States* (1948) was cast in the form of trip reports from several northeast state hospitals in the 1930s, and hardly what you would call an objective study. In purple prose it ripped into the overcrowding, the understaffing, the physical abuse, and the psychic torture in America's mental 'asylums'. A tireless self-promoter, Albert Deutsch learned from the fate of his earlier social history, *The Mentally Ill in America*, which, failing to scandalize anyone, brought about no lasting reform.

Together with a *Life* photo essay "Bedlam 1946" and Mary Jane Ward's autobiographical novel *The Snake Pit* (1946), swiftly adapted by Hollywood, the Deutsch exposé sparked a nationwide uproar and, eventually, policy change. For the best reasons and with the best intentions, it also sparked the most radical reform in social engineering mental health: deinstitutionalization. Half a century later, deinstitutionalization itself became denounced as the second shame of the states, as the chronically underfunded or simply unfunded services keep feeding mentally ill recruits into the armies of the homeless and into overcrowded jails.[15]

To readers of Kesey's novel, all this must seem like déjà lu. In a profound affirmation of the power of the written word, Joel Kassiola contends, in fact, that *Cuckoo's Nest* "can be more insightful and moving to political action than ten years of social scientific reports on the conditions in our institutions for the (judged) mentally ill" (68).[16] On the other hand, social-scientific reports can be no less moving to political action than Kesey's fiction—if you know where to look. One such place is a bookshelf sagging under the weight of studies by David Healy, of which *Mania* is only the latest in his case against pharmaceutical corporations.

These days neurobabble has replaced psychobabble as the fig-leaf hiding our ignorance of the etiology of mental illness, but nothing has changed about the corrupting practices of the Big Pharma and the venality of many top psychiatrists. Healy's scrupulously documented litany of fraud boggles the mind. Ghostwriting of medical publications by the PR sections of large pharmaceutical companies is only one symptom of the malaise. It goes hand in hand with the distortion or even outright suppression of ill-effects of psychotropic drugs, such as—ironically—the link between antidepressants and heightened risk of suicide.

Today most large-scale clinical trials are designed and administered by the pharmaceutical industry. As a consequence, they own the resulting data which are then regularly manipulated to extract profit from individuals afflicted with mental disorders. No one, it seems, pays much heed to basic research principles such as looking for negative (disconfirming) evidence. Big Pharma doctors the results that interfere with the branding of new 'diseases', and then uses those to market new designer drugs. The blues and reds moved up in the world. They are ultramarine and vermilion now, indispensable to quality lifestyle and priced to match.

While savaging the cupidity of the psychopharmacological industry, Healy focuses his anger on its most contemptible expression: the manufacture of bipolar disorder among children. Difficult as it is to believe, rating scales and diagnostic criteria are manipulated to bring more children into the fold, with the results that antipsychotic medication is administered even to one-year old infants. To put this in perspective, hardly any mental patients were diagnosed with bipolar disorder (manic-depressive psychosis) before 1920, and not many before the early 1960s when drug companies began to market the disease.

Also in the early 1960s, around the time when Kesey's novel appeared in bookstores, researchers from the University of Oklahoma launched a psychemical experiment on a different type of a nonverbal, nonconsenting subject. In the spirit of the times, they injected a three-ton bull elephant with LSD, ostensibly to study its brain chemistry with a view to treating mentally ill people. The dosage was proportionally elephantine: almost three hundred milligrams, or three thousand times the contents of a sugar cube. The experiment was a calamity. The animal went into a massive seizure and collapsed dead in front of the scientists.

Being somatically nonaddictive, acid does not really belong on the FDA's list of controlled substances (it was legal until 1966). This does not mean that it is harmless. Combined with antidepressants, it may bring on dissociative fugues and even psychoses, not to mention hallucinogenic effects that can last for hours. As emerged during the 1980s Rockefeller congressional hearings, however, the real harm comes not from the drug but from the CIA. Is anyone shocked any more by revelations of the agency's illicit LSD experiments on its own staffers, on military and government personnel, mental patients, doctors, and even members of the public?[17]

As Kaptain Kelp of the Merry Pranksters, Kesey himself was responsible for much of the hype about acid. Of course, the truth about hallucinogens—sought by the poetic descendants of Coleridge in a quest for neoplatonic inspiration—is much more prosaic. According to Kesey, the first three pages of *One Flew Over the Cuckoo's Nest* were dashed off on peyote and remained virtually unchanged in subsequent drafts. The comparison of the first draft and the final text exposes the mystification. To take the most salient example, the book's opening sentence, "They're out there," does not even appear until the sixth paragraph in the draft.

Far from being a drug-induced instance of automatic writing à la "Kubla Khan", the opening section bears witness to painstaking deliberation and revision. It carefully places the novel within the American literary tradition and its panoply of national myths. John A. Barsness puts his finger on this heritage by arguing that McMurphy is a quintessential American hero, a Jeffersonian native son born of the "nineteenth-century notions of the democratic frontiersman, made virtuous and pure by the beneficial influences of nature, absolutely free physically and morally from the debilitating corruption of European civilization" (432).

He is a Thoreauvian faux naïf roused by instinctive opposition to any form of authoritarian control. He is a self-reliant Emersonian, intuitive and wise despite being unschooled, moved into action by the quiet desperation of his fellow men. Guided more by gut instinct than by logic and reason, he personifies the virtues of the utopian revolutionary past and the manifest destiny of the future. He stands apart from conventional social norms and—a *sine qua non* in the (post) industrial and (ex)urban age—he is at one with nature which infuses him with virility and a zest for independence.

There is a thread of continuity between the mystique of life on the frontier, the Transcendentalist mysticism that struggled to offer an antidote to the Gilded Age, and the social revolution epitomized by the *Little Red Book* toting hippies. In *The Return of the Vanishing American* (1968) Leslie Fielder even went so far as to posit a rebirth of the Old West in the New West tripping on the corner of Haight and Ashbury. Never mind the tensions between the ethos of the prairie-schooner era and the consumerist culture of today. Self-reliance and escape from society belong as much to American history as to its intellectual mythology.

It is no accident that Kesey places his mental hospital in the Western-most state, the very name of which evokes the roughshod days of the Oregon Trail and the tangled history of the Oregon Territory. Symbolically, the American frontier vanished after the 1890 census, which reported that there was no longer any place in the country with less than two people per square mile. But the frontier persists as an idea in the American mind, resurrected time and again by national myth-makers. Like Kennedy's New Frontier—evoked at the time when most of the nation lived in the city—it may be a no-place but always a better place.[18]

But in the fifties and sixties, with no more physical frontier to escape to, many Americans simply tuned out and dropped out. Some, like Holden Caulfield, found refuge in loony bins. Retreating from the shopping mall, the prefab bungalow, the TV-dinner and other Babbitry of the American Combine, Kesey's lunatics also search for a better place, only to find it on Nurse Ratched's ward. Sixscore years earlier, Emerson warned every rabbit-man in America: "Society everywhere is in a conspiracy against the manhood of every one if its members" (17). Had he lived in the twentieth century, he might have penned *Cuckoo's Nest* himself.

ONE RABBIT, ONE VOTE

> "Didn't you explain the voting procedure to him, Doctor?"
> "I'm afraid—a majority is called for, McMurphy. She's right, she's right."
> "A majority, Mr. McMurphy; it's in the ward constitution."
> "And I suppose the only way to change the damned constitution is with a majority vote."
>
> Ken Kesey, *One Flew Over the Cuckoo's Nest*

The key hits the lock. It is early morning and the patients are not up yet. Only the ward aides go about their business as usual.

But today there is a new Admission, a big battle-scarred Irishman for whom the loony bin is a ticket out of prison work-farm. He is nothing like Harding, Bibbit, Bromden, and the rest of the rabbit-men on the ward. He cusses, laughs and gambles; he is loud, proud and fearless; and he will fight Nurse Ratched until she has him lobotomized. Before then, however, he will organize the patients into an effective opposition, test the limits of democracy in a series of votes, and effect a therapeutic cure that will leave the loonies self-reliant and free.

Kesey's storyline is a classical Freytag's pyramid. The rising action tracks Mac's victories over the Big Nurse, from the time she loses self-control over his sperm-whale shorts, through the ground-shifting votes to change ward policy, to the fishing trip that turns erstwhile rabbits into men. The climax comes in the wake of the drunken party, when the Big Nurse bullies Billy Bibbit into suicide, driving McMurphy to choke her.[19] In the denouement, with most of the Acutes gone from the ward, Chief Bromden smothers the life out of the vegetative hero and lights out for his native territories, on the way to Canada.

The events are narrated by the Chief who has tricked the Combine and the Nurse into thinking he is deaf and dumb. On the face of it, his account is far from reliable. Witness to systematic oppression on and off the ward, Bromden is given to imagining cogs, wheels, gears, and other machinery of mind-control in the Big Nurse's wicker bag. Yet he is also extremely perceptive. Always at the epicentre of events, his point of view strings them into a coherent whole. He tells us more about Mac than meets the eye, and what he says rings true. In fact, it is the only truth that makes sense of the Irishman's otherwise inexplicable actions.

Even as he was inspired by the tragic longing of the real men at the Menlo Park Hospital, Kesey's protagonist is pure fiction. For all the narrative realism—in search of which Kesey even arranged to undergo a clandestine electroshock—Mac is a figure of romances, of Sunday matinees, and Hollywood Westerns (before *The Unforgiven* broke the mold). Although a grifter, he is upfront about it which is, of course, another confidence trick. The successful con gives his mark what he wants, and on the ward everybody wants something: Bibbit self-worth, Harding manhood, Cheswick toughness, Bromden clarity.

Like Oscar Schindler, Mac grows from manipulator to saviour, developing a conscience that radiates outward to encompass all victims of institutionalized oppression. He is a man alone against the American Combine. He is an Ahab in sperm-whale shorts committed to a life-or-death struggle against his nemesis. He is Christ the Redeemer and a comic-book hero. He is a knight errant whose sacrifice restores order and fertility to the ravaged subjects of the Fisher King.

He is also the centrepiece of a political allegory about the blight consuming the nation, of which the mental ward is a reflection—a synecdoche. The Inside is kept in check with intimidation and repression, widespread spying and denunciations of inmates by inmates, all Eliotesque hollow men full of vacuum tubes, faulty switches in the social machine. Outside, the "nation-wide Combine" (181) is ruled by witch-hunts, loyalty oaths, Cold War militarism, and a culture of conformity that hatches look-alike Americans like insects in schools, families, the army, and the hospitals. After all, as the Chief explains, even though the Big Nurse controls the Inside, she works with a view to adjusting the Outside too.

Kesey has always insisted that, far from being a devil incarnate, the Nurse herself is a product, even a victim, of the Combine. In his words, she may have "worked for the villain and believed in the villain, but she ain't the villain".[20] His target, in other words, is far more systemic than any one abuser, no matter how degenerate she is. Nor is there much doubt what his target is. Of all the social problems modelled by the means of the ward, political disfranchisement gets the lion's share of attention. Only lunatics, after all, could live in a system that deprives them of the very right the country is supposed to be built on: democratic representation.

Starting with a canny political joke—McMurphy outcrazies the crazies by claiming he is going to vote for Eisenhower in 1960, when the two-time president cannot even run—*Cuckoo's Nest* fashions itself into a canny political allegory. It is more than the innuendo that you have to be mental to vote for four more years of Ike. Randle Patrick McMurphy stands for RPM, or so many revolutions per minute. Ironically, his revolution is no more than the exercise of the right to vote enshrined in the country's and the ward's constitutions. But it transforms him into a political

"... Randle Patrick McMurphy stands for RPM, or so many revolutions per minute. Ironically, his revolution is no more than the exercise of the right to vote enshrined in the country's and the ward's constitutions. But it transforms him into a political agitator of his constituents who, like Billy Bibbit, 'just don't think a vote wu-wu-would do any good' ..."

Figure 2.3   Direct democracy and (not so) simple majority: voting to change the Constitution.

agitator of his constituents who, like Billy Bibbit, "just don't think a vote wu-wu-would do any good" (117).

Even before his democratic awakening, Mac exhibits the pat manner of a professional politician. Watching him work the

Acutes with smiles, backslaps, and handshakes, the Nurse has an easy time insinuating a comparison to a candidate dispensing meaningless amities before elections to state Senate. His barnstorming crusade for votes makes this comparison to a campaign-trail politician even more accurate. Among others, it forces McMurphy to rethink his lobbying tactics after he loses the first vote, and widen his electoral base in the wake of the second vote by appealing for support to the Chronics.

Extolling the novel's political commitments, Jerome Klinkowitz describes McMurphy as no less than a democratic force aimed at "raising the consciousness of the people" (15). This promising thesis fizzles out, however, in a banality. The proletarian revolution of the mind consists, apparently, in little more than making the patients laugh at the vaguely evoked establishment. Interestingly, even as he highlights its political dimension, Robert Forrey places *Cuckoo's Nest* on the opposite end of the spectrum, damning it as "conservative, if not reactionary, politically" (222).

Robert Boyers is even more critical. Apparently, unable to "move political and social institutions" (447), McMurphy sublimates his political impotence via sexual liberation. Make love not revolution, maintains the critic, is all that can be salvaged from Kesey's political agenda. Right or wrong, no one could ever hope to reconcile these contradictory readings. Taken together, however, they leave no doubt that politics lies at the heart of Kesey's masterpiece. Indeed, in the words of a preeminent Polish theatre director, outside the United States *Cuckoo's Nest* "is immediately understood in political terms".[21]

Not by accident, Kesey's Inside is a scaled down prototype of the *political* world Outside. The ward has a president, a constitution, a democratic process, a ballot, a voting system (simple majority), a welfare system providing free housing and free 'Medicare', a law enforcement apparatus, and even class divisions between the Acutes and the disfranchised mass of the Chronics. Lest any reader overlook these parallels to the United States at large, they are reinforced by the deranged Colonel Matterson's incessant ramblings about the Republican Party and America the red, white, and blue . . . the watermelon . . . the peach . . . the plum.

The names themselves are a dead giveaway. Modelled on the twenty-ninth President of the United States, Warren Harding, President Harding of the Patients Council is also a political nonentity. The historical Harding's main title to fame is that his administration is regarded as one of the most corrupt ever. His platform, exemplified by the campaign promise of a return to 'normalcy', meant in practice non-interference with Big Business, political isolationism, belligerence towards 'lesser' nations, a repeal of taxes on excess profits, and turning of state parks over to loggers and oil men. Sound familiar?

If no one remembers the man, everyone remembers his slogan: "We want a period with less government in business and more business in government". It could hardly ring more ironic when, in the spirit of laissez-faire profiteerism, the latter President Harding rubber-stamps Mac's slaughter of the lambs in poker as the embodiment of the heart and soul of the country:

> I'm all for him, just as I'm for the dear old capitalistic system of free individual enterprise, comrades, for him and his downright bullheaded gall and the American flag, bless it, and the Lincoln Memorial and the whole bit. Remember the Maine, P.T. Barnum and the Fourth of July. (254)

Even as Doctor Spivey dispenses political banalities about the ward being a democratic community run by the patients, *Cuckoo's Nest* depicts a profound erosion of the principles of the government of the people, for the people, and by the people. Much as in *Walden Two*, the silent mass constitute a demotic majority at the mercy of a political system that leaves them powerless to change it, or even express themselves within it. An occasional vote on policy cannot, after all, hide the fact that the ward's constitution is merely a fishbowl exhibited to visitors on public relations tours.

Underscoring their collective impotence, Harding mockingly reassures his fellow institutionalized Americans: "We can even have a lobby in Washington" (228). Ironically, Washington is the Big Nurse's right-hand aide and one of the ward's most brutal oppressors. Even more ironically, in the course of the novel Mac actually petitions Washington, D.C., to examine the administration of electroshocks and lobotomy in government hospitals—to no avail. And, in the irony of ironies, McMurphy pans his own campaign to restore democracy on the ward as "a part of the plot to overthrow the government" (268).

As one of the leaders of the sixties' counterculture, Kesey knew full well that it is not easy to overthrow a government. Outside of taking up arms, the only way to do it is from within the system engineered to preserve the status quo. It is a classic Catch-22. It would take a different political system—such as, for example, the Swiss democracy, which enshrines constitutional change in its constitution—to allow itself to be changed into a different system. Little wonder that all kinds of political outsiders, from the Tamil Tigers to the Nepalese Maoists, prefer bullets to ballots.

But neither does constitutional framework safeguard democracy. In 1933 Hitler became Reich Chancellor legally and constitutionally—in the wake of which he legally declared an emergency, dissolved the constitution, and imposed a regime of internal oppression. Evidently, there was a chink in the political chain-mail of the Weimar Republic through which an anti-democratic arrowhead could pierce through.

Could anything of this sort come to pass in the United States? Does the Constitution harbour its own Trojan horse, a fatal design flaw that could one day precipitate a dictatorship? It does. Article V, which deals with constitutional Amendments, opens with the following proviso:

> The Congress, whenever two thirds of both Houses shall deem it necessary, shall propose Amendments to this Constitution, or, on the Application of the Legislature of two thirds of the several States, shall call a Convention for proposing Amendments, which, in either Case, shall be valid to all Intents and Purposes, as Part of this Constitution, when ratified . . .

Remember when your parents promised you a birthday wish, only to see you turn the wishing system inside out by

wishing for more wishes? This self-reflexive turn has a coun-
terpart in the keystone of American democracy. The Constitution allows itself to be amended *in any manner whatsoever*,
providing a specified majority so desires. In other words, it
grants wishes to all, even to those who one day might wish to
abolish the Constitution. All it takes is the votes of two thirds
of Congress or two thirds of the states to propose the abrogation of any part of the Constitution—or even all of it.

The political bar for this is high but not impossibly high,
as witnessed by no less than twenty-seven Amendments (only
one of which had been repealed—by another Amendment).[22]
The quorum could, for instance, table an Amendment to the
effect that a simple majority, such as on the Nurse Ratched's
ward, should henceforth suffice to table and ratify new
Amendments. It could even propose that one individual's
wishes become the wishes of the nation. Once ratified, such
an Amendment would constitutionally create an American
dictator who could then constitutionally pass an Amendment
banning further Amendments.

The Patriot Act—which contains provisions against opposition to the Act—is the best proof of the vulnerability of democratic institutions to authoritarian makeover. Authority, after
all, is no more than social legitimacy for making laws and
expecting them to be carried out without resorting to coercion.
In his classic analysis of the patterns of social domination, Max
Weber distinguished three pure types of authority. These are:
rational, which rests on the assumption of legality; traditional,
grounded in historical precedent; and charismatic, deriving
from an exemplary individual and the normative behaviour
ordained by that person.[23]

The Big Nurse, for example, has traditional and rational
authority invested in her. Mac represents charismatic authority—cult of personality, if you will. In *The Plot Against America*, Charles Lindbergh gets elected to the White House in 1940
entirely on the strength of his charisma. Have looks and fame,
will govern. By virtue of becoming president of the United
States, however, he assumes the mantle of authority that is at
once rational and traditional. The point of all this is that, all else

being equal, the type of authority alone may have a dramatic impact on the course of history.

Weber himself drew attention to the fact that political power based on charisma rarely survives over longer periods. A WWII partisan hero, Josip Broz Tito fought with the same ruthlessness to have himself anointed as the postwar political leader of Yugoslavia. Shored up with rational authority, for decades he kept a tight lid on the volatile Balkan ethnicities until his death in 1980. In the absence of his personal authority, however, a weak federal system spiralled into anarchy and civil war. Similarly, as soon as Roth's president Lindbergh bafflingly disappears, the vacuum spawns a paramilitary power-grab.

The displacement of traditional authority by charismatic, followed by the displacement of charismatic authority by rational is, in fact, a recurrent phenomenon. It is familiar from countless historical examples, richly satirized by Orwell in *Animal Farm*. Led by a charismatic leader, a sociopolitical revolution overturns an entrenched system. Fast-tracked to the highest office, the leader begins to arrogate to himself the previous authority's powers even as, symbolically, he divests himself of some of its trappings. Eventually, another revolution is needed to establish rational authority and democracy.

In *Democracy in America*, Alexis de Tocqueville identified a number of critical flaws which remain as true today as in 1835. Among them, the so-called tyranny of the majority got the top billing. Anticipating much of Foucault's discourse on power, the Frenchman observed that, even as social control under absolute monarchy is usually coercive in nature, in a democracy it takes the more or less subtle form of mind control. Far from being self-reliant, Americans are, as he phrased it, enslaved to the ethos of the majority—political correctness, in the contemporary idiom.

Once internalized, such behaviour is hard to eradicate, insofar as political unorthodoxy becomes a transgression against society itself. This, in turn, forges a further identification with the collective, despite rote invocations of self-reliance and rugged individualism. "Freedom of opinion does not exist in America"

(116), de Tocqueville observed famously. Conformity, he went on, pervades wherever centralized power effectively sublimates the grievances of the socially weak.

Even as the French writer diagnosed these conditions in nineteenth-century United States, Kesey found them unchanged in the twentieth. The quadrennial pageant of electing one of two candidates fielded by the right-of-centre and centre-right wings of the Demublican party does not, after all, guarantee Americans a say in the affairs of the country. Nor does the electoral college math which every four years threatens to mock the electorate's wishes. If a functional democracy is one that respects and reflects the political will of the voters, the American system is far from democratic. In fact, it is so badly designed that it openly defies the will of the voters.

Two presidential elections more than a century apart lay bare this democratic deficit.

In 1876 the Republicans fielded Rutherford B. Hayes, a decorated brigade commander of the Civil War. Against him ran Samuel J. Tilden, a Democratic reformer celebrated for taking on the Tammany Hall. Hayes's campaign was so shadowy that he was stuck with the nickname Rutherfraud B. Hayes. Perhaps for that reason, the clear winner in the popular vote (though not by much) was the Democrat. Consequently, in accordance with the will of the American public, he should have become president. Yet just because Hayes got a razor-sharp majority in the electoral count—185 to Tilden's 184—he was sent to the White House.

On the campaign trail the Republican party accused Tilden of contracting syphilis and alcoholism, while the Democrats charged Hayes with insanity and the murder of his own mother. Scurrilous dealings also characterized the presidential election of 2000, captured in a political cartoon depicting Uncle Sam with Florida hanging flaccid from his belly and a caption: "Electile Dysfunction". Al Gore edged Bush II in the popular count by more than half a million votes. By all reckoning, he should have become the forty-second president. The electoral math once again defeated the will of the people: Bush's 271 beat Gore's 266.

ELECTILE DYSFUNCTION

". . . Scurrilous dealings also characterized the presidential election of 2000, captured in a political cartoon depicting Uncle Sam with Florida hanging flaccid from his belly and a caption that read: 'Electile Dysfunction'. . ."

Figure 2.4   Uncle Sam in need of Votagra (2000).

On two occasions, the voting system made a travesty of the wishes of the American people. Other times it merely teetered on the brink of travesty. Take the twentieth century alone:

- in 1916, Wilson carried the electoral college but bested Hughes in the popular vote only by a little over 600,000
- in 1960, Kennedy edged Nixon by scarcely more than 100,000 votes
- in 1968, Nixon barely squeaked past Humphrey (in fact, if less than 25,000 voters had switched sides, America would have hailed a different chief)
- in 1976, with eighty million votes cast nationwide, Carter's margin over Ford was less than 2 percent.

This electoral mythomatics indicates that American democracy openly defies—or is in perennial danger of defying—the voters. America's electoral anomalies do not, of course, end there. Even when the popular and electoral ballots converge on the same candidate, the numerical discrepancy can be staggering. In 1944 Franklin Roosevelt secured 432 electoral votes against 89 for Thomas Dewey. The almost fourfold advantage would appear to testify to FDR's unassailability. The popular vote painted a very different picture. Dewey polled almost 90 percent of Roosevelt's numbers.

While the nation favoured the incumbent president only by a slim margin, the electoral math pulled a different rabbit out of the hat: a crushing landslide for the status quo. The 1952 ledger was equally lopsided. Adlai Stevenson's share of the popular vote was almost 80 percent of Eisenhower's, yet he drew less than 20 percent of Ike's electoral score. In 1992 Ross Perot spoiled Father Bush's re-election bid, split the conservative vote, and persuaded almost twenty million Americans to cast ballots for him. His electoral score? Zero. The voice of twenty million people was shut out by a winner-take-all plurality.

In Great Britain, the Liberal Democrats are also perennially punished by plurality. The party that wins a given constituency, be it only by a single vote, wins all of that constituency's political capital. Under plurality it is possible to get almost half of the nation's votes and yet win no parliamentary seats. Is this fair to the voters? Proportional representation, such as in Germany, guarantees 'third parties' their share of parliamentary seats and thus their share of political power. In contrast, the British and American systems punish third-party voters, in effect perpetuating a bipartisan monopoly.

Not to beat around the bush, the election of the most powerful public servant in the world is governed by a system that robs citizenry of their say in the process. The people elect Tilden over Hayes, or Gore over Bush, and the system spits out the wrong president. Where exactly is the democracy?

POLITICS AND POLITRICKS AS USUAL

> So this's how you work this democratic bullshit—
> hell's bells!
>
> Ken Kesey, *One Flew Over the Cuckoo's Nest*

James Madison remarked once that if men were gods, no government would be necessary. Well, they aren't, and it is. Still, being a necessary evil, politicians are not entrusted with permanent power, like Supreme Court justices are. And instead of being nominated, they are publicly elected. This presumes a formal system—an electoral rulebook, if you will—to convert voters' preferences into the politicians who will govern them. Naturally, as always in life, we cannot *all* get what we want. What any voting scheme does is vector individual preferences and convert them into a collective choice.

The simplest electoral system is a simple majority. Under the Big Nurse a simple majority—50 percent plus one vote—changes ward procedure, as per the ward constitution. When, on his second attempt, Mac rounds up all twenty Acute votes, he still falls short of a majority and has to hustle up one more vote from the Chronics. When Chief Bromden eventually puts up his hand (it is an open ballot), the Nurse declares the extra vote invalid: the polling station has closed. Here, two outcomes—change the ward rules to allow patients to watch the World Series or leave the rules intact—play the role of two candidates.

Because there are only two ward policies to choose from, a plurality (more votes than the opponent) is automatically the majority (more than half the votes), assuming everyone votes. When there are three candidates—as with W, Gore, and Nader in 2000—this need no longer be true. Depending on whether you approve of what the Supreme Court did with the Florida recount, Gore or Bush had the plurality by securing a handful more votes than his rival. Neither had the majority, i.e., more than 50 percent of the total, owing to the spoiler candidate, Ralph Nader (who polled 2.7 percent nationally).

For most people the concept of democracy is virtually synonymous with elections that are reasonable, fair, and open. The trick is to devise a voting scheme that is reasonable and fair, and that guarantees everybody a chance to get involved in the political process. Amazingly, the current voting system, assumed by most Americans to be the best of all, is actually one of the worst when it comes to electing public officials. Other electoral alternatives are demonstrably superior to the winner-take-all plurality of 'one person, one vote' entrenched in the United States.

One popular alternative is the ranked ballot whereby voters rank political candidates in the order of preference, and the system tallies the scores. Another is a series of round-robin pairing-offs between all candidates, whereby the one who wins every two-way contest wins the election. Another system allows voters to indicate their favourite together with their second (and third, and so on) choices, and then progressively eliminates the least popular candidates while redistributing their votes. Yet another scheme breaks free from one-person-one-vote, allowing citizens to cast 'approval' votes for every candidate they like.

Each of these electoral systems—Borda count, Condorcet winner, Instant Runoff Voting (IRV), and approval voting—is sensible and fair. Each can be (and has been) shown to be *more* sensible and fair than the system Americans currently use to elect their presidents and other officials.[24] Yet, in a shocker that many people cannot get over, each may elect a *different* president. Suppose for a moment that each system takes the same stack of ballots, tallies them, and selects the CEO of the United States. Each might elect a different president in a process that is, in each case, reasonable, democratic, and fair.

So, who *da* Man? The answer is that there is no answer. Asking by means of the ballot a different question to the electorate, each system elicits a different answer and elects a different politician. The will of the people, expressed by their votes, *doesn't change*. Nor does anyone tamper with the ballots. Just because a different—but absolutely fair—voting system is in place, a different politician will be sent to the Oval Office. Much as there is no unique democratic system of government, there is no unique democratic voting outcome. The truth about voter preferences is not out there. It's all in the rules.[25]

This does not mean that the electorate is blundering in the desert, or that people's votes are random or arbitrary. What it does mean is that the American system is insensitive to what a better voting scheme could elicit. And a better voting scheme—better even than plurality, Borda, Condorcet, IRV, or approval—does exist. It is called range voting, and it might be the answer to the anomalies plaguing the current system and the above alternatives. Exotic as it may sound, range voting is not something that you might do only when in Texas. If you have ever rated books on Amazon, films on IMDb, video clips on YouTube, or consumer products on eBay, you have already cast a range vote.[26]

The inefficiency of the American electoral system is one thing. As Kesey makes abundantly clear, affording citizens their proper role in the political process is another. Seemingly distinct, the two issues come together in the case of vote splitting. After all, you can get the entire nonvoting majority in the country off the couch and into the voting booth and still make no difference at all, exactly as if all had stayed home. How? Split their votes right down the middle. If 50 percent vote pro and 50 percent vote con, a giant leap for voter participation will have zero effect on the election.

In *Walden Two*, Frazier spells out the political cost of vote splitting. "Do you think we'd be so foolish as to vote half one way and half the other? We might as well stay home" (183). In the real world, Los Horcones has long experimented with forms of government involving the highest numbers of people in decision making. Having tested democracy in all shapes and hues, they decided that it does not promote the values they seek. Any system of government that resolves policy issues by voting, they concluded, is inherently adversarial:

> We found that negative, competitive statements occurred frequently. Members in the minority on a vote said things like "they have made a poor decision" or "I'm sure that solution will fail" . . . However, when the decision of the majority turned out to be correct, the minority did not show their approval. Winning or losing the vote seemed to become more important than making a correct decision.[27]

Perhaps. It is, after all, human nature to be adversarial when it comes to power and social hierarchy, and politics is all about power. But it is equally in human nature to be cooperative and look for win-win solutions that benefit all. The lack of interest in organized politics proves that there is something wrong with American politics, not with the American people. It is the faulty system that keeps people away by means of—for starters—the electoral college, the need to register to vote, or holding elections on working days.

Look again at Los Horcones. Given the opportunity to have a direct say in the affairs of the community, the communards exercised it without hesitation. So adamant was their involvement, in fact, that apparently nothing could change their convictions. Direct democracies, from Periclean Greece to modern Switzerland, prove indeed that people are intensely interested in politics and power—so long as it's people's power. The difference is crucial. When Pericles founded democracy in Athens in mid-fourth century BC, it was only to establish his own power base independent of the hereditary aristocracy and landowners who might oppose his imperial designs.[28]

His *demokratia* put an end to the privileges of the Aeropagus, transferred the legislative power to the Assembly, and enfranchized the adult male minority to participate in public affairs. Women, slaves, and foreign-born Athenians were excluded outright and, while most public officials and jurymen were selected by lot, the poor could ill-afford to hold office because they needed to make a living. Power to the people meant in practice power to Pericles and the people at the top.

Still, if imperfect then, two and a half thousand years later democracy should be as reliable as Apple's OSX. Of course, it isn't. But that does not mean we should stop getting people educated about politics and getting them involved in the process, much like Mac's revolution aims to. It does not mean we should stop experimenting with other forms of voting than plurality in order to let the voice of the people be heard more clearly. And it does not mean we should not tweak the American democracy, if need be by borrowing from others.[29]

After all, if dictatorships tend to be drearily alike—look no further than Chavez's Venezuela—across the world democracies offer a gamut of solutions when it comes to devolving power to the people.

The purest form of democracy is direct rather than, as in the United States, representative. You might think that the complexity of modern states exceeds the capacity of citizens to oversee their business. But you would be wrong. Direct democracy in the twenty-first century is not merely achievable but practiced with ringing success—foremost in Switzerland. Swiss local, cantonal, and federal-level referenda take power away from politicians and put it in the hands of regular folks in a type of *demokratia* unpracticed in America since the popular assemblies of the settlement-era.[30]

Europe and North America may seem worlds apart, but there are a number of historical affinities between Switzerland and the United States. After all, when the Pilgrims set sail for the New World, in a gesture as religious as political they carried with them the Geneva Bible. The 1620 Mayflower Covenant is permeated, in fact, with the spirit of Calvinism. Killjoy repression and other-group directed intolerance aside, within the fold Calvinism was, as a matter of fact, one of the most fair-minded and egalitarian religions ever.

In practice, much of this democratic spirit can be traced to accountability. Much like modern Switzerland, the church was not governed by an individual but by a group. Uniquely, when the conclave became deadlocked, input was solicited from outside this inner power circle, bringing *more* voices into the forum. Even more remarkably, the supervisors assigned to oversee different city sectors had to be approved by the people. Given these ideals and practices, it is little wonder that the Declaration of Faith passed in Geneva in 1537 inspired most of the covenants of the New England Puritans.

In the nineteenth century it was America's turn to transform the political history of the Swiss. In 1848, when Switzerland was modernizing its constitution, it adopted the American bicameral system to ensure political representation at the federal level and to the individual cantons. Thus the Swiss Federal Assembly corresponds to the U.S. Congress while the Swiss National Council and the States Council correspond, respectively, to the House and the Senate.[31]

Like in the United States, Swiss states are organized differently and retain different rights (in keeping with Article 3 of the Swiss Constitution). Delegating all powers to the cantons, the article means that the assumption of a nontrivial political role by the state requires a constitutional Amendment, to be ratified by the people and the cantons. On paper, things are similar in the United States. In the Tenth Amendment, all powers not expressly delegated to the federal government by the states in Article I, section 8—which delineates the powers of Congress—and not expressly denied to the states in Article I, section 10, devolve to the states or to the American citizenry. In practice, this constitutional directive is skirted by the U.S. government's assumption of implied powers.[32]

A word about government: Switzerland is ruled by a Federal Council of seven ministers who form the country's top executive body. Council (*Bundesrat*) elections, whereby each minister is elected by the combined two chambers of the federal parliament, take place every four years. The Swiss government, in other words, is elected by the parliament. Given that Switzerland enjoys proportional representation, the parliament comprises many parties, all of which are minorities. In practice this means that each councillor gets elected by the opposition, which ensures that all are compromise candidates known to work across party lines.

The parliament also selects the president and the deputy president from the seven ministers. They not only continue to hold their day jobs (e.g., foreign affairs, defense, finance), but—unlike in America—*do not wield any extra power.* They are elected, if you like, to pose for photo-ops with foreign dignitaries during state visits. Moreover, presidents are rotated annually so as not to accrue undue power. Consequently, every minister can count on becoming president every seventh year in office. Since there is no term limit, s/he can also count on having to forge multi-party compromises with past presidents since competent ministers tend to serve a long time.

So much for the government. Now for the key ingredient: democracy. The fundamental difference between Switzerland and America is the role of citizens in political decision-making. The cornerstone of Swiss democracy is the referendum. The 1848 Right of Referendum binds the government to put *any* act of parliament to national vote, provided 50,000 people so demand within 90 days of its passage. Direct democracy is further enshrined in the 1891 Right of Initiative. It grants *any* citizen the right to propose a constitutional Amendment, provided he secures the support of 100,000 others within eighteen months.

Reminiscent of the agora of the ancient Greek republics, Swiss municipal, cantonal, or federal referenda embody democracy at grassroots level.[33] Ordinary citizens like McMurphy can propose just about any change if they obtain enough signatures. Conversely, inasmuch as the parliament proposes rather than disposes, laws already ratified can be subsequently rejected by people's vote. In short, the government rules by the consent of the nation. It's people's power all the way. If a requisite number of signatures is obtained within a given time period, there *must* be a vote.

Since the foundation of modern Switzerland under the 1848 constitution, there have been more than 150 referenda on constitutional Amendments, and tens of thousands of cantonal and local ones. In the same period Californians voted in more than a thousand referenda—but with a dramatic difference. In the U.S., referenda are limited strictly to the municipal and state level. Franklin and Jefferson may have wished to delegate power to the people but, in spite of the lip service paid to the idea, today's 'federalists' are chary of surrendering power to Mr and Mrs Doe.[34]

The problem may, once again, lie in the Constitution. Larry Sabato makes no bones that, for all its genius, quite a few of its provisions are simply outmoded. Having been framed for a much less complex nation and times, they are in urgent need of reform.[35] And until they are reformed, the dysfunction and unfairness that have crept into American politics will remain. Radical as the notion may appear today, the original framers of the Constitution expected it to be regularly revisited and revised to reflect the country's changing needs. Yet, outside the Bill of Rights, it has been amended just seventeen times in 230 years.

Unlike the United States or Canada, where so much power is concentrated in one-person offices like the presidency, every echelon of the Swiss government is a group. As delegates of the people, these public bodies reflect the multiethnic, multilinguistic, multireligious, and multicultural nature of the country.[36] Having said that, the largest political group in Switzerland are the voters. The rights they enjoy mean that they are routinely asked to sign on to political initiatives. Sign-up sheets work their way through streets, offices, even shops, before they are

"... The largest political group in Switzerland are the voters. The rights they enjoy mean that they are routinely asked to sign on to political initiatives. Sign-up sheets work their way through streets, offices, even shops, before they are carted off to local, cantonal, or federal governments, usually in full view of the media ..."

Figure 2.5   People's democracy at work: empirical scientists have shown that direct democracy and other forms of citizens' partici- pation contribute to social stability and individual happiness.

carted off to local, cantonal, or federal governments, usually in full view of the media.

A referendum that follows may be on a *formulated* initiative, meaning that the group wanting the change has already formu- lated the text of the proposed law. This is not common, as it risks mistakes that could result in it being struck down by the consti- tutional court. More typically, people submit unformulated ini- tiatives which politicians then whip into bills. Of course, elected officials attempt to influence the vote with counterproposals and by promoting their views in the media. There are also popular political shows such as *Arena* which, instead of muscle-bound wrestlers, star-party bosses and parliamentarians who go head to head armed with posters, pamphlets, and pie-charts.

All constitutional Amendments require a double 'Yes': a simple majority of the popular and cantonal vote.[37] In practice this means that such proposals face formidable obstacles before they become law, which contributes to Switzerland being rather slow to change (women did not acquire the right to vote until 1971). Another contributing factor is the inclusiveness of the system which solicits input from any and all parties, chambers, commissions, NGOs, unions, citizens' groups, and so on, in order to hammer out a compromise. As a consequence, Switzerland's laws are a curious mosaic of progressive conservatism and pragmatic idealism.

Before every constitutional vote, citizens receive an election guide the size of a novelette (covers are also used) which includes all the information one could wish for to make an informed decision. Among others, it includes summaries of the initiative and—if there is one—of the parliamentary counter-proposal; lists of benefits and hazards; tabulations of costs; full legal texts; editorials by the pro committees; counterarguments by the executive branch; and the breakdown of the parliamentary vote on both proposals. This being Switzerland, the parliamentary vote is simply a recommendation and not a binding decision.

Significantly, direct democracy presumes an educated populace capable of grasping nuanced political issues. Given that any matter of state may be submitted to the vote of the people, in Switzerland no effort is spared to produce discerning citizens. Unlike the States—where forty-five million are functionally illiterate—the Swiss political system presumes literacy.[38] In the same spirit, voting in a referendum is made easy. It takes place on weekends (albeit most people vote by post) and there is no need to register. If you're a citizen and over eighteen, you can cast your ballot.

This isn't to say that there is no voter fatigue about mundane issues. Some referenda feel like neverenda, political footballs kicked about in empty aisles. But if you approach people with a sign-up sheet to stop trees being felled along a local road, for Sundays to be made car-free, or for the military to be abolished, they respond en masse. In fact, participation is highest in referenda initiated by regular folks or by local organisations, as opposed to political parties or lobbies. Typically, the Swiss system yields a compromise. Initiatives often go too far, but the fact that they are brought in the first place goads politicians to enact changes. Sometimes these changes suffice for the original initiative to be withdrawn.

Whichever way you look at it, the key element of Swiss democracy is the delegation of power to the people. Politicians are not power-brokers but executors of the nation's will—revocable delegates who wield authority by virtue of the mandate of the people. And, as such, they are largely left to themselves. It is commonplace to see the country's politicians shop for *Lebkuchen* in a corner bakery. Top executives walk alone or use public transport without getting mobbed or shot at. Unlike America, assassinations are unknown because, to terrorize the country, you'd have to assassinate those who wield the power— the electorate.

Granted, Switzerland is small and the United States is big. The former has less than eight million, the latter more than three hundred million people. In area Switzerland is smaller than Vermont and New Hampshire combined, or roughly 10 percent of California. What works for a small country may not be feasible in a colossus like America—or so argue the skeptics. Saturated as it is with phones, mobiles, and internet terminals, however, not to mention the post office and the voting booth, the United States could institute national referenda with relative ease.

America is not too big for real democracy. It lacks not the technology but the political will to embrace constitutional referenda and other instruments of citizens' participation that directly contribute to political stability and personal happiness.[39]

JESUS WAS A SAVIOUR

I'm doing all I can to try to build a better world.

Ken Kesey, "Ken Kesey Was a Successful Dope Fiend"

Jesus was a saviour, but in his historical time he was regarded by the powers that be as a rabble-rouser and a Zealot revolutionary. Grandiose as the comparison is, Kesey does not hesitate to intimate parallels between Jesus and McMurphy who—when led to his spread-armed crucifixion on the electroshock gurney—asks for a crown of thorns. To the inmates Mac is, of course, a saviour. To the Big Nurse he is a rabble-rouser. To the penal and medical system he is a violent offender and a mentally disturbed patient. Like in Kurosawa's *Rashomon*, everything depends on your point of view.

In *One Flew Over the Cuckoo's Nest* the point of view meshes so closely with the events that, when Milos Forman asked Kesey to abandon the narration from the Chief's perspective, the writer refused to work on the screenplay.[40] The considerations of point of view transcend, however, the confines of the ward. A mere diagnosis of mental abnormality has repercussions that transcend medical semantics insofar as it engineers social policy as effectively as more overt forms of social control. In today's Nigeria, colonial-era laws still allow courts to jail the mentally ill for any length of time, sometimes for life. Just like under Stalin, many of the incarcerated are political adversaries pure and simple.

American social history supplies equally poignant examples of noncoercive social conditioning. Homosexuality was regarded as a psychiatric disease almost until the end of Nixon's presidency. Then, in 1973, the American Psychiatric Association gave notice that there was no scientific evidence that being gay was a mental illness and removed it from its diagnostic glossary of mental disorders. In one day, gays ceased to be deviants in need of psychiatric treatment. In one day, following this medical u-turn, a sizeable percentage of American society went from being abnormal to normal.

On the other hand, if homosexuality was no longer a psychiatric illness in the United States, it was still sufficient to classify people as mentally ill outside it. It took the World Health Organization almost twenty years to agree with APA's diagnosis. Their *International Classification of Diseases* dropped homosexuality as a mental illness only in 1992.[41]

If you can't cure them, you can kill them. In 2010 Uganda made world headlines by debating a law that punishes so-called aggravated homosexuality with death. Against genetics and evolutionary science, the parliamentarian who tabled the bill argued: "It's not an inborn orientation, it's a behaviour learnt—and it can be unlearnt. That's why we are encouraging churches and mosques to continue rehabilitating and counselling these people."[42] The rehabilitation will be permanent. The death penalty is sought for 'serial offenders' and for engaging in homosexual acts with a disabled person or anyone under eighteen.

If you scoff at this crude attempt at social engineering, remember that the devil does not often flaunt his horns. In 2004 a Bush II initiative called New Freedom Commission on Mental Health produced a report which requested compulsory mental health screening for all American children, starting with preschoolers.[43] Although no such program has been instituted, grants have been issued and pilot programs set up in sites across the country. Given the history of clandestine CIA experiments, real-life cuckoo's nests, and real plots against civil liberties in America, isn't it something to be concerned about?

3 You'll Never Make a Monkey Out of Me

or

Altruism, Proverbial Wisdom, and Bernard Malamud's *God's Grace*

ONE FINGER ON THE BUTTON

> An outline for a novel is the equivalent of a scientific hypothesis.
>
> Bernard Malamud, lecture at Harvard University

In 1982, a couple of unlikely bestsellers gnawed at America's conscience and at the root of its thermonuclear politics. On the face of it, they could hardly have resembled each other less. Where *God's Grace* trucked in exuberant fiction, *The Fate of the Earth* dished out fact upon sombre fact. Where Bernard Malamud raced a slalom course between out-of-this-world fantasy and tableaux miracles, Jonathan Schell hewed to the canons of Montesquieu. Where the novelist peopled the Earth with talking primates, the essayist let political and military history speak for itself.

Deep down, however, both books could have flowed from the same quill dipped in an inkwell made from a Cold War missile casing filled with radioactive blood. In austere and unflinching detail, both elaborated counterfactual scenarios of nuclear doomsday. Much as in his follow-up essay, "The Unfinished Twentieth Century" (2000), Schell looked death squarely in the eye, inventorying the after-effects of a thermonuclear thanatos syndrome. So did Malamud in the last novel published before his death in 1986—the darkly comic and allegorically realistic *God's Grace*.

"It may be one of the most important works of recent years", wrote Walter Cronkite for the back cover of *The Fate of the Earth*. Almost as an afterthought he added: "there still may be hope to save our civilization". Whether he had read *God's Grace* or not, he may have been speaking about it, for there is no mistaking Malamud's dread for the fate of the Earth. Figurative and whimsical where Schell is solemn and factual, he also begins his tale in the wake of a "thermonuclear war between the Djanks and Druzhkies, in consequence of which they had destroyed themselves, and, madly, all other inhabitants of the earth".[1]

God's Grace paints a front-seat picture of the global Armageddon: tsunami floods, radiation everywhere, the implosion of the biosphere so catastrophic that even cockroaches perish, and the life in death of the last human on Earth. Calvin

"... There is no mistaking Malamud's dread for the fate of the Earth. Figurative and whimsical where Schell is solemn and factual, he also begins his tale in the wake of a 'thermonuclear war between the Djanks and Druzhkies, in consequence of which they had destroyed themselves, and, madly, all other inhabitants of the earth'. . . ."

Figure 3.1 The fate of the Earth: a thermonuclear (hydrogen bomb) explosion.

Cohn, a paleologist, eludes the Bomb and the wrath of the Almighty by virtue of conducting research at the sea bottom. In the afterglow of the holocaust, he and Buz—a young chimp prodigy he discovers on the surface vessel—drift for weeks before getting shipwrecked on a tropical island, their Ararat and purgatory.

Like other protagonists of post-apocalyptic narratives, from *A Canticle for Leibowitz* to *The Day After*, Cohn takes it as his duty to rekindle civilization from nuclear ashes. There is only one problem. As God rumbles from on high, piqued at finding him alive, he is the only human to survive the Second Flood. Unfazed, Cohn transfers his promethean designs onto Buz and others of his kind who begin to appear on the island. The Lord seems to approve for, equipped with an artificial larynx, Buz miraculously masters human speech. No less miraculously, he teaches it to others.[2]

A new world Adam, Cohn gives names to the newcomers and, displaying a resourcefulness that would make Robinson Crusoe proud, proceeds to engineer a chimpanzee society. Not to replicate the errors of the past, in lieu of a political constitution he lays down seven Admonitions for the post-human age in the hope of steering his communards toward a better life. Daily he lectures to the grooming apes on history, sociobiology, and altruism. Impatient at the pace of progress, he even monkeys with evolution by begetting a child with a 'womantically' inclined female, Mary Madelene.

Yet the more he educates the apes under the Schooltree and presses them to obey the dictates of brotherly love, the more nature rears its head, dragging the community towards anarchy. Little by little, the quasi-Edenic garden—on which even insect-pollinated trees get pollinated in the absence of insects—devolves into a primeval jungle. Hostility, racism, and eventually cannibalism write the closing chapters of the communal history. In the final scene, the prodigal son Buz leads captive Cohn up the mountain to slay him in a reversal of the story of Abraham and Isaac. At last, humanity is no more.

However dissimilar on the surface, Schell and Malamud are one in intent. Both speak to every American, Russian, Chinese, or Gabonese who hopes for the survival of his sons and daughters. Both are hard-nosed realists about our chances to avoid self-extermination, horrified that Ecclesiastes' sun that also rises may be made of runaway neutrons. Both resort to every weapon in their narrative arsenals to make sense of a long procession of American administrations which, even as they ratify disarmament and non-proliferation treaties, upgrade their nuclear stockpiles in a political game of chicken played with one finger on *the* button.[3]

Both, in short, interpret literally Albert Camus's admonition from his 1957 Nobel lecture that the purpose of the postwar generation of writers is to save the world from destroying itself. In a world menaced by nuclear annihilation, warned the French laureate, there is no shortage of modern-day grand inquisitors seeking to establish the kingdom of death. To overcome this threat, the writers must, "in an insane race against the clock, restore among the nations a peace that is not servitude, reconcile anew labour and culture, and remake with all men the Ark of the Covenant".[4]

Crucially, the relation between *God's Grace* and *The Fate of the Earth* is the opposite of *God's Grace* and *Walden Two*. On the surface, the fictional communities conceived by Skinner and Malamud teem with similarities. Both are small and isolated farming groups founded and dominated by alpha-male American scientists. Both leaders are, at the same time, insiders and outsiders. Both engineer their societies from the bottom up, even as neither relinquishes top-down control. Both abjure violence, putting their faith in positive reinforcement instead. Both, in their separate ways, go back to nature to better human nature.

But apart from the knack for telling a good story, what separates a literary masterpiece from a behaviourist pamphlet is evolution. Where Skinner disregards the behavioural aspects of human adaptations, Malamud makes our genetic carry-on the centrepiece of his plot. Where Skinner's social engineers cure everyone of such primal instincts as parental investment, status seeking, gossip, cheating, envy or jealousy, Malamud lets them run their course. Taking issue with the closing of the American mind, he even has his protagonist educate the apes on, the Descent, Advent, Ascent of Man as Darwin and Wallace had propounded the theory of species and natural selection; adding a sketch on sociobiology, with a word about the nature-nurture controversy. (152)

God's Grace questions our degree of autonomy from the ancestral *Homo* insofar as the latter is the progenitor of so many behaviours of the modern human. This anthropological—not to say sociobiological—perspective is no mere poetic licence. A lifelong teacher and professor of literature, in preparation for the novel Malamud became a student of evolution. Even as he steeped himself in Thoreau's *Walden*, he steeped himself in primatology, paleoanthropology, and evolutionary psychology, reading everything from Louis Leakey's *Unveiling Man's Origins* to Jane Goodall's *In the Shadow of Man*.

In a radical step for a writer of fiction, he even spent a year at the Stanford Center for Advanced Study in the Behavioral Sciences, absorbing the essentials of within-group and between-group selection. Having done his homework, he makes it clear that evolution is an ideal vantage point from which to contemplate human society and morality. All would-be social reformers who discount the bedrock of biology have only so much, or rather so little, chance of success. Armed with the latest in sociobiological research and the oldest of folk wisdom, I set out to prove him right.

FROM CHIMPAN-A TO CHIMPAN-ZEE

I am a pacifist.

Bernard Malamud, marginal note in
unfinished novel *The People*

In the decades before *God's Grace*, Malamud had jump-cut from writing about a late-comer baseball sensation, Italian petty hoodlum turned grocer, tsarist Jew, and libidinous college professor to earn-his-wings angel, Black Power militant, middle-aged biographer of D.H. Lawrence, and other equally unpigeonholable creations. On the way, he had experimented with everything from impressionist imagism to stream-of-consciousness to almost scientifically rectilinear prose. But if he had been taking creative chances all his life, in *God's Grace* he is gambling for the jackpot.[5]

It is not even that he populates the story with sapient chimpanzees, a five hundred-pound Jewish gorilla, and an irascible God who enjoys pelting Cohn with lemons as a reminder of who is the boss of all bosses. It is not even that on page one he kills off everyone on the planet save for one man who, as foretold by the Creator, is also working under a death sentence. But, in an eyebrow-raising variant on 'last couple on Earth', he has his hero copulate with an ape who bears him a humanzee baby which is then killed and devoured by other chimps. Meanwhile, all this lunacy is textured out of a kaleidoscope of genres, from the evolutionary parable to post-apocalyptic survivalist drama to theosophical burlesque.

These protean designs proved too much for the critics, most of whom pooh-poohed Malamud's turn toward fantasy, clearly expecting another melancholy serving of matzo-ball realism. Many asked aloud why a National Book Awardee and Pulitzer Prize winner would sabotage his career with so lowbrow a fare as a beast fable.[6] Few paused to acknowledge that fantasy, especially with allegorical overtones, boasts a pedigree stretching from the Sanscrit *Panchatantra* and the Arabian *One Thousand and One Nights* to Spencer's *Faerie Queene*—to say nothing of Aesop, La Fontaine, and Br'er Rabbit.

"I write fantasy", Malamud shrugged off the barbs, "because when I do I am imaginative and funny".[7] And funny he is, even if it is slapstick sometimes. When Cohn contends with the Almighty, only to be knocked senseless by a pillar of fire in front of the petrified apes, Buz declares the spectacle, ahem, a knockout and casually inquires about the next episode. Much of Malamud's comedy owes, in fact, to such intermingling of high drama and almost Pythonesque irreverence. It may be the end of the world as we know it, but it is deflated by the rolling vernacular in which Cohn and Buz negotiate their priorities.

"Not all of us are eager to be reminded how close man has come, through his own madness, to the end of time," pointed out the author. "So, I wanted a little laughter in this serious book".[8] Try as you might, however, to look on the bright side of life after doomsday, *memento mori* is never far from sight. Cohn's island may be the new cradle of life, but it is littered with bones of animals that perished in the Second Flood. Just like the paleolithic fossils Cohn painstakingly excavates near his cave, they foreshadow his own mortality and the extinction of the human race.

All allegories feed on symbols, ur-tales and archetypes, and *God's Grace* is no exception. Not surprisingly, the encyclopedic (not to say Miltonic) range of its intertextual hyperlinks begins with the Bible, especially the book of Genesis. Playing more roles than Dan Castellaneta does on *The Simpsons*, at various points in the story Cohn becomes God, Adam, Cain, Abraham, Jacob, Noah, Moses, and Job, to name a few. At other times he cameos as Everyman, suffering redeemer Jesus, proto-storyteller Homer, and stranger-in-an-estranged-land Gulliver. Most of all, he is Robinson Crusoe and the latter's real-life prototype, Alexander Selkirk, who eked out several years on a barren island off the coast of Chile.

Another trove of allusions comes from Shakespeare, whose *Works* Cohn salvages from the sinking vessel. At once an island Prospero to Buz's Caliban and a Julius Caesar to his Brutus, Cohn also reprises the role of 'Womeo' in his starcrossed union with Mary Madelyn. Other allusions radiate to some of the iconic narratives of modern culture. One such is Golding's *Lord of the Flies*, in which an island commune degenerates into ritualistic murder. Another is Orwell's parable of talking animals who struggle to wrest power from the human. Another still is the man-made apocalypse in *Cat's Cradle*—and behind all looms *The Planet of the Apes*, with its cast of sapient, English-speaking chimps.[9]

Yet the parallels go only so far. If Malamud's chimps are the new meek to inherit the earth, they look like God's second mistake—if only he would admit it. If only. The Almighty who presides over the Second Flood is autocratic and short-tempered. As the biggest player on the globe, he enjoys cowing Cohn with divine muscle and thunder. Yet he is also a dispenser of grace, however stingy it may appear to the survivors. Having misspent his assets on unregenerate humanity, he is willing to re-invest them in the great apes. After all, they survive the holocaust even though, being morphologically like humans, they should have perished.

Better still, he creates a lush island on which they can try their hairy hand at civilization. Despite dismay at Cohn's survival, he even dispatches a Samaritan gorilla to save him from sure death of radiation. Why? The answer lies, perhaps, in Cohn himself. He has always been short and, after the radiation sickness, his bowed legs get even more crooked, chimp-fashion. Like his protégés, he is trim and muscular, and prolonged exposure to the sun leaves him with a deep brown tan. Losing his hair, he grows a short beard and, to complete the picture, becomes a devout fructivore. His make-over is completed in a vote with which Buz and his conspecifics make him honorary chimp.

The transformation only externalizes Cohn's chimp-like traits. One day, of course, the metaphor turns flesh when the island becomes haunted by an albino ape believed to signify trouble for the community. Ultimately, suggests Malamud, this is what we are: white apes chained to our adaptive heritage. Vying with Buz, Cohn vies with his moral limitations no less, so much so that even his name reflects this struggle. Before he changes it to Calvin, his name used to be Seymore, and this conversion from See-More to one of the staunchest dogmatists in religious history foreshadows the blind spots he will exhibit in the island protectorate—notwithstanding all his intelligence and adaptability.

The adaptive value of intelligence is unquestionable. It is the best solution for surmounting the contingencies of life on earth. But even though mental agility and plasticity enabled us to become the top predator of all times, they've exacted a heavy price. Sounding for all the world like Walker Percy in an existential mode, E.O. Wilson diagnosed it as a psychological exile of humankind.[10]

Some of our inner unrests, pathologies and neuroses, proposed the sociobiologist, may be the toll levied by evolution for cutting us to the front of the line. Considering how badly we behave toward each other and even toward ourselves, was the toll worth paying? Ironically, we are the sole species capable of even contemplating the question. For Blaise Pascal and other thinkers of the Enlightenment this alone would have sufficed to answer it in the affirmative. In an interview entitled, fittingly enough, "Century of Thanatos", Percy was equally forthright: "Better to be a dislocated human than a happy chimp".[11]

It is not hard to see why. Our hyper-intelligence may be the source of countless social problems, not to mention the existential itch that, once experienced, cannot be scratched out. But if you do not like this *sui generis* part of human evolution, what is the alternative?

And yet, to pay for the evolutionary ratchet that produced the intelligence explosion in the early hominids, we may have mortgaged our future. The same big brains that served us so well against predators, glaciations, food shortages, and other ecological IQ-tests are responsible for the nuclear means of exterminating life on earth—and for the lack of political will to ensure we can't. Viewed in this light, shared intentionality, which begot intelligence, which begot culture, which begot science, which begot the H-bomb, may be the ultimate Trojan horse. Little wonder that Cohn plans a key lecture,

> beginning with the Holocaust that I mentioned yesterday; all that Jewish soap from those skeletal gassed bodies; and not long after that, since these experiences are bound to each other, the Americans drop the first atom bombs—teensy ones—on all those unsuspecting 8 a.m. Japanese crawling in broken glass to find their eyeballs. I could say more but I haven't the heart. (154)

Since 1945 we have lived, worked, and played in the shadow of atomic arsenals and their delivery platforms: ICBMs, long-range bombers, and boomer subs (today we would add suitcases). Why worry about it anew? Because the

Bush II administration revitalized nukes as a viable military and political option. It did so, despite the fact that the 1968 Nuclear Non-Proliferation Treaty has by now been ratified by all countries of the world bar three. Israel, Pakistan, and India still live by Groucho's quip of not wanting to belong to the club that would have them for a member.

In 2001, the United States torpedoed the creation of inspections regime at the Biological Weapons Convention and pulled out of the Anti-Ballistic Missile Treaty. In 2004, it opposed inspections and verification measures proposed by a new international treaty banning production of nuclear weapons materiel. Most damagingly, perhaps, it abandoned the norm-based approach to non-proliferation. It decided, in other words, to junk the principles of equality that have up till now been the mainstay of all international agreements. Some states, in America's eyes, would now officially be more equal than others.

In practice, that has always been the case. Israel, which has nuclear strike capability, has never faced serious repercussions. Iran, which does not (yet) have the nukes and is a signatory to the non-proliferation treaty, has been treated like a pariah. In 2006, however, Bush swayed Congress to okay sending civilian nuclear technology to India, despite the awkward fact that halting the spread of 'nucular' materials was the keystone of his foreign policy. With one stroke of a pen, the president burnt three decades of America's non-proliferation policy on the altar of a geopolitical counterweight to China. Did somebody say 'nuclear arms race in Asia'?

In the wake of the 2010 Measures to Further Reduction and Limitation of Strategic Offensive Arms, the combined number of strategic warheads fielded by the Djanks and the Druzhkies will stand at over three thoussand (not counting tactical nukes which are the mainstay of America's current R&D). Since one is enough to vaporize a whole city, there are not enough cities on Earth to be the targets of these bombs. Tellingly, as late as 2009 the doomsday clock of the *Bulletin of the Atomic Scientists* stood at five minutes to midnight. That was two minutes *closer* to Armageddon than in 1962 when Khrushchev and Kennedy eyeballed each other over Cuba.

It is five minutes to midnight.

How close is humanity to catastrophic destruction? The Doomsday Clock conveys the time remaining and monitors the means humankind could use to obliterate itself. First and foremost, these include nuclear weapons, but they also encompass climate-changing technologies and new developments in the life sciences that could inflict irrevocable harm.

"... 'The Americans drop the first atom bombs—teensy ones—on all those unsuspecting 8 a.m. Japanese crawling in broken glass to find their eyeballs. I could say more but I haven't the heart' / In 2009 the doomsday clock of the Bulletin of the Atomic Scientists displayed five minutes to midnight. That was two minutes closer to Armageddon than in 1962 when Khrushchev and Kennedy eyeballed each other over Cuba ..."

Figure 3.2   Dying of radiation burns in Hiroshima (1945) / Promo for the *Bulletin of the Atomic Scientists*.

Culture is an evolved mechanism for effecting response more rapidly than genes can. But culture can be massively maladaptive. One nuclear war can undo aeons of selection for intelligence. "I worry about technology rampant," confessed Malamud on many occasions. "I fear those who are by nature beastly."[12] To the extent that we cannot shed the adaptations that occasionally make us behave like proverbial beasts, that fear will always be real. But are we really doomed to the mercy of our biological appetites—the four F's of evolutionary survival: fighting, fleeing, feeding, and reproduction?

The question of freedom has dominated Malamud's fiction since his first novel, *The Natural*.[13] It has also dominated the sporadic interviews he had granted in his lifetime. How much freedom do we have? How far does it extend? What do we do with it? The suppressed premise of these questions is the almost truistic acceptance that moral responsibility exist only to the extent that people (or sapient chimps) possess free will. Despite libraries of theodicean treatises, of course, no one has resolved the logical and moral paradox of omnipotent God and human freedom of choice.

In *God's Grace* the paradox returns as a parable on moral freedom and the biological nature of Man. Who was *really* responsible for the nuclear war and the Second Flood: the Almighty or humankind fashioned in his image? Who *really* failed in Cohn's commune: the self-serving man or the all-too-human apes? What is a human being: a moral and therefore culpable agent or a muppet agitated by God's invisible strings? "The book asks, in a sense, a simple question", summed up Malamud. "Why does man treat himself so badly? What is the key to sane existence?"[14]

Death, he might have added, combs everybody with one comb. The savage primitive, selfish and self-serving, is the face of humankind for whom civilization is merely a napkin with which to dry out the fangs. But wait a minute. Aren't we a little more two-faced than that? Aren't people capable of remarkable feats of cooperation, coordination, and collaboration? Even waging war requires millions of individuals to act in concert, each critically dependent on another. True, this is not yet altruism, but it is a radically different type of behaviour from 'every man for himself'.

Moreover, full-bloodied altruism is not hard to find even on the battlefield. The 2008 headline about a Royal Marine who threw himself on a grenade to save his mates is just one of many examples of such seemingly maladaptive behaviour. Even as his buddies dove for cover, a reservist lance corporal in an Afghanistan reconnaissance patrol jumped onto the tripped booby-trap grenade to absorb the blast with his pack and body armour. The gods must have been smiling that day for, incredibly, he suffered only severe shock and a nosebleed.[15]

Naturally, not all that glitters is gold. Willing to give up his life for his mates, the soldier was a willing participant in neo-colonial occupation of other human beings in this dusty corner of the Middle East. It is erroneous, or at least overly generous, argue many moral philosophers, to speak of altruism the radius of which is so narrow. If Cohn's eutopia is anything to go by, Malamud agrees.

George, the black gorilla, is the object of virulent hatred by the chimps, with the Jesus-loving Buz in the lead. A passel of emaciated baboons become a live meat market for Esau and his otherwise civilized cohort. Baboons, rants the alpha-male in a verbal analogue of a Hitler moustache glued to the lip of a Southern redneck,

> are dirty, stinking, thieving monkeys, interfering into ev-erybody's business. They breed like rats and foul up all over the clean bush. If we don't control their population they will squat all over this island and we will have to get off. (224)

If his rationale is as grotesque as it was in the Third Reich and in the Jim Crow Dixieland, so are the behaviours it attempts to justify. The mere proximity of the 'black' monkeys drives the supremacist chimps into a frenzy of predation at the end of which they polish off every morsel of bushmeat stripped from a baboon child.

Caught red-handed, one chimp soldier who has only been following orders defends himself: "Esau told us that baboons don't belong to our tribe". To Cohn's exasperated reproof that God wants all to live at peace with strangers, he counters with: "What for?"[16] Clearly, Cohn's colonists put little stock in the proverbial golden rule of all moral codes: *Don't do onto others what is hateful to you*. In this, however, they are only too human. German colonists in Namibia also denied the humanity of the indigenous Herero people, calling them baboons while exterminating them left and right in the first genocide of the twentieth century.

And yet, gripped by pessimism to which he repeatedly con-fessed in the years before his death, Malamud hung on to hope. "My premise", he told Joseph Wershba in 1958, "is that we will not destroy each other. My premise is that we will live on. We will seek a better life. We may not become better, but we will seek betterment".[17] It may appear wishful to look for a counterfoil to Armageddon in the words from the coldest years of the Cold War. But at the bottom of every Pandora's box rattles a persistent, if muted, hope that tomorrow may not turn out to be the day after.

HUMAN MORALITY, PRIMATE SOCIALITY

> It seems entirely possible that chimpanzees, as they progress in their evolution may, if their unconscious minds insist, incite molecular changes that will sooner or later—sooner, I hope—cause them to develop into a species something like man.
>
> Bernard Malamud, *God's Grace*

Before violence and aggression scuttle the communal experiment, Cohn sets up seven Admonitions on the face of a mountain. These quasi-Mosaic edicts are to safeguard the principles that the social engineer sees as essential to a politically just and spiritually enlightened society. Like the Christian injunctions against the seven deadly sins, they are a distillate of the dual nature of his endeavour. On the one hand, they reflect the nobility of his eutopian aspirations. On the other, by the very fact of being posted, they testify to the need to redirect the truant onto the path of virtue.

1. We have survived the end of the world; therefore cherish life. Thou shalt not kill.
2. Note: God is not love, God is God. Remember Him.
3. Love thy neighbour. If you can't love, serve—others, the community. Remember the willing obligation.
4. Lives as lives are equal in value but not in ideas. Attend the Schooltree.
5. Blessed are those who divide the fruit equally.
6. Altruism is possible, if not probable. Keep trying. See 3 above.

7. Aspiration may improve natural selection. Chimpanzees may someday be better living beings than men were. There's no hurry but keep it in mind.[18]

In interview after interview, Malamud cited his formative influences to be World War II, the Holocaust, the racial strife in America, and the threat of nuclear war. All of these concerns are reflected in the blueprint for the primate community. The spectre of nuclear winter, lit by the embers of atomic blasts, drives the First Admonition. The Second Admonition replaces the Christian mantra of 'God is love' with an elliptical reminder that God is the ultimate unknown. So much for invoking his will as an excuse for bigotry and war—or for arming American troops in Iraq and Afghanistan with rifle sights stencilled with biblical references.

With Russia and the United States separated only by eighty-five kilometres of Bering Strait, the Third Admonition is a reminder that ICBMs have shrunk the world to the size of a neighbourhood. Grafting the Schooltree onto the biblical Tree of Knowledge, the Fourth exhumes the ghosts of John Scopes and the 1925 Monkey Trial. The Fifth Admonition to distribute resources equitably rings with especial force in the United States where the wealth of the top 1 percent exceeds that of the bottom 95 percent.[19] The Sixth goes after the geopolitical divisions that often limit the right to peaceful coexistence only to those who share our patch of dirt.

The Seventh Admonition, however, seems different. Talking about natural selection, it seems to veer away from politics and anything else we might term culture. Or does it? Malamud thinks not, leaving no doubt that the separation between the alleged genetic determinacy and cultural indeterminacy is a red herring:

Cohn lectured on the development of the great apes and ascent of homo sapiens during the course of evolution. He had several times lectured on natural selection—the maximization of fitness, someone had defined it—a popular subject with his students. It promised possibilities if one made himself—or in some way became—selectable. (187)

If the apes wish to become more selectable, they can do something about it instead of waiting for adaptive behaviours to grind themselves out over eons. Put differently, social engineering can guide natural selection in a co-evolutionary *pas de deux*. Culture is, after all, an adaptation. For a very long time now, it has been changing the genetic character of human populations via multilevel selection. On second thoughts, Cohn's lecture about the road to eutopia being paved by social engineering and evolution is far from an anomaly. All seven Admonitions make as much sense from a sociobiological as from a sociopolitical point of view.

The First Admonition reflects the core precept of moral codes worldwide: thou shalt not kill. Naturally, from the biblical Yahweh commanding the Israelites to smite their enemies to modern nations butchering one another in the name of democracy, killing has always been legitimized under certain circumstances. Self-sacrifice is an established fact, but altruistic tendencies are on the whole notably less intense than the impulse for personal and genetic survival. If people get hungry enough, they murder and eat each other. If newly dominant males kill the displaced leader's offspring, they have adaptive reasons for doing so.

Against this background Malamud's beast fable is once again nuanced and true to life. The raid on Cohn and the butchery of his child are perfectly consistent with predation, signifying that deep down the chimps may regard the human as a different species. Conversely, if they see Cohn as a chimp, their behaviour makes equal adaptive sense. By deposing the dominant male and by getting rid of his progeny, they induce Mary Madelyn into estrus. Significantly, throughout all this, the apes are murderous but highly cooperative. Their behaviour is not prosocial but it *is* highly social.

The Second Admonition attempts to prise morality away from doctrinal religion. "The world isn't ready for simple pacifism or Christian humility" (93), shrugs Frazier in *Walden Two*, and he could be Malamud's spokesman. Indeed, historically religion has been a flashpoint for hatred and intolerance, fragmenting us into sects and factions, only to pit one against another. And yet, religion can also be the source of one of the most *inclusive* tribal identities. In this case, however, the marker is not genetic but cultural.

Religion can act like a centripetal force, herding individuals toward the common centre. There is no one blood family on earth that is a billion strong, but there are more than a billion Catholics (roughly the same as atheists) united under the Fisher Ring. With God as the overarching tribal leader, religious systems often paper over the genetic differences of the believers. Black and white Methodists, Ashkenazi and Coptic Jews, Iraqi and Saudi Shiites kneel side by side because, even as they fence off non-believers, their religions give them a cultural group identity.

The Third Admonition is the moral golden rule, vividly paraphrased by a Pashto proverb: *Pinch yourself to find out how much it hurts others.*[20] It is there to counter the adaptive distinctions we always make between the in-group and the out-group. After all, from corals to shoaling fish, ants, termites, rodents, flocking herbivores, and primates—not to mention species that aggregate in family groups—social and colonial animals dominate the world. To survive alongside one another, all must have evolved ways of determining friend from foe and of knowing what to do with either.

Because morality evolved to harmonize in-group attitudes, it is biased in favour of those who are with us. As David Berreby documents in *Us and Them* (2005), sharp distinctions between those who are insiders and outsiders are bred into our genome. Social animals are often xenophobic and hostile to strangers of the same species who live outside the territorial and social boundaries of the group. It is far from a matter of just giving trespassers the evil eye. Individuals who stray into others' territory open themselves to attacks that may be lethal. Unprovoked aggression of this sort has been reported for almost all social species.[21]

The Fourth Admonition reflects the species-specific demands made by intelligence, culture, and social life. Human evolution selected for prolonged childhood, the longest in any animal that ever lived on planet Earth, for a very good reason. The amount and the complexity of sociocultural information to be absorbed by every new member of our species demands brains of the size that could not possibly fit into any birth canal. Solution? Produce smaller brains—although already pushing at the limits of female anatomy—and lengthen childhood.

The Fifth Admonition fosters prosocial behaviour through emphasis on egalitarianism and resource sharing. Looking out for number one (individual fitness) may be a number-one priority for most individuals most of the time, but behaviours that are good for me are seldom good for the group. But groups also compete with one another, and the more cohesive they are internally, the better chance they stand of outcompeting the competition. This yin-and-yang of multilevel selection means that the selfish gene cannot be the whole story.

This is not to say that there is a gene for cooperative behaviour, let alone for altruism. But the conceptual nucleus of modern biology has been taken to be synonymous with Dawkins's famous meme for far too long. We are survival machines, wrote Dawkins, programmed to replicate our twisted strands of genetic code. We may do so with the aid of the group or even by contributing to the welfare of the group, but with the ultimate goal of multiplying copies of our DNA. If acts of altruism and selflessness occur on the way, they occur only to the extent that they serve the continuation of the gene beyond the individual currently carrying it.

The Sixth Admonition does not merely encourage a reinterpretation of the selfish gene in more prosocial terms—it demands it. Self-sacrificing behaviour is, after all, not incompatible with self-serving behaviour, even though much of the time they may be only reluctant bedfellows. Put differently, self-sacrifice is not necessarily maladaptive, having emerged from the same evolutionary pressures that produced such forms of social exchange as favouring kinfolk and reciprocal back-scratching. There is, in short, no need to look outside evolution to explain why 'me first' is not always an enemy of 'we first'.

Evolution is about adaptation but not *just* about adaptation. The Seventh Admonition reinforces this point by stressing the interplay between genetic and social factors.[22] Biology has moved on from the days when Darwin's cousin, Francis Galton, framed the nature-nurture dialectic. Today his thesis and antithesis look more like the 1948 Escher lithograph of one hand drawing another in a closed loop. This is because, in all likelihood, gene-culture coevolution was the twin Rolls-Royce engine that lifted hominids from the plains of Africa to the heights of scientific, artistic, and material sophistication we enjoy today.

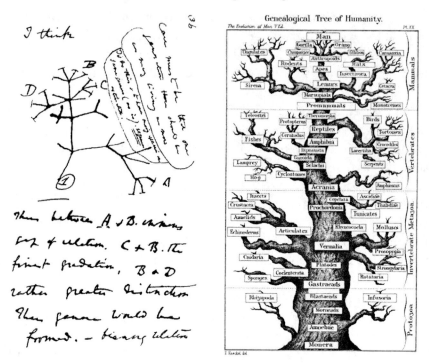

"... In all likelihood, gene-culture coevolution was the twin Rolls-Royce engine that lifted hominids from the plains of Africa to the heights of scientific, artistic, and material sophistication we enjoy today ..."

Figure 3.3   Darwin's first sketch of an evolutionary tree from his *First Notebook on Transmutation of Species* (1837) / Classic genealogical-teleological tree of humanity.

How did it happen? Even if the details are still subject to debate, some facts are beyond doubt. The most evident among them is that humans are adapted for culture in ways that apes are not. The crucial difference here is our adaptation for understanding other agents as *agents*, i.e. intentional beings. This allows us to share a point of view—and thus information—by drawing attention to intention. Evidence suggests, in fact, that, in conjunction with theory of mind, this shared ('we') intentionality is what drove human cognition. The result? The ratcheting up of learning skills and the explosion of culture.[23]

The key factor in cultural evolution is its fantastic rate. Molecular genetics shows that *Homo sapiens* separated from apes some six million years ago. Fossil records suggest that for the next four million years we continued as very ape-like australopithecines. Our uniquely human ability to attribute beliefs and intentions is therefore likely less than two million years old. This is a very short time for any cognitive adaptation to emerge. On the other hand, something did manifestly select for human cognition in spectacular ways. *You* are the living proof of that. What was it?

Given the speed and the ratcheting effects of this cognitive evolution—perhaps we should say revolution—there is really only one agent of change to fit the job description: culture. Material and symbolic culture is, after all, influenced by biological imperatives and, in turn, biological traits are influenced by cultural selection. Without culture in the picture, conclude Richerson and Boyd in *Not By Genes Alone* (2005), "we can't explain why our societies are so different from those of other primates, the emotional salience of tribal-scale human groups, or their importance in social organization and social conflict" (235).

Genetic variation among groups—especially mixed groups—can't explain variation in group behaviour. The experience of partitioned nations, from (East) Germany to (North) Korea to (Northern) Ireland, is unequivocal in this respect. So is cross-cultural adoption, whereby children effortlessly adopt the new culture and not that of their genetic parents. Nor can ecological factors be the answer. First of all, all environments on Earth have by now been altered by culture, so that even if the hypothesis were right, it would be wrong. Secondly, the ecological hypothesis would predict similar behaviours in similar environments, which is not always the case.

This is not to say that ecological factors never select for behaviour. Harsh environments regularly yield raiders (Vikings, mountain peoples of Spain). Seasonal environments yield cultural adaptations to do with food preservation and storage. Arid ecologies promote group behaviour necessary to complete irrigation systems. On the other hand, there is a whole spectrum of examples which cannot be accounted for by purely ecological factors. Among them, the customs and patterns of domination between Dinka and Nuer tribes and Yankee vs. Southern culture of honour are by now canonical.

Genetic and cultural selection have walked hand in hand since at least the early Pleistocene. The result is civilization as we know it: Fatman and Little Boy, the Big Mac, the Lindy hop. That still leaves the question of what evolutionary mechanism acted as the cognitive ratchet. The recently discovered mirror neurons—so-called in distinction to canonical neurons—look more and more like a link between natural selection and the evolution of culture. This is because, as we are learning, mirror neurons directly detect and simulate other people's cognitive and emotional states.[24]

That's right: cognitive *and* emotional states. Take a triadic structure: you, me, and an object—or some relation between objects, or anything else—you want to draw my attention to. Intentional actions and indicated structures, as it turns out, speak directly to our evolved brains. The latter detect intentions even before 'we' do, and process them with unerring alacrity. It is not, in other words, a case of 'humankey see, humankey do'. Eerily, mirror neurons are attuned to intentions behind movements, the purpose of gestures. You could say that they *understand their meaning* in terms of goal-directed actions.[25]

At the cortical level, the brain does not work by tracking motor activity. It does not work, in other words, in terms of extending a forelimb and closing digital protrusions around a tapered cylinder resting a couple of feet away. It works in terms of reaching for a banana in order to eat it. How do we know? Because when the exact same action is repeated in another context—for example, miming the original gesture without actually grasping anything or even without intending to—nothing in the brain fires and nothing activates. Somehow our evolutionary 'wet' chips are able to grasp other intentional beings' minds.

It is important to remember that all this happens without any reflective or inferential mediation. It is an automatic and immediate cortical understanding in the heat of the moment—a looking-glass reflex of our evolved brain. But there is more. The discharge of these neurons is eerily similar when actions are performed and when they are merely observed. Mirror neurons are voyeur neurons, primed to activate if you burn yourself with scalding water or if you only witness my own injury and distress. And it is not just cognition, either.

When I see you frown, look around, and spread your hands while elevating your shoulders, I can reasonably surmise that you are puzzled or lost. But a long time before that I am ready to offer help, because my brain—to be precise, my visceromotor system—understands and feels your discomfort before 'I' do. It's the ultimate case of what-you-see-is-what-you-get. When I see your pantomime of helplessness, my brain not only *knows* that you are disoriented or discomfited, but *feels* it. This is crucial because morality hinges on empathy, on the capacity for putting yourself in other people's shoes.[26]

Training is one conduit of moral virtue. Aristotle spent years pounding the precepts of goodness into Alexander, who then went to pillage most of the known world. But the rudiments of morality appear to be preloaded into humans. Empathy, the feeling of the feelings of others, is after all the foundation—to many philosophers a precondition—of altruism.[27] Altruism, in turn, is the foundation of groupish behaviour and thus of society as we know it. Naturally, in everyday parlance altruism comes bundled up with goodness. Not so in biology, where it is defined operationally rather than in reference to any intrinsic features.

Regardless of the motives or intentions behind it, if an action that benefits others is costly to the performer, it is considered altruistic. This can include even paradigmatically hostile or aggressive behaviour. Bees that die after stinging, or army ants that get eaten before their numbers can overwhelm the prey, are highly altruistic but hardly benevolent. Both are out to kill. Just because actions benefit someone else's survival, they must not, therefore, be regarded as good in some transcendent moral sense. By the same token, however, selflessness must not be excluded from the overall economy of social life.

Economists, political scientists, and sociologists often reduce us to rational utility maximizers, conspicuously leaving out the human dimension, the capacity for disinterested self-sacrifice. To gauge what is wrong with this picture, look no further than Adam Smith. Hailed in America as a prophet of wealth-maximizing laissez-faire, Smith was more nuanced a thinker. Not only did he publish a whole book on altruism, but he maintained in *The Theory of Moral Sentiments* that Man has capacities "which interest him in the future of others, and render their happiness necessary to him, though he derives nothing from it" (9).

Armed with these caveats, let us look at altruism again. Suddenly it seems to be everywhere. Far from an esoteric trait of the likes of St. Francis of Assisi or Mother Teresa, benefiting others at cost to self dominates the social landscape. Granted, just because we are all altruists does not mean that all instances of self-sacrifice are equal. But there is no denying that, sometimes at least, we act out of other-directed motives. Or is there? Cynics can always find alternative reasons for even the most altruistic acts. A soldier smothering a fragmenting grenade with his body earns, after all, not only posthumous fame and decoration, but a pension for his family.

On this interpretation, his apparent altruism might be a roundabout kind of kin selection. The *esprit de corps* or brotherhood in arms—especially in small, tight-knit, frontline units—could also activate self-sacrifice as a sublimated form of 'kin' selection. But what about families who report felonious kin to the police in the knowledge that the latter will be sent away for life or to the chair? Theodore John Kaczynski, aka Unabomber, was not caught as a result of a years-long FBI investigation. His brother recognized the terrorist's writing style and opinions in the latter's manifesto and tipped the Feebs. What was in it for him, in the absence of financial reward? Heartlessness does not explain anything since, in many cases, families turn in kin whom they love and support during the trial and later in jail.

All this counterevidence, however, may be missing a larger point. As Janet Radcliffe Richards points out, if you raise the bar too high no one will ever be able to jump over. A Doubting Thomas, who always suspects everyone's motives, writes even the possibility of altruism out of the social equation. In contrast, Richards's implicit and Donald Broom's explicit position is that self-sacrifice is not incompatible with self-interest. Naturally, many moral philosophers may find much amiss with this thesis. Genuine morality, they will remonstrate, demands an extension of the willing obligation to the entire human race.

Wouldn't it be nice? I put more stock, however, in Remarque's (echoed by Stalin) remark that while a single death is a tragedy, a million deaths is a statistic. We would have to be a very different species to empathize with abstractions such as humanity with the same intensity as with personal acquaintances. This is not to mention the fact that, by these standards, a Martian anthropologist would have to conclude that practically all people are immoral, given that we ordinarily limit our radius of good will to the inner circle of family, neighbours, and associates. So do, for that matter, chimps and bonobos.[28]

More to the point, however, our Martian anthropologist would see human and animal morality as continuous, no matter how far removed from each other on the spectrum. Not the *same*, of course—not by a long shot. He would not conclude that moral judgments that apply to the Nuremberg trials should apply to animal predation or aggression. But neither would he waste his time dusting our frontal lobes for God's fingerprints. Human morality, he would conclude, is as much a consequence of evolution as is our brain architecture, anatomy, propensity for counterfactual thinking, and even our proverbs.[29]

THE BOOK OF PROVERBS

> Cohn said he thought to be human was to be responsive to and protective of life and civilization.
>
> Buz said he would rather be a chimp.
>
> Bernard Malamud, *God's Grace*

Morality is a trait emergent because of a basic fact of existence. Just like many other organisms, we have always needed others to watch out backs in the struggle for survival. The position that evolution made us moral could not, however, be more at variance with the Christian view that people alone possess moral sense by the grace of God. According to the church, even as it makes us human, morality separates us from animals—even those closest to us, the great apes. Moral sense could never be mistaken for moral instinct. We are our primate cousins' cousins, but not when it comes to altruism.

Nonsense, counters Malamud, making the relation between evolution and morality the backbone of the Admonitions. Not for nothing does his hero urge the apes to "evolve into concerned, altruistic living beings" (146). Moral sense is not a veneer that somehow (how exactly?) emerged via non-evolutionary processes. We are altruistic as a consequence of the same selective pressures that have made us egocentric. Adaptively, it is not difficult to see why. Cooperative and altruistic units tend to outperform self-oriented individuals. To quote the Spanish proverb, *Three helping each other are as good as six.*

And herein lies the rub. Egoism betters individual fitness, but altruism betters group fitness. Something does not add up, and this something has an analogue in Gödel's incompleteness theorem.[30] The brilliant if highly eccentric mathematician proved that no system past a certain (quite low) threshold of complexity can be shown to be consistent. It could, in other words, be utter nonsense and you would never know—unless you climb to a hierarchically higher level. Therein, indeed, you can prove to your satisfaction that the first one is (or isn't) trustworthy. But if you think you just got out of paying for lunch, forget it.

The second level lets you verify the consistency of the first, but at a price. Now to determine that the second floor is soundly constructed, you need to climb to the third; for the third to the fourth; and so on, ad infinitum. It is a variant on the chicken-and-egg regression. To make your chicken hatch consistent eggs, you have to verify that the chicken itself is in working order, which means verifying the egg from which it came from, and so on and on. Nature iterates this yin-yang architecture independent of scale because, at its most fundamental, mathematics is a fractal.

Why bother? Because multilevel selection is another fractal. Think of it as a recursive function of two evolutionary vectors: pro-individual and prosocial. When competition between individuals gets suppressed, you get internally cohesive groups—which then begin to compete against one another. In other words, even as within-group cooperation suppresses the 'me first' vector for the sake of 'we first', competitive behaviour reappears at the next level up in the biological hierarchy. Within-group selection gives way to between-group selection, which then acts as the primary agent of change.

From the earliest and most primitive eukaryotes all the way up to the earth's biosphere, all the intermediate stages iterate this fractal architecture.

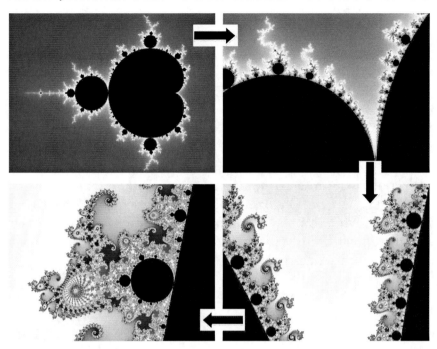

"... Nature iterates this yin-yang architecture independent of scale because, at its most fundamental, mathematics is a fractal. Why bother? Because multilevel selection is another fractal ..."

Figure 3.4   Mandelbrot set: iterating the fractal architecture independent of scale.

One factor that would seem to cast doubt on multilevel selection is inter-group migration in primates (and presumably in early humans). If groups are so fluid as to be practically nonexistent from the genetic standpoint, there is little for group selection to work on. Unlike apes, however, we cooperate within units that far transcend family groups, or even the one hundred to one hundred fifty strong forager-hunter band sizes. Instead of relying on genetic markers, *cultural* group identity relies on symbols—language, customs, ideology, religion, and so on. As such, it is largely independent of inter-group migration.

Groups with a higher coefficient of altruism will tend to outcompete rivals and spread the groupish genes. Self-serving behaviour has not, of course, ceased to exist. Far from it—if only because my interests are best served if everybody except me is altruistic. At every level 'me first' behaviour is, therefore, watched over by the local police. At the lower levels, for instance, the job is handled by the immune system. Most of the time our cellular organelles, their aggregates (cells), and *their* aggregates (internal organs) do work well as a team, which is good because their 'heave ho' has to synchronize if we are to live.

Naturally, aggregates of organs that we call human beings also engage in competition against other aggregates. Still, even players on a pro-basketball team who vie for individual fame and contracts unite to compete against other teams. Guess what? The yin-yang vectors reappear at the next level up. Teams of players who competed against one another as the Knicks and the Sixers unite into Team USA to compete against other national teams. In principle, this process could go on forever because its architecture is so fundamental (as for Gödel's theorem, in my opinion, it holds true everywhere in the universe).

Individual egoism twines with altruism within a group, which twines with competition against other groups, which twines with altruism within groups of groups, which twines with competition against other groups of groups, and so on, independent of scale. Multilevel selection permeates our lives because it is a fractal present at every level of existence. This includes, notably, the level at which we daily forge our destinies: the world of people and societies, of selfish prerogatives and social norms. And if our selfish prerogatives and social norms appear to be in constant tension, it is because they mirror the vectors that shape our lives.

We are moral creatures even if only because we are so often immoral. Do you recall the communal goodwill and unity within Walden Two—and the starkly different attitudes that dominate its dealings with other communities?

> If we buy up half the farms which do business in a particular town, we control the town. The feed dealers, hardware stores, and farm machinery salesmen depend on us. We can put them out of business or control them through our trade. The real estate values in the town can be manipulated at will, and the town itself gradually wiped out. (215)

Unwittingly, Skinner perfectly illustrates between-group rivalry by which evolution also acts on populations. Assemblies of individuals evolve into organisms when within-group selection is suppressed. More altruistic groups with a higher coefficient of cohesion tend to outperform groups rent by internal strife and spread their groupish genes.

Assuming the evolutionary vectors of morality are really as deep-seeded as I claim, shouldn't there be some evidence of them going back to the beginning of recorded history? But where might we, literary scholars, even begin look for such evidence? Paleoanthropologists have it easy: they dig for fossils to ascertain who we were and how we lived. Could literary scholars do some excavating of their own among literary fossils? But what would such literary fossils even look like?

The answer has been staring us in the face for as long as there has been recorded memory. There is, indeed, a body of verbal artifacts preserved since times immemorial and available for examination, though not in musty musea but in the canons of folklore. Like hemoglobin cells, these living fossils continuously course through the arteries of our civilization, some evergreen, some falling into disuse, continuously testing their fitness against the times. They are, as you must have guessed by now, proverbs.

Although no book of proverbs has ever won the Nobel Prize in literature, it is not a reflection on their literary and social value. A better gauge to their wit and wisdom than the blatantly politicized votes of the Swedish Academy (which, like in *Cuckoo's Nest*, use simple majority) is the judgment of one of the fountain-heads of our culture: the Old Testament. The Book of Kings records that Solomon—the epitome of biblical wisdom—bequeathed three thousand proverbs capturing the principles of a good life in a good society. Even more suggestively, the very Book of Proverbs refers to itself as a manual for living.[31]

Proverbs are, indeed, the wit of one but the wisdom of many. The reason we cite them almost daily is precisely because they compress so much wit and wisdom into such a compact delivery platform. Granted, it is not always easy to separate proverbs from other miniature forms: apothegms, aphorisms, epigrams, maxims, adages, *bon mots*, or dicta. Some distinctions, however, can be made on the basis of features associated with oral transmission. Having been passed from generation to generation, many proverbs are cast in a form that lends itself to easy memorization.

Brevity and pith are high on the agenda (*In the friendship of asses, look out for kicks*: Behar). So is symmetry (*What's yours is mine, what's mine is my own*: Tamil). So are parallelism and parataxis (*Where the power, there the law*: Russian), or chiasmus (*A stranger, being a benefactor, is a relative; a relative not conferring a benefit is a stranger*: Burmese). Other features, not always preserved in translations, are rhyme (*In time of test, family is best*: Burmese) and alliteration, often augmented with a caesura (*Be good with the good, bad with the bad*: Latin). Finally, personification and metaphor (*Relatives are scorpions*: Tunisian).

If some proverbs appear anachronistic, it is because they reflect pre-urban environments. They express prosocial sentiments or interpersonal obligations in reference to farm life (*If the cattle are scattered, the tiger seizes them*: Burmese), produce (*Nine measures of grain for relations, but ten for strangers*: Tamil), or domestic animals (*When the cat and mouse agree, the grocer is ruined*: Iranian). But even if their vehicle is out of date, their tenor isn't, because social dynamics has not changed much at all. To retool Michael Ghiselin's often quoted words, scratch today's urbanite and watch a pre-urbanite bleed.[32]

Proverbs are ultimate self-help manuals for dealing with social contexts. Handed down from generation to generation, they are time capsules buried in the minds of speakers of a language. Some are cast in the form of observations (*Lying and gossiping go hand in hand*: Spanish). Others as admonitions (*Do not stretch your feet beyond your carpet*: Lebanese) or commandments (*Love thy neighbour*: Greek). Others still incline toward paradox (*A pair of women's breasts has more pulling power than a pair of oxen*: Mexican). All seek to engineer behaviour by retrofitting the social skills of individuals.

But there is a problem. Some proverbs directly contradict others. While the Italians caution that *A short tail won't keep off flies*, the Koreans retort that *If the tail is too long, it will be trampled on*. More familiar advice to look before you leap flies in the face of a reminder that he who hesitates is lost. Clearly, proverbs can be cherry-picked to suit the need of the moment, and it is worth asking why it should be so. One answer is obvious. Proverbs are not logically consistent axioms for living in a group because different tactics are useful in different situations. Just as there is no one adaptation that will work in all ecological systems, there is no one social behaviour that will work for all individuals for all times.

Instead of explaining these self-contradictions away, however, I think we ought to put them in the spotlight. Proverbs encapsulate the wisdom of societies, predating even the dim beginnings of recorded history. Their transmission over countless generations attests to their tactical value as behavioural recipes. Consequently, proverbs can be examined for evidence of evolutionary pressures acting on human agents living in a group.

Specifically, to the extent that proverbs reflect deep-seeded economies of human life, some of them *ought to* be self-contradictory. Since human behaviours are theorized to be the sum of the selfish and groupish vectors, and since proverbs tap into deep and constant facets of human nature and social dynamics, human verbal artifacts ought to reflect this tension. Some proverbs, in other words, ought to reflect the interests of the individual, campaigning for 'me first' and pointing out the risks of trucking with others. Others should champion 'we first', extolling the benefits of cooperation and altruism and flailing the antisocialist.

Let me firm up these remarks into testable predictions. The first three are general and perhaps self-evident. In any statistically viable sample, we ought to find:

1. a great degree of overlap and redundancy among proverbs from diverse cultures and geographical regions, detectable especially in advice aimed at adaptive behaviours
2. a great number of proverbs dealing with kin (families, relatives, marriages, husbands and wives, parents and children, siblings, etc.), communal life (neighbours, friends, social leaders, visitors, strangers, etc.), and social intercourse (exchange, debt, borrowing, fairness, reputation, etc.)
3. a preponderance of men's point of view, detectable in proverbs dealing with men-women relationships, such as in marital or love-related advice.

My database included proverbs from sundry cultures and regions of the world—over forty thousand entries in all.[33] In all three cases, the null hypothesis proved void: the findings were consistent with the predictions. There *is* a massive redundancy across cultures. We reinvent the wheel over and over again, so much so that all proverbs cited in this chapter have equivalents in other cultures. Everyone has his version of *When in Rome, do as the Romans do*, or in ancient Bihar: *Suit your appearance to the country*. Everyone, including Egyptians almost four thousand years ago, has his version of the golden rule: *Do for one who may do for you, that you may cause him thus to do.*

These and countless other examples attest that human nature respects no national boundaries. Folk wisdom comes from insight repeated from one society to another, indexed by its transcultural and transpersonal character. For historical reasons, biblical and classical sources have been disseminated more widely in our Western civilization. But they are animated by the same sentiments that animate proverbial wisdom from regions outside the sway of the western world, such as Persia and South-east Asia, and from peoples that have retained their nomadic or agrarian way of life.

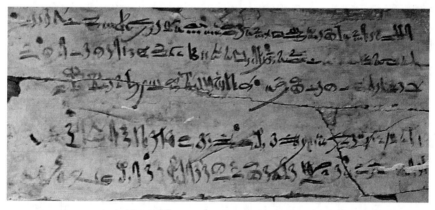

"... Everyone, including Egyptians almost 4,000 years ago, has his version of the golden rule: *Do for one who may do for you, that you may cause him thus to do* ..."

Figure 3.5   Egyptian scribe's exercise tablet from *The Instructions of Amenemhat* (circa 1500 BC) that advises: *Be on your guard against all who are subordinate to you . . . Trust no brother, know no friend, make no intimates.*

Proverbs, moreover, are mirrors of our evolutionary priorities. In line with my predictions, communal life and social intercourse dominate the agenda. Many, indeed, are preoccupied with lineages, blood, hereditary characteristics, incests, marriages, weddings, quality of wives, resemblance of children to parents, and so on. At the same time, they mirror the patriarchal hierarchy of social position and transmission of (oral) knowledge. One hilarious result of this man's point of view is, as I discovered, a venomous hatred of mothers-in-law in all cultures and not a word about fathers-in-law!

My two other predictions are more specific and considerably less self-evident. Both attempt to tease out the adaptive tension between the egoistic 'me first' and altruistic 'we first' vectors:

4. in the case of proverbs dealing with social life, there ought to be direct contradictions between egoistic sentiments and prosocial ones (reflecting the selective pressures of within-group and between-group selection)
5. at the same time, there should be a significant quantitative preponderance of prosocial proverbs over egoistic ones (reflecting the need to police self-serving and anti-social behaviour).

Once again, the data proved to be remarkably consistent with the predictions. Proverbs dealing with social life display stark and direct contradictions. Limitations of space allow me to include only a small sample below, but I have deliberately mixed in proverbs from around the world in order to exemplify the transcultural nature of the 'me first' versus 'we first' tug-of-war. None of these examples, I reiterate, are one-off anomalies. All without exception have equivalents in many—in some cases all—other cultures. In quite a few cases, in fact, polar opposites can be found within one and the same culture, as in the opening examples from Burma and France:

By association with whatever friend safety diminishes (Burmese), but *By association with whatever friend safety increases* (Burmese)

A sin that is hidden is half forgiven (French), but *Clean conscience makes a good pillow* (French)

Everyone lays a burden on the willing horse (Irish), but *A voluntary burden is no burden* (Italian)

Friendship is friendship, but money has to be counted (Russian), but *Mutual confidence is the pillar of friendship* (Chinese)

If you would be well served, serve yourself (English), but *Nobody can rest in his own shadow* (Hungarian)

If all men pulled in one direction, the world would topple over (Yiddish), but *A boat doesn't go forward if everyone is rowing his own way* (Swahili)

Nature forms us for ourselves, not for others (French), but *In a village divided against itself even a monkey will not abide* (Tamil)

Old promises are left behind (Maori), but *There is no virtue in a promise unless it be kept* (Danish)

Love your neighbour, but don't pull down the fence (German), but *A near neighbour is better than a distant cousin* (Italian)

A good bone never falls to a good dog (French), but *A good name is the root of wealth* (Vietnamese)

Love thy neighbour, but don't let him into your house (Maltese), but *Love thy neighbour* (Greek)

Better one true friend than a hundred relations (Italian), but *An ounce of blood is worth more than a pound of friendship* (Spanish)

A long continued loan usually confers ownership (Irish), but *A loan, though old, is no gift* (Hungarian)

Be particular about your conscience and you will have nothing to eat (Chinese), but *Honest fame awaits the truly good* (Latin)

Pardon one offence, and you invite many (Latin), but *It is more noble to pardon that to punish* (Arabic)

A patriot is a fool in every age (English), but *He serves me most who serves his country* (Greek)

Trust not the many minded populace (Greek), but *The voice of the people is the voice of God* (Latin)

Revenge is the pleasure of gods (French), but *Revenge is a tree that bears no fruit* (Dutch)

The troubles of a stranger aren't worth an onion (Yiddish), but *Do good regardless of consequences* (Chinese)

If it's not your worry, don't hurry (Polish), but *He who lives for himself is truly dead to others* (Latin)

Your partner is your opponent (Egyptian), but *A thing is bigger for being shared* (Gaelic)

The malice of relatives is like a scorpion's sting (Egyptian), but *Your family may chew you but it will not swallow you* (Arabic)

Proverbs are not circulated by individuals but by groups. As such, they ought to reflect the needs of groups, i.e., extol prosociality and condemn egoism. I found this, indeed, to be the case. Moralistic advice against putting on airs, not repaying debts, forgetting obligations, breaking one's word, oppressing the less fortunate, not sharing wealth, being lazy, gossipy, vindictive, deceitful, envious, jealous, hypocritical, materialistic, exploitative, godless, and so on, is the norm. From thousands upon thousands of examples, I can reproduce but a handful. Most should be familiar in spirit, if not in word, again testifying to their transcultural character:

An ape's an ape though he wears a gold ring (Dutch)

If one does not counsel one's brother, one will share in the misfortune (Yoruba)

If the family lives in harmony, all affairs will prosper (Chinese)

They don't unload the caravan for one lame donkey (Iranian)

The career of falsehood is short (Pashto)

A chief is known by his subjects (Hawaiian)

A bad coconut spoils the good ones (Swahili)

Cheerful company shortens the miles (German)

The confession of a fault removes half its guilt (Tamil)

Courtesy that is one side cannot last long (French)

A common danger produces unity (Slovakian)

A good deed bears interest (Estonian)

A single finger cannot catch fleas (Haitian)

Give a little and you gain a lot (Pashto)

Charity begins at home (English)

A good man protects three villages; a good dog, three houses (Chinese)

The staves of ten men make the load of one (Behar)

Though you go fifty miles for it, you must have society (Tamil)

Love thy neighbour as yourself (Bible)

Do not go to his house if he does not come to yours (Tunisian)

Society is ancient as the world (French)

Credit is invisible fortune (Japanese)

If a countryman of mine gets beaten I am thereby weakened (Chinese)

Given the deep-seeded predisposition to take care of number one, however, it should be mirrored in behavioural advice that casts doubt on truck with others. Oftentimes family, neighbours, and social groups can be less than trustworthy or easy to live with. This ought to be reflected in advice *against* being prosocial. Again, in terms of propositional logic, this makes little sense. If I enjoin you to *p*, I should not enjoin you to ~*p*. But socially and evolutionarily it makes perfect sense. Evolution works on what it gets, and what it gets in this case is different levels of natural selection.

At different times, individualism and altruism make adaptive sense, and both ought to be common enough to be noticed and warned against. To put it cynically, social norms are enforced for each individual's benefit. You are *always* better off when all others are altruistic. The rational strategy is to trumpet social norms while evading them. You get the credit for being a good guy and benefit from the effect it has on others, but you also reap whatever benefit might accrue from cheating (so long as you are not caught).

The number of antisocial sentiments, however, ought to be significantly smaller than the number of injunctions against egoism. Although, for illustrative purposes, my sample below is the same as the prosocial proverbs above, the numerical disparity between the two groups is enormous and unmistakable. My estimate is that the ratio of proverbial prosociality to egoism is between 10:1 and 100:1, and almost certainly closer to the higher value.

Prosocial policing is, in other words, very much in evidence at the level of behavioural advice bequeathed by one generation to the next. It is needed to counter egoistic sentiments, such as:

The best neighbours are vacant lots (French)

A man is a tiger in his own affairs (Tamil)

People seldom wish that others prosper (Yoruba)[34]

The camel carries the burden, the dog does the panting (Turkish)

If you do not ask their help, all men are good natured (Chinese)

Better to be alone than in bad company (Spanish)

To accept a favour is to lose your liberty (Polish)

Everybody collects coals under his own kettle (Finnish)

To live is either to beat or to be beaten (Russian)

A stolen orange is better tasting than your own (African Bemba)

If you want to please everybody, you'll die before your time (Yiddish)

We all love justice in the house of others (French)

There are only two good men—one dead, the other unborn (Chinese)

Unguarded property teaches people to steal (Lebanese)

Relatives are friends from necessity (Russian)

Self-preservation is the first law of nature (English)

When you go out to buy, don't show your silver (Chinese)

If everyone swept in front of his house, the whole town would be clean (Polish)

A good man is always made to toil (Tamil)

Kind hearts are soonest wronged (French)

Too much trust breeds disappointments (Philippines)

Fence your own vineyard, and keep your eyes from those of others (Greek)

The first time it's a favour, the second, a rule (Chinese)

My study of the adaptive origins of social proverbs is but a small brick in the wall of evidence corroborating the neo-Darwinian account of human affairs. But such corroboration testifies, once again, about the necessity of incorporating the evolved human nature into the eutopian design. Naturally, proverbs reward study not only as evidence for human peleomorality but as literary artifacts whose authority and resonance make themselves felt in any number of social contexts. One of them is, in fact, American politics as exemplified by the fiery abolitionist oratory of the 1872 American vice-presidential candidate, Frederick Douglass.[35]

Douglass, it turns out, relied heavily on biblical proverbs to strengthen the social and moral sentiments in his abolitionist polemics. Biblical sources boosted the authority of his philippics while adding the cachet of employing generations of folk wisdom in the fight against slavery. In general, as authoritative collective statements, proverbs are well suited to being used as moral and political weapons, a lesson not lost on generations of American presidents always in search of that folksy touch.

AS THE GREENLAND ICECAP MELTS

> The human race needs the novel. We need all the experience we can get.
>
> Bernard Malamud, in "A Talk with Bernard Malamud"

It is a common fallacy that having a 'gene for obesity' means that you are fated to gorge yourself on Mars bars. Because genetic characteristics determine your future, goes the story, you can hope to be a model, but the best you will ever do is waddle down the runway in an Armani muumuu. Not so. First of all, there is no gene for anything. Phenotypes are induced by constellations of genes interacting in ways that still largely elude us. Second, behaviour is genetically underdetermined. There is latitude for contravening the expression of some genes—for example, by exercise or dieting.

How does this pertain to God's grace and American utopia? The selective pressures of evolution endowed humans with a predisposition to detect patterns in the inkblot of life. Studies document that we are wired to integrate information, sometimes at the cost of seeing something in nothing. There is no doubt about the adaptive value of integrating a predator's face out of twilight shrubbery. At times, of course, a pair of burning eyes and a row of ivories would be concocted by an overactive brain. But the brains that played it safer got to live longer. *Better safe than sorry*, indeed!

This predisposition to find patterns and meanings reappears in other areas of life. Neuroimaging studies especially document something interesting about the parietal lobe—the region of the brain designed to detect where our physical body ends and the outside world begins. Meditation, mantra-induced trance or intense prayer can suppress this adaptive mechanism. The result is a sense of dissolution of self, coupled with a feeling of oneness with God or the universe. Believe it or not, the perception of God's grace and everything else it subjectively entails may be a by-product of the adaptive biology of the brain.[36]

This is not, however, the end of the story. In 2009 *Evolutionary Psychology* reported a bombshell: a strong antagonistic correlation between eutopia and popular religiosity. The data are eloquent. Countries with the lowest levels of social dysfunction—measured by rates of homelessness, unemployment, abortion, teen pregnancies, STDs, homicide, incarceration, divorce, and seventeen others—are invariably the most secular. Countries plagued by social problems, such as the United States, are the most religious (as reflected in frequency of prayer, church attendance, self-confessed belief, etc.).[37]

Behind this correlation hides causality. With the easing of socioeconomic problems, religiosity withers, and vice versa:

social dystopia turns on the religious tap. Such on/off devotion, not to mention the ease with which large populations abandon belief in God when conditions improve, challenge the view widely held in America that religious practice is the bedrock of existence. Rather, religion is a flexible coping mechanism. When social and economic dysfunction reaches certain levels, people deal with the trauma by turning their eyes towards heavens.

This does not necessarily mean that we have no evolutionary predilection for God—for seeing the supernatural in the natural.[38] It does mean, however, that biology is not deterministic of behaviour. Newsflash! You can still be a model. The news is even better for social engineers. Working in concert with sociobiologists, they can exploit our adaptive predispositions to counter the social ill-effects of the maladaptive ones. This includes America where, at least among Republican and Tea Parties, it is politically incorrect to admit that religiosity is less effective at engineering better social conditions than are government programs.

The giant social experiment that is the United States has always fascinated the world, not least because during the past century America has emerged as the leader of the Western world. Malamud's novel is a painful antidote to any such chutzpah. Never mind America. Humanity itself gives little indication that it is fit for the job. Even as evolution's unfinished experiment has favoured the sapient *Homo* to develop intelligence and civilization, we may not have been the optimal choice. Global stewardship demands global perspective and global consciousness, neither of which is much in evidence.

No need to look further than the 2009 climate conference in Copenhagen. While political leaders drowned their inaction in planet-saving rhetoric, scientists pegged the rise in global temperature at 1–6° Celsius by the century's end. Never mind the upper range, argued the optimists. Never mind the lower range, argued the pessimists. Believe who you will, but if one side right, the Second Flood will not come with a nuclear bang. It'll come with barely a whisper, as the Greenland icecap melts, as Antarctica slides into the ocean, and as rising seas drown coastal resorts where tourists fan themselves with copies of Margaret Atwood's *The Year of the Flood*.

4 We Better Kill the Instinct to Kill Before It Kills Us

or

Violence, Mind Control, and Walker Percy's *The Thanatos Syndrome*

D-I-S-A-S-T-E-R

> Where does one start with a theory of man if the theory of man as an organism in an environment doesn't work and all the attributes of man which were accepted in the old modern age are now called into question: his soul, mind, freedom, will, Godlikeness?
>
> Walker Percy, *The Message in a Bottle*

In *Leviathan* Thomas Hobbes depicted society in a state of war of all against all. Three centuries later, in *On Human Nature*, Edward O. Wilson agreed that people are innately aggressive. Much like rationality, however, aggression is not a mono-axial or even homogeneous trait. Wilson's biological and anthropological data led him, in fact, to distinguish seven types of aggressive response. Beside the familiar varieties, such as territorial, hierarchical, sexual, hunting, defensive or related to weaning, the sociobiologist identified a uniquely social trait: "moralistic and disciplinary aggression used to enforce the rules of society".[1]

There is nothing new about the need to engineer human society so it does not succumb to aggression—and the need to correct it when it does. The oldest Sumerian tablets in existence contain myths of messianic sacrifice for the fallible mankind in need of redemption. The epic narrative of the cruel king Gilgamesh of Uruk, the gods-sent redeemer Enkidu, and the Mesopotamian Noah, Utnapishtim, overflows with such lapsarian imagery, subsequently codified by the entire Judeo-Christian tradition. Genesis 4:1–16, in which Cain slays Abel, is the archetypal parable of humankind falling prey to aggression.[2]

Interestingly enough, already the Old Testament suggests that a corrective intervention into human behavioural programming might engineer violence out of existence. As a punishment for wrongdoing, Cain is banished to wander the earth. But to make sure that the sentence is not cut short by a summary retribution on the murderer, the Almighty brands a mark on his forehead that inhibits homicidal urges in all who might have otherwise aggressed him.[3] The implication is clear. Much as in *The Thanatos Syndrome*, violence may be rewired out of our system through some form of mind control.

Today we would be more inclined to take the sociobiological rather than the theological route to explain the essence of *la bête humaine*. Charles Darwin would have approved of research in adaptive anthropology, behavioural ecology, and evolutionary psychology which approaches morality as a form of compromise among competing spheres of genetic self-interest. As Robert Wright sums up the essence of such research in *The Moral Animal* (1994), by and large human beings "tend to pass the sorts of moral judgments that help move their genes into the next generation."[4]

Although couched in the language of evolution, the idea that our moral sense is rationalized instinct is nothing new. After all, natural laws evolved by societies worldwide are strikingly alike in their commandments, starting with 'thou shalt not kill'. There is, naturally, a very good reason behind it. The overwhelming majority of known foraging societies, which provide the closest approximation to what our hominid ancestors may have been like, wage constant war against one another.[5] This belligerence is such a constant that some ethnographers consider it a factor in the evolution of cooperative behaviour.

As chimpanzees amply prove, stalking and killing requires a great deal of coordination and cooperation among members of the raiding party. Nor does such division of labour need to be explicitly articulated. On the contrary, the ability to work together in order to wage hostilities appears to be in our primate genes. No wonder that, with Plato in the lead, philosophers theorizing the nature of just and fair society felt obliged to come to grips with our instinct for aggression and the need to contain it. Ironically, then, generations of blueprints for utopia come armed with passages on how to control the dark side of the human ape.

Broadly speaking, the relation between utopia and human nature comes in two flavours. The optimistic variety is represented by Thomas More who affords that a radical change of social governance will bring about a beneficent change in human behaviour. Much as one might wish it were otherwise, More clearly puts the cart ahead of the horse. The Waldenite experimental communities alone show that the biology of the horse cannot be taken out of the equation—quite apart from begging the question of how and why the transition to the perfect society should arise in the first place.

The more cynical (or realistic) view of human nature insists that *it* must be changed before any utopian blueprint can succeed. The question here concerns the nature and the extent of these putative modifications. As *Walden Two* and its real-life spinoffs make clear, efforts to engineer humans into Eloi are destined to fail as long as they fail to come to grips with evolution. It is, of course, evolution that fuels human aggression. But this does not mean that we are condemned by our genetic architecture to violence, murder, and war. Such a 'program' would make no sense since no single behaviour is adaptive across all possible ecological niches.

Propensity to violence, territoriality, and xenophobia are undeniably what is needed in certain environments. In others, however, it may become maladaptive and, by dint of between-group selection, lose ground to more benign behaviours. Take, for example, modern Belgians. In as cold-blooded a display of democide as any, in the span of one generation Belgian colonials exterminated between five and fifteen million (estimates vary) native inhabitants of the Congo Free State. Today, however, they are a model of cooperation and peace, with Brussels the political symbol of the united, non-bellicose Europe.

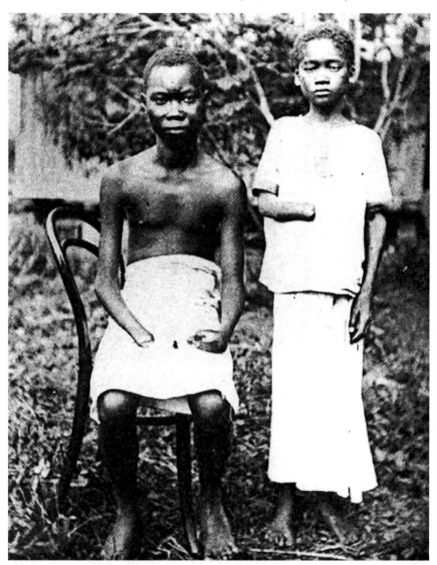

"... In as cold-blooded display of democide as any, in the span of one generation Belgian colonials exterminated between five and fifteen million (estimates vary) native inhabitants of the Congo Free State ..."

Figure 4.1   Congolese children with their hands amputated for failing to meet work quotas (circa 1900).

From the evolutionary standpoint, it is possible to give peace a fighting chance by creating habitats in which it could thrive. But what if we had the technological means to go after aggression directly? What if there was a medical or pharmacological key to lock away human fangs and claws? This, in essence, is the premise behind the experiment in social engineering detailed in *The Thanatos Syndrome*. The project's medical honcho can hardly contain himself when ticking off the benefits to the half-skeptical and half-awed protagonist:

> "What would you say if I gave you a magic wand you could wave over there"—he nods over his shoulder toward Baton Rouge and New Orleans—"and overnight you could reduce crime in the streets by eighty-five percent?"
>
> I wait, knowing there is more.
>
> "Child abuse by eighty-seven percent?"
>
> "You mean you've done it by—"
>
> He waves me off. "We've done it—the numbers will be out next month—but let me finish. Teenage suicide by ninety-five percent. Ninety-five percent, Tom."
>
> "Yes?"
>
> "Wife battering by seventy-three percent."[6]

Yet, even as Percy grants that one day we will have the tools to engineer aggression out of humankind, he realizes that our record of harnessing technology for society's good spells d-i-s-a-s-t-e-r. Advocates of eradicating war and murder may be hard put to see the downside, but any putative de-aggression would afford endless opportunities for making things worse instead of better. For one, whoever eluded the procedure would wield total control over a population of sitting ducks. That alone guarantees that millions would try it. Worse, unless de-aggression was universal and irreversible, any rational individual or government *ought to* try it.

The consequences of such asymmetry are allegorized again in the book of Genesis. While Adam and Eve are unable to do or even conceive of doing harm, the serpent is not, making them easy dupes for his machinations. But suppose that one day de-aggression could be implemented on a global and permanent basis—say, by means of a water-soluble compound released into the world's rivers and oceans. The lifting of the purely fiscal burden that war and aggression put on law enforcement, health care, and the penal and judicial systems would be manna from heaven.

More importantly, we would no longer suffer abused children, victims of rape and domestic violence, shell-shocked or dead soldiers, civilians maimed by weapons of war, victims of murder, tortured prisoners, lynched scapegoats, ethnic cleansing, and democidal mass graves. For a small planet on which a minor war (3,000–30,000 dead), major war (30,000–300,000 dead), massive war (300,000–3,000,000 dead) or mega war (3,000,000–30,000,000 dead and above) on average every fourteen months is a historical constant, this is one supposition not to shrug off too lightly.[7]

My working premise comes from the words of Lazare Ponticelli, France's longest surviving veteran of World War I. In an interview shortly before his death at the age of 110, he summed up the wisdom for the ages in four words: "War is completely stupid." War and its blood kin, democide, are more than stupid: they are horrendous. In the twentieth century alone, they killed as many as two hundred million people, mostly civilians. They laid indiscriminate waste to nations, economies, and cultures. It would seem we should be willing to pay any price to rid ourselves of war and violence. But, given a chance, would we?

THE MORE THINGS CHANGE,
THE MORE THEY STAY THE SAME

> Weimar leads to Auschwitz.
> Walker Percy, in "The Art of Fiction XCVII"

In 1961, at the ripe age of forty-five, Walker Percy began his literary career with a slim existential novel entitled *The Moviegoer.* Edging past Joseph Heller's *Catch 22* to capture the National Book Award, it found a place in the hearts of so many that it has never been out of print. In France, where Percy continues to enjoy high esteem, it has even become part of the national school curricula. Twenty-six years and six books later,

Percy's belletristic career came to an end with *The Thanatos Syndrome*. The last book published before his death in 1990, it easily smashed the popularity of even *The Moviegoer*.[8]

Praised from *The Atlantic Monthly* to the *USA Today*, within two weeks of publication this thinking person's medical thriller climbed the national bestseller lists, becoming a dual main selection of the Book-of-the-Month Club. Not an easy feat for a story that is in equal parts a philosophical fantasy, a detective yarn, and a Southern comedy of manners. In a 1984 interview, asked about *The Moviegoer*, Percy characterized it as "a novel of ideas as well as, I hope, a good novel in its own right".[9] There is no better way to describe *The Thanatos Syndrome* than to say it is a novel of ideas and a good novel in its own right.

The story reintroduces psychiatrist Tom More, protagonist of Percy's 1971 realistic fantasy, *Love in the Ruins*.[10] His namesake is, of course, Thomas More, statesman for all seasons and author of *Utopia*. Asked about the connection, Percy had some warm words to say about his hero:

> My ideal is Thomas More, an English Catholic . . . who wore his faith with grace, merriment, and a certain wryness. Incidentally, I reincarnated him again in my new novel and I'm sorry to say he has fallen upon hard times; he is a far cry from the saint, drinks too much, and watches reruns of M*A*S*H* on TV.[11]

Love in the Ruins left all the critics ready to peg Percy as a contemporary Southern moralist scratching their heads. The plot was set in a futuristic post-Auto Age, with vines sprouting in Manhattan, wolves roaming Cleveland, old political parties defunct, and the entire country glued to stereo-V. Against the backdrop of the American bicentennial, Tom More set out to diagnose the psychic state of the union in the latter days of the second millennium after Christ. With the hilarious if ruinous aid of the Devil himself, he identified the pathologies afflicting the nation as intellectualized alienation and mindless consumerism.

Thanatos picks up the thread of More's life in Louisiana after a two-year stretch in a minimum-security jail for trafficking methamphetamines to truckers. Home from the clink, he begins to notice strange things around him. Odd words, odd behaviours, odd sexual habits, spikes in intelligence combined with loss of verbal aptitude. . . and everyone tail-wagging happy. Much as *The Invasion of the Body Snatchers*, the spooked hero begins to investigate these transformations. In a playful homage, Percy even sneaks in a reference to "a stealing of people's selves, an invasion of body snatchers" (33).

When not busy asking questions about the nature of human existence and human nature, *Thanatos* is a pitch-perfect detective story. Dr Lucy Lipscomb, a young and attractive cousin of More's, plays Della Street to his Perry Mason in their investigation of the etiology of the syndrome. As they struggle to stay under the radar of a sinister conspiracy, the plot dishes out all the ingredients of a first-rate cliffhanger, from the morass of clues and red herrings to the round-the-clock surveillance, run-ins with the police, and the nail-biting expedition to rescue local schoolchildren from a gang of pedophiles.

To their shock, the amateur sleuths tie the syndrome to a rogue experiment in social engineering. Masterminded by Bob Comeaux, chief physician at Fedville clinical complex, and John Van Dorn, scientist *extraordinaire* at the local nuclear facility, the clandestine Blue Boy project diverts heavy sodium from the reactor's coolant system into the water intake of local residents, effecting dramatic changes in behaviour.

One of those is the attrition of people's linguistic faculties. In severe cases it actually retards their communication to the level of five year olds, with lapses into third-person chimp talk ("Mickey like", "Donna want"). Offsetting this verbal regression is a twenty percent increase in general IQ and computational abilities, and an almost photographic retrieval of information. Overnight students discard calculators, local bridge players attain master rankings, and athletes perform at unheard-of levels.[12]

There is also a new type of casualness in sex, a kind of placid, almost simian copulation. But the factor that troubles More the most is a certain loss of 'self'. On the plus side, his patients no longer suffer from depression, rage or guilt. On the other hand, their existentially anxious but, for all that, human agency gives way to a sort of good-natured animal placidity.

But the Blue Boy experimenters do not stop there. Doctoring the resident population with Na24 ions, they effect a dramatic breakthrough in violent crime and other American scourges. Overnight there are no more infants in trash bins, no back-alley abortions, no venereal diseases, no teenage pregnancies, no epidemic spread of AIDS. All this is accomplished by pushing the female menstrual cycle into chimp-like estrus. The cure is radical but the societal gains, as the Blue Boy doctors and scientists point out, are incalculable not merely in fiscal terms but in social cohesion and quality of life.

More than anything else, they effect a staggering—in some aspects almost complete—inhibition of aggression. Bob Comeaux is at his most persuasive when rattling off the benefits for the Louisiana State Prison Farm and its "ten thousand murderers, rapists, armed robbers, society's assholes, who would as soon kill you as spit on you" (194). Incidence of murder, knifing, and homosexual rape drops to zero. Admissions for violent crime are down by two-thirds. Outside in the streets there is no violence, gang warfare or gun-toting machismo. Instead of stalking the 'hoods, young black hoodlums flock to apprentice in trades.

Here and there a discordant note creeps into this symphony of social good. One such is episodes of rogue violence in some of the treated individuals. Another is Comeaux's almost proprietorial pride in the "darkies" who, plied with sodium, happily work the cotton fields of the prison farm like in the good ol' days. Still, the benefits must be very real if even Max Gottlieb— More's old friend from *Love in the Ruins*—joins Blue Boy. The opportunity to cure aggression and violence at a stroke must be irresistible if this kind Jewish doctor overlooks the legacy of the betterment programs of the Stalinists, the Nazis, the Maoists or the Khmer Rouge.

Even though the scientists who administer the treatment do so without the authorization of the FDA, there is no reason to believe that anything would have been different if the feds were on board. One reason, in fact, why Comeaux goes ahead with Blue Boy is his confidence that, when presented with a *fait accompli*, Washington will adopt and expand it. Knowing what we know about federal programs that covertly infected American soldiers with syphilis just to monitor the progress of the disease, his faith in the government seems entirely justified.[13]

"I would like to cure epilepsy, cure mental disturbances, and construct a better world", proclaimed José Delgado, one of America's technical wizards who revolutionized research in neurology in the fifties and the sixties.[14] Giving a short shrift to phenomenology and other 'soft' dimensions of the psyche, Delgado—like Comeaux—advocated engineering American society wholehog. This was to be accomplished using techniques developed with the funding from the Office of Naval Research and the U.S. Air Force. Who wouldn't be skittish at the promise of a shortcut to utopia?

Conspiracies are, after all, not figments of Percy's imagination. Watergate, Irangate, and Iraq-gate have shown that renegade cliques can insinuate themselves into the highest echelons of America's policy-making. Moreover, they can operate for the longest time without detection and, for most of the culprits, with complete impunity. Despite what most people believe, the internet-fuelled information glut plays straight into the hands of political conspirators. It allows them to bury toxic secrets under terabytes of factoids while restricting access to sensitive scientific information.

Naturally, Percy is too complex a novelist to reduce visceral unease about social-engineering to a standoff between the axes of good and evil. Reprehensible as they are, the tactics of the Blue Boy engineers arise from a genuine sense of impending doomsday. Even More is sympathetic to Comeaux's distress at the country rent by plagues of almost biblical proportions. "We're talking about the decay of social fabric. The American social fabric . . . from the destruction of the cities, crime in the streets, demoralization of the underclass, to the collapse of the family" (265).

There are, of course, horrendous statistics to back him up, and the fact that the Fedville technocrats focus on curing symptoms rather than causes only adds to the atmosphere of a crisis. It is true that the last words of the novel—"Well well well"—signal the structure of comedy. After all, even though *The Thanatos Syndrome* deals with such heart-rending issues as covert behavioural engineering and sexual abuse of children, all ends well and without a single loss of life. Retribution is exacted but in a restorative and integrative manner of Menander rather than in an Aeschylean climax of violence.

The good-natured comedy of Southern manners hides, however, a *cri de coeur*. In a legal precedent of *Doe vs Dade*, the Supreme Court in *The Thanatos Syndrome* legalizes the termination of children up to eighteen months who, for genetic or medical reasons, are unfit to function in society. The historical referent for this fictive pedeuthanasia is clear. In the 1973 pro-choice milestone of *Roe vs Wade*, the United States Supreme Court ruled that state laws banning abortion in the first six months of pregnancy violated the 14th Amendment—and were as such unconstitutional.

An orthodox Catholic, Percy accuses American doctors of killing millions of unborn children with the backing of the medical and legislative establishment. Taking cue from More's *Utopia*, however, he plays his own devil's advocate by incarnating his views both in Tom More, a medical scientist, and Father Smith, a Catholic priest. Outwardly antithetical, both embody different aspects of Percy's life as a trained physician and member of the Roman Catholic church. Thus, when Father Smith confronts his alter-ego, Dr. More, the author also confronts himself:

> You are a member of the first generation of doctors in the history of medicine to turn their backs on the oath of Hippocrates and kill millions of useless people, unborn children, born malformed children, for the good of mankind. (127)

Strikingly, this apocalyptic indictment issues from the mouth of a decrepit cleric given to bouts of catatonia and outlandish behaviour. Like Graham Greene's whiskey priest, he is a speaker of words anguished enough to deserve such an anguished preacher. Tortured by what he sees as the devaluation of meaning and especially the meaning of human life, Father Smith removes himself to a remote fire-tower where, like Simeon Stylites, he passes his days looking for signs of fire and of God's grace. A lapsed Catholic on top of being a lapsed priest, he fears he is also a lapsed human being.

In a confession that forms the moral centrepiece of the novel, he owns to adulating the Nazi Germany during a visit in the 1930s. Had he been German and not American, he tells More, he would have likely joined the Hitlerjugen and the SS. Percy himself resided in Germany in 1934, where he experienced the nation's single-minded fervour under the newly elected Chancellor. In a post-publication interview, he plumbed the depths of this self-knowledge. "Does anyone imagine that we are not capable of doing what the Germans did, or what the Russians did—given the proper circumstances?"[15]

Worldwide, eugenetic programs have only too often proven to be pretexts for eliminating society's marginals by means of abortion, sterilization, or 'mercy' killing. But although the most systematic of such campaigns was instituted by the Nazis, the purification of the Aryan stock started on the instigation of the medical and humanitarian elites of the democratic Weimer Republic. Inevitably, the social Alphas arrogated to themselves the right to terminate the Gammas: the retarded, the autistic, the chronically ill, the genetically inferior (and, soon, the politically subversive).

Weimar, indeed, leads to Auschwitz.

Befitting an artist with a medical degree from Columbia and pathological training from Bellevue, Percy referred to his brand of the philosophical *roman* as the diagnostic novel. Not surprisingly, the diagnosis of insanity and its relation to the social norm lies as close to the heart of *The Thanatos Syndrome* as *Cuckoo's Nest*. Just like Kesey, Percy is convinced that some of our neuroses, psychoses, and depressions are more than ailments

"... But although the most systematic of such campaigns was instituted by the Nazis, the purification of the Aryan stock started on the
instigation of the medical and humanitarian elites of the democratic
Weimer Republic. Inevitably, the social Alphas arrogated to themselves the right to terminate the Gammas: the retarded, the autistic,
the chronically ill, the genetically "inferior" (and, soon, the politically subversive). Weimar, indeed, leads to Auschwitz ..."

Figure 4.2   President of the Weimar Republic, Paul Von Hinden-
burg, and the democratically elected Adolf Hitler (1933).

pure and simple. They may be resources for learning from our
inner selves which tell us things of value in these strange and
sometimes pathological ways.

Indeed, it would be impossible to guess which writer said:
"What interests me as a novelist is not the malevolence of
man—so what else is new?—but his looniness".[16] Both invert
the relation between the normal and the abnormal in the manner of Saul Bellow's *Herzog* in which, overcome by existential
absurdity, a lone man acts in accordance with his conscience
only to be branded a fool, if not a disturbed eccentric. The
trope dates back at least to the Elizabethan drama where the

royal fool often plays the role of idiot savant, speaking truths punishable in the mouths of others.

Father Smith, who preaches to his gasping parishioners that pedeuthanasia on even the most humanitarian grounds is murder, utters things no one would for fear of being branded a lunatic. Madness is, of course, a convenient label for any unorthodoxy—even as one person's madness is another's gospel truth.

Social hypocrisy frequently impedes the calculation of the true costs of maintaining lives that, through no fault of their own, contribute nothing to society: the vegetative, the comatose, the mentally ill. No politician has the guts to acknowledge that, crippled by the expenses of looking after them, the state may be unable to aid others in need: the poor, the aged, the senile, the handicapped, the unemployed, the single parents. Which lives are more equal in this unforgiving zero-sum calculus? Which of them should be funded and which neglected?

The convicted criminal Tom More and the semi-lunatic Father Smith are typical Percy creations, meant to provoke questions about who really is insane or socially unfit. Do all people disposed of in mental asylums, or else by painless and humane euthanasia, really deserve to be labelled as abnormal? Aren't they perhaps, as the psychiatrist R.D. Laing wondered in *The Divided Self*, blessed with a vision so penetrating that it blinds the rest of us to its sense? Aren't the truly socially unfit those who would engineer the mentally unquick and the genetically malformed out of society?

In one of its greatest ironies, the same modern age that turned the sanctity of life into a political (and thus secular) sacrament also killed more people than in the entire history of the world combined. If only for this reason, questions about social engineering are as much political as scientific. Science and technology have, after all, put the means of extermination of human life on earth in the hands of a few dozen politicians and generals. Without science and technology, the outreach of these and other would-be reformers would be perforce limited to the people with whom they come in direct contact.

Consider the popular variety of voluntary indoctrination: psychotherapy. Patients enter psychiatric counselling in the hope of being behaviourally modified out of undesirable personality traits. However, given the finitude of resources, a psychiatrist could never help more than a handful of patients. But a miracle waits in the wings. Armed with fruits of pharmaceutical science, he can change behaviours on a greater scale than one-on-one consultation ever would. Peddling uppers to truck drivers who fall asleep at the wheel, Tom Moore amplifies his outreach a thousandfold.

If the task of a psychotherapist is to strike a healing chord with a patient, science is the amplifier that, like in a Band Aid concert, can spread that chord for the benefit of millions. Like every amplifier, however, it can also distort it beyond recognition. All power corrupts and, insofar as science and technology bestow power, they corrupt. Give him a source of heavy sodium and a water delivery system, and watch a eutopian engineer morph into a remorseless techno-wizard. Tom More himself is jailed for doing out of the best intentions what he accuses the Blue Boys of doing—illegally doping people.

Bob Comeaux, who turns a hundred thousand residents of Louisiana into unwitting guinea pigs (or rather, laboratory chimps), is only a fictional character. But he is a professional twin of that other über-physician and psychiatrist, Ewen Cameron. The resemblance is all the more conspicuous in that more than one of Cameron's associates insisted that he truly cared about the welfare of his patients, even as he focused exclusively on their symptoms. A former staff psychologist even noted: "He abhorred the waste of human potential", even as he concluded: "For him, the end justified the means".[17]

Our civilization has chased the fox of science too deep into the foxhole to even think of going back. What is alarming, however, is not our dependence on science but our lack of scientific knowledge which all too often manifests itself in its outright dismissal or, worse, unhealthy reverence. This serves straight into the hands of political and social engineers enamoured of all-or-nothing fixes precisely in contexts that beg for nuance and vision. God knows what's going to happen if, like Comeaux, one day we discover a fix for that part of our nature responsible for violence, aggression, and war.

Natural selection is a matter of inclusive fitness—inclusive of the genetic material a given individual shares with kin—and group selection. Although not all human actions directly enhance reproduction or survival, from the standpoint of individual gene-carriers the ultimate good is just that: the propagation of genes. To the extent this clashes with the good (self-interest) of others, it often clashes with our willingness to accept their welfare as equal to our own. The history of the world, right up to today's gory headlines, leaves no doubt about *that*.[18]

But what if one day we come up with a technology to impose a worldwide *pax humana*? Biological imperatives are not, after all, life sentences without parole. More than any other species we are capable of giving nature the slip. Our sexual hunger, to take one example, is more unquenchable than that of most animals, yet most of us manage to maintain committed relationships. True, there is no pill yet to induce monogamy. But just like it's worth contemplating what would happen if there *was* one, it is worth contemplating a scenario where the faucet of aggression could be turned off—just like that.

PEACE OF MIND OR PIECE OF MIND?

> Literature discovers and knows and tells, tells the reader how things are, how we are, in a way that the reader can confirm with as much certitude as a scientist taking a pointer-reading.
>
> Walker Percy, "The State of the Novel:
> Dying Art or New Science?"

The difference between us and the Spartans who tossed their malformed or sickly infants over the cliff is not human nature but rather the technology at our command. Even though attempts to construct a better society are as ancient as recorded history, it was the scientific and particularly medical innovations of the Enlightenment that laid the foundations for modern social engineering. Equipped with the technological armoury of the industrial revolution, and fortified by the fledgling science of psychology and then sociology, planners set forth to engineer happier nations and states.[19]

Eminent among them was the drafter of the Declaration of Independence, Thomas Jefferson, who—with Franklin's approval—included pursuit of happiness in the set of fundamental human rights. On any count, it was a startling move. Unlike liberty and equality, happiness is a bird of a very different feather inasmuch as it comes with the guarantee of failure. Liberty can be mandated and, if need be, won in battle. Equality can be mandated and, if need be, enforced. But mandated happiness, if such a thing even makes sense, reeks of totalitarian control. One can be born equal and free, if you will, but no one is born happy.[20]

If social engineering is a planned intervention in society's institutions to improve people's lives—or at least to improve the conditions for the improvement—the right to pursue happiness has some odd corollaries. If happiness is a carrot dangled in front of citizens' noses as they pull society's collective cart, those who ever get to it should stop pulling their weight. Less metaphorically, one person's happiness can make others unhappy. Dick Cheney's or David Koresh's utopia is not mine, not to mention that short-term personal gratification rarely aggregates into lasting social welfare.

Moreover, as research on happiness, economics, and public policy shows, personal satisfaction is hardly even "connected to what most people would deem moral".[21] Jefferson's project of aligning personal happiness with social good will never get off the ground unless it acknowledges that mapping individual utilities onto social welfare requires coming to grips with our evolved behavioural predispositions—our nature.

As Skinner knew, aversive control is popular with inexperienced enforcers because its results are immediate. At the same time, it is highly ineffective unless permanently in place. More effective and stable is nonaversive control which does not incite resistance by the simple expedient of deferring ill consequences into the future. Nonaversive techniques are also superior from the controller's point of view since they make it hard to devise counter-strategies. This is especially so when power is depersonalized or dispersed, making it unclear who the controlee should escape from or counterattack.

There is no reason why new techniques of control should resemble the old. Aldous Huxley pointed out as much in his 1946 foreword to *Brave New World*:

> Government by clubs and firing squads, by artificial fam-ine, mass imprisonment and mass deportation, is not merely inhumane (nobody cares much about that nowadays); it is demonstrably inefficient—and in an age of advanced tech-nology, inefficiency is the sin against the Holy Ghost. A really efficient totalitarian state would be one in which the all-powerful executive of political bosses and their army of managers control a population of slaves who do not have to be coerced, because they love their servitude. To make them love it is the task assigned, in present-day totalitarian states, to ministries of propaganda, newspaper editors and school-teachers.

Propaganda and education are effective because, as de Tocqueville noted, they facilitate the internalization of the established social ethos.[22] So is and so does normative leg-islation which forges social obedience under the rule of law. Of course, in the case of resistance or open dissidence, social order can also be maintained by means of para/mili-tary coercion. Finally, social compliance can be enforced by means of a direct somatic intervention into citizen's minds, sang by Roger Waters on *The Dark Side of the Moon*: "you raise the blade, you make the change, you rearrange me till I'm sane".

These four techniques of social control split into two groups: voluntary, which relies on indirect internal conditioning, and involuntary, which relies on external force or direct control of the subject. Propaganda, education, and other species of indoctrination effect compliance indirectly, and are thus non-coercive. So is normative legislation—the breach of which, however, is enforced by fine or imprisonment, bringing it in line with para/military control. At the other end of the spec-trum lies somatic engineering: mind control.

Starting from the Hobbesian premise, where it is human nature that stands in the way of utopia, governments routinely induce compliance in populations. Democracies typically resort to non-coercive propaganda which makes it easier to deflect blame onto dissidents. If McMurphy did not foment revolt by exercising the constitutional right to vote, the patients would get their TV privileges back. If the Palestinians acquiesced to the West Bank settlements, their lives could return to 'normal'. The Socialist Party of America had only itself to blame for being the target of Wilson's Sedition Act—the very same that legalized the party's persecution.

This is not to say that acceptance of any social authority is automatic. Max Weber himself was adamant on this point: "That subjection to military discipline is formally 'involuntary' while that to the discipline of the factory is voluntary does not alter the fact that the latter is also a case of subjection to *authority*" (213). This is a crucial point: one must not regard voluntary and involuntary control as necessarily separate from each other.

As a matter of fact, Percy's thought experiment is brilliant precisely because it deliberately blurs the line between the external and internal modes of control. In his scenario, Louisiana residents have no inkling of what is being done to them, or even that anything is. They just 'spontaneously' stop committing crimes, have more sex, and talk in chimp syntax. None are aware that they are being experimented on, and none would care even if they were told they were.

In *The Thanatos Syndrome* the technology that engineers people's behaviour works by engineering their psyches. In Orwell's *1984* external and internal control are equally intertwined. When Winston Smith is released at the end of the novel, it is not because he bamboozled the regime into believing he loves Big Brother but because he *really* loves him. Under involuntary (coercive) duress, Smith internalizes the totalitarian ideology, thereby also internalizing the external mode of control.

And yet the distinction between the external and internal modes of social control is crucial. The notion of behaviour control via invasive techniques may be anathema to a population disposed to hand over its constitutional rights to controls applied externally. No matter how undemocratic, the anti-terrorist platform of the Bush II's administration put the government outside the somatic divide. For most Americans this sufficed to sustain an illusion of freedom from thought police. Few appreciated what Percy models by means of *The Thanatos Syndrome*, namely that external and internal techniques need not be categorically distinct.

This is not to equate George W. Bush's "war on war" with Orwell's vision of totalitarian compliance, or with Percy's scenario of societal de-aggression. But deep inhibitors—not least the right to liberty engraved in the U.S. Constitution—would need to be overcome before any form of somatic engineering could become socially acceptable. I will defer to the next section the question of whether mass-compliance technology of de-aggression could be accepted by the public and the government. For now, I want to assess the feasibility of a somatic top-down control system.

None of the technologies described below should be taken to imply that they are in any way inevitable or even desirable. My goal is merely to dispel the default assumption that it can't happen here. After all, corrective interventions into our heads have been taking place for thousands of years, although on a scale limited heretofore by our primitive technology. Trepanning has been practiced in almost every culture we know, from the ancient Egyptians throughout the middle ages, as depicted from Hieronymus Bosch's *The Cure of Folly* to Hieronymus von Braunschweig's *Handywarke of Surgeri*.

In 1943 Tennessee Williams's sister Rose underwent a lobotomy that, as his journals reveal, left him racked with guilt. With computing and neurological equipment getting more sophisticated, however, surgical intrusion soon gave way to subtler techniques. In 1975 the first mind-reading system became operational at Stanford Research Institute. It relied on the discovery that EEGs show distinctive patterns that correlate with individual words, no matter if the words are vocalized or merely thought. In short, the Stanford system recognized words by monitoring a person's thoughts. Unvoiced, silent thoughts.[23]

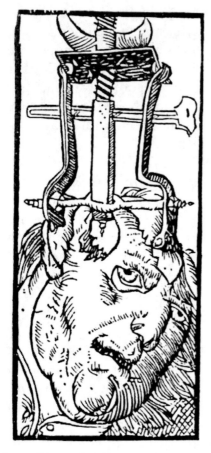

". . . Corrective interventions into our heads have been taking place for thousands of years, although on a scale limited heretofore by our primitive technology. Trepanning has been practiced in almost every culture we know, from the ancient Egyptians throughout the middle ages, as depicted from Hieronymus Bosch's *The Cure of Folly* to Hieronymus von Braunschweig's *Handywarke of Surgeri . . .*"

Figure 4.3   Engraving of a trepanation by Peter Treveris in Hieronymus von Braunschweig's medical treatise *Handywarke of surgery* (1525).

The key factor here is the gradual collapse of barriers between the brain and the increasingly potent technology. Organic or inorganic, new techniques are clearly pointing to—rudimentary at present—integration of human and nonhuman systems. This will likely take the form of chip implants, especially when issues of miniaturization, capacity, durability, and migration are resolved.[24] In the United States subcutaneously dog-tagged infantry, parolees from the penitentiary system, amnesiacs, paraplegics and quadriplegics, prostate-cancer suspects, and other chronic patients are the current beneficiaries of this technology.

The futuristic Veri-Chip is already in mass-production. Embedded under the skin, no bigger than a grain of rice, this scannable device from Applied Digital is not yet an active chip with enough switch-gates to control the human brain, but the first step in this direction has already been taken. Brain prostheses in the form of a chip hypothalamus, tested in California, are even more to the point. These devices are still far from controlling the complex theatre of emotions enacted in the nucleus of the brain. Yet they are already capable to some degree of controlling functions such as mood, memory, and awareness.[25]

The difference is crucial for, whereas previous devices, such as cochlear implants, only stimulated brain activity, the chips currently tested in primates—the last stage before moving on to humans—actually replace brain tissue. For the first time, central brain regions dealing with cognitive functions, such as learning or speech, run on circuitry. The system reads neural signals in the brain, processes them, and conveys the output to brain tissue in another area. "It proves you can take out a piece of a central brain region", sums up the project's leading scientist, "replace it with a chip, and get it to operate as it did before".[26]

Researchers from Cyberkinetics Inc. are implanting chips in the skulls of paralyzed patients. These tiny brain-embedded computers detect neural activity which occurs when people think about moving a limb. Quite simply, the chips "read their thoughts."[27] BrainGate devices embedded in patients' brains detect relevant intentions, send these to a computer to decipher and thereby allow the paralyzed humans to think their TVs on and off, as well as adjust channels and volume. Similar brain-machine interfaces enable monkeys (soon to be tested on humans) to think their paralyzed limbs to move.

In each case scientists are able to intercept and interpret brain signals and convert them into electrical impulses that subsequently control muscles. Mind-reading becomes even more literal when it comes to the hippocampus, the part of the brain central to memory formation and long-term storage. Today it is possible to see in real time how images, for example, are stored and recalled in the brain. The principle is simple. Neurons (place-cells) in the hippocampus activate when you move around. This allows controllers to detect what your brain is up to by reading your thoughts off the scanning equipment.

This is possible because, as it turns out, brain patterns activated in a bathroom are different from those in a concert hall, jail cell, church, and so on. By monitoring brain activity—say, by means of a chip implant—scientists can tell where you are *independent of whether you want them to know.* More advanced studies have broken the thought 'content' barrier in even more spectacular ways. At the Max Planck Institute for Human Cognitive and Brain Sciences in Germany even abstract concepts, such as the feudal connotations of a medieval castle, can now be distinguished with an impressive three-quarter success rate.[28]

In the context, the researchers' collective assurance that reading people's most intimate thoughts is still a long way off is highly significant.[29] Never mind the inexactness of the time frame. Whether it takes a decade or a century, their implicit confidence that it is bound to happen is the most compelling reason to re-examine our complacent assumption that it can't happen here. Can minds be forced to divulge secrets? Can thoughts be monitored—literally read off a monitor? The futuristic aura that surrounds such questions is really a red herring insofar as the answer is an unequivocal 'Yes'.

The future is already here. It may seem like risible fiction to claim that, working without human supervision, today's machines monitor and read people's thoughts as well as make life-or-death decisions in America's courts of law. But it isn't. Enter brain fingerprinting, a forensic technique that matches crime scene evidence with the evidence stored in the suspect's brain. Conventional fingerprinting works by matching fingerprints. DNA 'fingerprinting' matches biological samples with the DNA of the suspect. Analogously, the new technique detects recognition of crime-scene images as only the perpetrator could see.

Brain fingerprinting is direct but non-invasive. It works by detecting the electrophysiological effects of information processing in the brain, measured from the scalp with multifaceted

USING BRAIN WAVES TO DETECT GUILT

Brain fingerprinting uses brain waves to test memory. A crime suspect is given words or images in a context that would be known only to police or the person who committed the crime.

HOW IT WORKS
A suspect is tested by looking at three kinds of information represented by different colored lines:

— **Red:** Information the suspect is expected to know.
— **Green:** Information not known to suspect.
— **Blue:** Information of the crime that only perpetrator would know.

NOT GUILTY	**GUILTY**
Because the blue and green lines closely correlate, suspect does not have critical knowledge of the crime.	Because the blue and red lines closely correlate, suspect has critical knowledge of the crime.

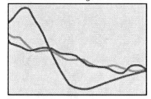 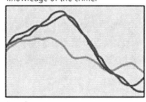

For more information see: www.brainwavescience.com.

SEATTLE POST-INTELLIGENCER

". . . Brain fingerprinting is direct but non-invasive. It works by detecting the electrophysiological effects of information processing in the brain, measured from the scalp with multifaceted electroencephalographic response analysis (MERA). Involuntary recognition triggers neurological patterns detectable by the computer, which can then confirm that the subject did or did not witness the murder scene as only the killer could have. And confirm is does, to date with *one hundred percent accuracy*—so much so that it trumps eyewitness testimony in courts of law . . ."

Figure 4.4   Brain-fingerprinting test on serial killer James B. Grinder which established his guilt and sent him to jail for life / Brief primer on the principle of taking "latents" off the brain.

electroencephalographic response analysis (MERA). Involuntary recognition triggers neurological patterns detectable by the computer, which can then confirm that the subject did or did not witness the murder scene as only the killer could have. And confirm is does, to date with *one hundred percent accuracy*—so much so that it trumps eyewitness testimony in courts of law.

Brain fingerprinting hinges on brain information triggered by specific stimuli. A specific electrical brain-wave response is emitted by the brain within a fraction of a second when an individual recognizes and processes a stimulus that is significant or noteworthy. Crucially, the process is not affected by the mental disposition or emotional state of the tested person and, as such, is not open to manipulation. The system is, in other words, unerringly selective, picking out only the information sought by the controller from the free-flowing beehive of cerebral activity.

Equally to the point, the entire system is under complete computer control. Input of the visual stimuli, recording of electrical brain activity, the mathematical algorithm that compares the responses to the stimuli and produces a determination of 'information present' or 'information absent', the statistical confidence level for this determination—all are taken out of controllers' hands. At no time are human biases permitted to affect the results. Let me spell this out. Mind-reading systems that solve crimes and exonerate death-row inmates, and thus indirectly make life or death decisions, operate today legally and without human input.

More in line with Percy's thought experiment is the treatment for dystonia, a condition that causes painful and disabling muscles contractions and, as a result, abnormal movements or postures. In severe cases, the only remedy is deep brain stimulation by means of surgically implanted electrodes. Working like a cardiac pacemaker, the implants deliver electrical pulses to the affected areas of the brain to block the disabling signals. Here, mind control is achieved by blocking out select neural impulses. Will future research allow such selectivity as to block out aggression?

Until recently implants have been too large to use in very young children, but no longer. Miniaturization has gone into nano-dimensions, rubbing shoulders with research into molecular biology where DNA is not merely the carrier, but the processor of information. Using complex biochemistry, scientists can now 'write' logic programs in evolution's code in a way analogous to computer programming.

DNA has been previously tapped for its computing abilities, albeit only for simple numerical operations. In contrast, the latest systems running on deoxyribonucleic acid—as opposed to silicon circuitry—are capable of solving knotty problems in logic. Using protein molecules to represent facts and rules of propositional logic, researchers pose questions and receive correct answers. Fed a molecular rule of a classic syllogism ('all men are mortal') and a molecular fact ('Socrates is a man'), the DNA computer answers the question 'Is Socrates mortal?' in the affirmative.

But even this is just *hors d'oeuvre*. These days the device tackles convoluted queries involving multiple rules and facts and solves all with flying colours. Next in line? "Programmable autonomous computing devices that can operate in a biological environment".[30] Translated into plain English: nano-computers inside a cell.

Percy's idea of sedating the neocortex with heavy sodium is sheer fantasy. But eerily enough, even today there exist techniques that are remarkably similar. Oliver Sacks, researcher, clinician, and model for the hero of *Awakenings*, is not anyone's idea of a fantasy monger. Yet, as he documents, transcranial magnetic stimulation (TMS) allows a brief inhibition of physiological functions in sundry regions of the brain. Zap the brain with a magnet and the result is an improvement in algebraic (computing), graphic (drawing), and verbal (proofreading) skills.[31]

Emotions, too, can be manipulated using, for a change, subliminal carrier technologies. The Silent Sound Spread Spectrum (S-quad or squad) is one method gradually emerging from the shadow of military secrecy. With the aid of teraflop supercomputers, it is now apparently possible not only to analyze EEG patterns of various human emotions but to replicate them—in other people. Hit a button and, presto: now you feel it, now you don't. Seemingly at will, the controllers can use emotion signature clusters to "silently induce and change the emotional state in a human being".[32]

The button-hitters may be aided by a neurological mechanism we share with our closest primate relatives. Emotional contagion is a process whereby the emotional state of one individual can induce a parallel state in others. Such 'herd instinct' is an important component in propagating emotions because emotional contagion is evolutionarily adaptive. It is easy to understand why. When you're potential prey, it helps to flee first and ask questions later. This is precisely why, when one animal gets spooked, mass panic can sometimes spread like brushfire.[33]

Here, then, is a recipe to make a Pentagon or a Kremlin general salivate. Find a raging, berserk, homicidal individual. Record his emotion signature pattern. Then use the squad carrier frequencies to induce the same state in your soldiers. Ironically, the technology is as frightful as promising for, if violence and aggression are ever to be relegated to history books, identification of neural signatures associated with aggression may be a necessary step to develop an effective inhibitor. More likely, of course, given the distinctive DARPA signature on the project, the military will study it with a view to brainwashing soldiers into monomaniacal aggressors.

This is but one reason why most of us would squirm about letting anyone go inside our heads and start flipping neuronal switches. Conversely, the very notion of tweaking aspects of personal identity such as mood, memory, and cognition may be too repugnant for many to accept the emergent technologies. Or would it? Fear and repugnance were also widely predicted to keep people away from heart surgery which, the alarmists said, would diminish the integrity and personhood of the patient. Nothing like that has come to pass, and it is at least conceivable that it may be no different with brain implants, mood changers, and personality-modifying chips.

There is nothing necessary, either, about requiring consent for a somatic procedure from the concerned citizens. Individuals deemed incapable of making decisions for themselves have routinely been subjected to medical interventions by society. In a less autocratic scenario, the build-up towards direct control of aggression could be so imperceptible, so paved for by education and propaganda, that it could happen without anyone realizing what is at stake. Pilot project could be so beneficial—or made to appear so by, say, Big Pharma PR departments—and so free of side-effects that any holdovers would appear to be lunatics.

Finally, the entire program of de-aggressing (or hyper-aggressing) a target population could be implemented surreptitiously. Just like in Percy's Blue Boy, ambitious social engineers could simply place a population before a *fait accompli*. This is assuming that the affected citizenry would even know that they have been rewired. Mind control past a certain level of sophistication would almost certainly permit control of the subjects' awareness of whether they are controlled. Like the Manchurian candidate, you could be brainwashed into believing that you have not been brainwashed at all.

After all, how would you know if you didn't know?

CAUGHT BETWEEN THE DEVIL AND HIS ADVOCATE

> Then be the devil's advocate. Attack us from your own experience. Name one thing wrong we're doing.
>
> Walker Percy, *The Thanatos Syndrome*

When the Blue Boy social engineers defend their draconian measures, aggression and violence top their list of justifications. America is inundated by a crime wave so unstoppable, remonstrates the chief scientist, that "We can't go out in our own streets" (218). Given that the suppression of violence is the lynchpin of Percy's thought experiment, it is time to consider a range of responses to a technology that curbs or even eradicates aggression. Rather than tying myself down to a specific scenario, however, I want to extrapolate a general set of precepts that will remain valid irrespective of the actual methods of reaching the Grail.

My premise is that the technology capable of blocking aggressive response in human beings (primates? mammals? chordates?) will become available at some point in the future. What then? With mind-reading and mind-controlling systems in the wings, and with more questions than answers about the consequent hazards, would we elect to rid ourselves of aggression and violence should the opportunity arise? Would we rush into adopting it regardless? Should we? And if so, under what conditions?

Leapfrogging technological specifics in order to focus on social-engineering constants, here are some preliminary answers. In what follows I use a term 'betrization' to denote any, invasive or non-invasive, procedure capable of disabling violence and aggression by virtue of modifying our neural 'hardware'. The term, coined by Stanislaw Lem in *Return From the Stars*, is doubly apposite. First of all, like in *The Thanatos Syndrome* or in Ira Levin's *This Perfect Day*, Lem's scenario is premised on a universal de-aggression accomplished by means of a medical procedure. Second, the term connotes the eutopian goal of engineering a better society.[34]

What arguments, then, could a devil's advocate mount against betrization, and what could the advocate afford in the way of a reply?

Devil's Advocate: Betrization creates the ultimate shooting gallery, turning humanity into so many clay pigeons for those who could evade the procedure.

Advocate: This is the crux of the matter. "Why don't you use some?" (196), asks Tom More of Bob Comeaux, who misses no opportunity to extol the virtues of ingesting heavy sodium. It turns out that Comeaux did use the treatment on his psychiatric patients and even on his closest family—but, tellingly, never on himself. And for a very good reason. By submitting to the treatment, the controller not only loses all power but automatically becomes vulnerable to whoever refuses to follow suit. In Anthony Burgess's *A Clockwork Orange*, no sooner is the youth-gang leader conditioned into defenceless non-aggression than he becomes savagely victimized by his unbetrizated former friends. For the same reason, the urge to beat the real-life procedure would be irresistible. Anyone who eluded the peacemaker or developed an effective antidote would rule the Earth.

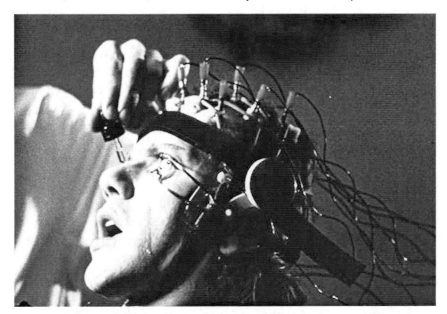

"... In Anthony Burgess's *A Clockwork Orange,* no sooner is the youth-gang leader conditioned into defenceless non-aggression than he becomes savagely victimized by his "unbetrizated" former friends . . ."

Figure 4.5   Direct and invasive: in the hot seat in Kubrick's 1971 Oscar-nominated film.

In Walden Two and then in Beyond Freedom and Dignity Skinner did not foresee further need for safeguards than the expedient of making the controller a member of the group he controls. Other Skinnerians were far from so sanguine. Roger Ulrich's ruminations in "Some Moral and Ethical Implications of Behavior Modification" are particularly pertinent. "Years back I attended a conference at Stockton College in New Jersey where we discussed aggression. Ken Moyer was describing some of the recent research that used brain stimulation and lesions to control aggression, along the lines suggested by the work of Heath, Delgado, and others. During the course of his talk, I wondered to what extent the people who implant electrodes in the brains of others would be interested in undergoing the operation themselves" (44).

Thomas More might have argued that a world advanced enough to undertake betrization would be one that has moved beyond a knee-jerk quest for supremacy. More likely, a civilization advanced enough to develop the technology would also have the foresight to ensure that no one could crook the wheel. Like a Cold War doomsday machine, the implementation of de-aggression would have to be taken completely out of human hands to safeguard every individual and government from a real or manufactured crisis that could be used to override the pacifist effects. Put differently, no sane government or person should embrace the technology unless it came with an ironclad guarantee of being instituted simultaneously and irreversibly worldwide.

Clearly, to have any chance of success, anyone wishing to persuade others of the benefits of betrization would have to be ready to undergo the procedure. Of course, he and anyone else might still try to beat the system, hence the sole effective safeguard of making the procedure work would be to make de-aggression inescapable. In practice, this would mean making it effective on a planetary scale—not forgetting astronauts, submariners, explorers working like Calvin Cohn on submersibles, people on respirators (in the case of airborne agent), and so forth.

Devil's Advocate: Even if implemented successfully, betrization could never work since everyone would immediately start looking for an antidote, even if only out of fear that everyone else was.

Advocate: Herein lies the second technological Grail. De-aggression would have to be made not only inescapable but irreversible—and not only at the time of implementation, but for ever. If this seems like an insuperable condition, there may be a way around it. Once in place, betrization might be able to bootstrap nonaggression into perpetuity given that one would first have to become unbetrized to want to be unbetrized and aggress others.

The really interesting scenario is if the technology is developed and controlled by a small group of people: a single state or even a lone research group. Would they be morally justified in implementing it on their own cognizance, without consulting the rest of the world? Would they opt to surreptitiously de-aggress only their foes, or would they proceed to save us from ourselves, so that, awakening one morning, we would find war and murder an obscene relic preserved only in daily papers, newsreels and history books? In *Walden* Two, in a rare poignant moment, Frazier confronts Castle with this very question. "Suppose you suddenly found it possible to control the behavior of men as you wished. What would you do?" (240). Well, what would *you* do?

Devil's Advocate: Betrization strips humanity of an innate part of its evolutionary heritage, rendering it at best incomplete and at worst deficient.

Advocate: The same evolutionary heritage gave us teeth which, without a moment's thought, we subject to medical intervention (extractions, fillings, braces, and so on). We have already prolonged the average span of human life to more than twice what it used to be in the hunter-gatherer ecosystem. We have reversed clinical death, separated Siamese twins, decoupled sex from procreation, performed caesarean births, cured certain forms of epilepsy using electrode implants, allowed infertile couples to have children—all of which, while beneficial and widely accepted, are no less 'unnatural' than betrization. Generally speaking, it seems that we are—and ought to be—willing to improve on nature as long as the results are beneficent. So much for the incompleteness thesis. Although the deficiency argument is addressed below, it may be worth noting that abusive spouses or stalkers 'de-aggressed' by a restraining order are not deficient because of the court's intervention (which is no more than a response to the underlying cause) but because of the underlying cause, i.e., their unacceptable threat of aggression.

Devil's Advocate: Betrization might be the first step down the slippery slope of gradually improving humanity until it bears no semblance to what we are today.

Advocate: The australopithecine bore no semblance to what we are today yet no one could argue that the change was not for the better—quite literally since *Australopithecus afarensis* could not argue, period. In reality this argument is about endorsing an invasion of biotechnology into the human body and, as such, has been answered above.

Devil's Advocate: Betrization makes us less human. As Tom More and Father Smith might have put it, in psychological terms it robs us of 'self' and in theological terms of soul.

Advocate: American plantation slaves—to take only one example—taken by force and subjugated by violence, would see this self-serving appeal to human self or soul in a very different light. Furthermore, our conception of what is human, even as reflected in our conception of human rights, differs dramatically from century to century and from society to society. Denying the power to aggress, to kill and maim, betrization makes us and our souls not less but more human. It also steers us from force towards peaceful means of conflict resolution in all aspects of our lives, from territorial disputes to armaments negotiations to marital quarrels.

Devil's Advocate: By taking aggression out of the gamut of human responses, betrization makes life less colourful and perhaps even devalues the significance of emotional response.

Advocate: With the elimination of the menace of physical harm, emotions become not less but more central. Betrization frees a range of emotions normally controlled by fear, among them a feeling of relief from violence or reprisal, safety in strange company or alien environment, empowerment to stand up to injustice (which, significantly, de-aggression would not cure), or even the luxury of undergoing such a paradigmatically violent emotion as anger. Already Aristotle questioned the connection between anger and cognate emotions and physical violence in "On Anger." It could well be that humanity cured of aggression could enjoy getting emotional over things, only this time without destructive consequences.

Devil's Advocate: As Malamud might have put it, betrization usurps the divine prerogative of, in effect, creating a new species.

Advocate: The historical roots of this response can be traced to the Judeo-Christian world view according to which humans beings were created by a transcendent but personal God in his image. Because this act is said to have directly imbued human life with value, anything that challenges the parameters of that life becomes suspect or even immoral. Yet this is like trying to close the stable doors after the horses have escaped. In countless ways we've been playing God since time immemorial. The list of our apparent usurpations is endless, from the headline-grabbers like cloning, abortion, or euthanasia (all decried for their godlike hubris), to the less contentious inoculations, fertility treatments, and organ transplants, most of which are legal and widely accepted. In principle de-aggression is no different from surgical brain lesions to treat epilepsy, medicating serotonin levels during depression, or immunization campaigns against polio or smallpox. Even though not everyone is at (equal) risk from disease, vaccinations are administered to all anyway as a preventive measure.

Devil's Advocate: Betrization robs us of freedom by taking choice out of our hands.

Advocate: All that betrization takes away is our licence to kill. In general, our freedoms are checked in a myriad ways considered beneficent by society. We are asked to refrain from violent or otherwise antisocial behaviour, to attend school up to a certain age, to abide by laws legislated by politicians, to do jury duty, and so forth. Under the state motto of Live Free or Die, New

Hampshire residents are neither free to aggress and kill, nor inclined to scrap the laws that take these freedoms away. Freedom is not an absolute goal but rather a means to a good life, valued to the extent that it doesn't harm others. If anything, betrization *increases* our range of freedom by giving us the freedom to live without fear. In a broader sense, it is unlikely that any form of de-aggression could eradicate our physical and even metaphysical freedom since, both as individuals and as a societal aggregate, we are computationally too intractable to ever become predictable to ourselves.[35]

Devil's Advocate: Betrization robs humanity of goodness, inasmuch as you need the bad to appreciate the good. An existentialist like Tom More might even argue that it is the act of choosing that is of value, not being good itself.

Advocate: Bloodshed and pain are not necessary to appreciate life without bloodshed and pain, just as I don't need my eyes plucked out to appreciate the beauty of colours. In most cases a choice between lesser or greater good suffices to appreciate the comparative value of goodness. In general, our innate capacity for counterfactual thinking, hypothetical reasoning, and fiction-making enables us to appreciate the relative value of sundry acts and states.[36] It must be reiterated that any form of behavioural control that would dam aggression would not be a panacea for social ills such as unemployment, mendacity, racism, industrial disputes, moral indifference—or for mishaps that have no basis in hostility, such as accidents, personal failures, group or romantic rejection, and others. In any case, the bloodshed and pain in the world around us resulting from too many people choosing not to practice goodness casts doubt on this 'no-good-without-the-bad' deontology.

Devil's Advocate: Betrization is tantamount to eugenics, a practice perennially abused along racial, ethnic, or nationalistic lines by would-be reformers of humanity, typically in the name of progressivist and humanitarian ideals.

Advocate: This is true. Karl Binding and Alfred Hoche's *The Release of the Destruction of Life Devoid of Value (Life Unworthy of Life)* provided a classic defense of a massive program of mercy killings under one of Europe's leading democratic republics. Alternating juridical arguments with medical cost-benefit analyses, it recommended painless termination of incurable cases against their will. Closer to home, American values and principles have on occasion been every inch as totalitarian and anti-libertarian. In the twentieth century, forced sterilization programs were carried out in the land of the free in order to improve the purity of the American stock. Far from decried, they were supported across the political spectrum, from Charles A. Lindbergh on the right to the political Left who also succumbed to the allure of cleansing the nation's genetic pool. Jack London was a fervent Socialist agitating for social equality and an equally fervent cultist of Nietzsche's superman.

Yet eugenic principles need not be condemned en masse. "Who's going to argue about knocking back crime, suicide, AIDS, and improving your sex life— any more than you'd argue about knocking back dental caries by putting fluoride in the water" (217), points out the chief scientist behind the Blue Boy project. Vitamin and mineral supplements, nutritional regimens, or fluoridation of toothpaste are only some ways in which we medicate entire populations hoping for positive results. Merely because any technology can be misused is no reason to reject it out of hand. X-rays can be deadly, yet are employed to save lives.

In his unpublished Second Book, Hitler envisaged for Deutschland the necessity "to raise the value of its people in racial terms and to bring them into the state-form most appropriate for that purpose".[37] The association most people still make when thinking of social engineering is with social Darwinism, eugenics, and the so-called behavioural genetics which prospects for differences between racial and ethnic groups (e.g., differences in intelligence). Not for nothing did Hitler approvingly cite America's support of eugenics in his early stump speeches. Be that as it may, virtually all perversions of eugenetic ideals—be they the Nazi Reich's or the sterilizations performed in North America or in Asia—hark directly to their selective nature. By default, universal de-aggression would be immune to this objection.

Devil's Advocate: However unlikely the event, betrization puts us at the mercy of any nonterrestrial civilization wishing to take advantage of our inability to defend ourselves.

Advocate: There is no logical argument to refute this objection. For reasons detailed above, de-aggression would have to be global and irreversible. No matter how fancy the intellectual footwork, the bottom line is that by pacifying the Earth we would be playing the odds with cosmic invasions. All the same, there are solid scientific grounds for assigning a negligible probability to the latter. Those stretch from the, at best, extremely low psychozoic density in the Galaxy, the forbidding distances between stellar objects (*pace* special relativity), the finely calibrated fit of life on Earth to the conditions on our planet, to the lack of any credible motivation for a galaxy-faring race to invade a small rock circling an average second generation star in the boondocks of the milky nebula. On the same scientific grounds, an alien race would almost certainly be non-humanoid. This means that, if betrization inhibits aggression towards humans but not all species, humanity ought to be able to rise against alien invaders. All seems to depend on how selective our tools of social control would be.

More likely—and more fraught with danger—would be the development of fully autonomous robots and military drones. If you yourself cannot drive an explosives-rigged truck into innocent bystanders because you have been de-aggressed, could you order a robot to drive the truck instead? Issuing a direct command to a machine to aggress other humans might or might not be feasible, depending on our scenario. But how about ordering a truck to plough through a busy sidewalk regardless of how many people are in it?

We must also consider the possibility that machines themselves might become capable of aggressing humanity unless betrizated. In one sense, at least, this may not be a far-out idea. The crucial factor is the necessity of extending de-aggression to robots which (who?) might exhibit agency and a gamut of volitional drives. After all, volitional autonomy in machines almost inevitably entails some form of evolution—and vice versa.[38] This entails, in turn, that the behavioural parameters that characterize humans (including the ability to be violent and harm others) might apply to droids, borgs, and bots. If so, an equivalent procedure for autonomous machines—those that could conceive and execute acts of violence—will be needed to remove such a threat.

Devil's Advocate: Betrization could never work because our intellectual processes are inherently uncontrollable. In the short run, involuntary thoughts about forbidden subjects might lead to frustration and nausea, and in the long run to paranoia and neurosis as—striving to avoid thoughts that trigger negative feedback—one would inevitably be thinking about them.

Advocate: Neither in Percy's, Lem's, nor Levin's scenario does de-aggression work through conditioning, which might be prone to these side-effects. Instead, in all cases betrization inhibits the ability to conceive performing a violent action. Assuming that betrization could be made universal and simultaneous, it would render acts of physical violence literally inconceivable and nip the problem in the bud—no bad thoughts, no bad consequences.

There would, of course, remain mementos in the shape of armaments, historical records, works of literature and art, and living memories. Would those need to be 'betrizated', i.e., expurgated of violent content, too? Without a volume of future neurology or history textbook in hand, it is difficult to prognosticate, though there may indeed be a need for different books and films for the new generation. Interestingly, Skinner himself remarked that, after a thoroughgoing remake into a new society, the contemplation of the classics of human art might be impeded, if not outright impossible. "If we founded an experimental community and raised children in the way that is described in Walden Two, when they grew up and read Dostoyevsky they wouldn't know what in the devil he was talking about".[39]

Devil's Advocate: Betrization would impoverish art—perhaps stifle the creative spirit in the arts and even sciences altogether—by diminishing the range of human emotions and responses available for contemplation and by diminishing the risk-taking ability needed to blaze trails and strike out in a-paradigmatic directions. Significantly, it might also block a range of responses to art.

Advocate: It would be a great pity if a Shakespeare, a Tolstoy, a Joseph Wambaugh or a John Woo could not ply their art after betrization. Still, it is not immediately certain that the inability to perform (or conceive performing) violent acts in real life would entail the inability to conceive them for artistic reasons. Assuming it would, it is indeed possible that some types of art or entertainment might no longer be read and enjoyed. So what? The history of literature, art, and entertainment is strewn with forgotten movements and forms—forgotten because they no longer serve our current aesthetic and social values. Grand Theft Auto and other violent video games elicit impassioned calls for their elimination even in our ultra-permissive age.

Having evolved to serve specific needs of a specific society, the art of any historical period reflects the conditions it was created in, and the betrized civilization may not have any need to read about past acts of aggression or military campaigns. Pain, suffering, and misfortune will always exist in the world and always inspire art that wishes to speak of the existential or merely humdrum trials and triumphs of the human spirit. Conflict, even on such a basic level as between the individual needs and desires and those of the collective, will always remain. By and large, as far as competition goes—for example in sports, or in artistic or intellectual pursuits—there is no reason to suspect that betrization would be any hindrance. It is aggression and physical violence that is the target of the procedure, not the desire to pit one's skills or knowledge against another. One might still lose a championship series, be trounced in a public debate, or denounce a superpower's policies without, however, fearing a bloody vendetta or a military occupation.

THE SILENCE OF THE LAMBS

> The twentieth century, which should have been the greatest triumph of civilization of all time. . . has been the most murderous century in all of history.
>
> Walker Percy, in "Walker Percy Talks
> About Science, Faith and Fiction"

In *The Silence of the Lambs*, pressed by Hannibal Lecter for a personal detail of her life, the FBI agent speaks of her father's last days in a hospital. Fittingly for a book preoccupied with violence and death, Clarice Starling's father was read to on his deathbed from a classic American poem, *Thanatopsis*. Like Dylan Thomas, the poet meditating on mortality aims to sustain and soothe the reader on the last journey either of them will ever undertake. His closing lines advise: "approach thy grave / like one who wraps the drapery of his couch / about him, and lies down to pleasant dreams".

Death is a catalyst and intensifier more powerful than any drug. Paradoxically, even as death forever threatens to put an end to existence, it gives meaning to—it authenticates—the experience of life.

Creating life without violence and war, de-aggression has the potential to dramatically alter the phenomenological experience of life and art. Would Percy necessarily embrace it? Would he endorse a world where the existential toil of imposing meaning onto a meaningless universe is partially replaced by a hi-tek procedure? A similar kind of phenomenological doubt fuelled Kesey's critique of fix-'em-once-and-for-all militant feminists. Sounding for all the world like Tom More, he asked:

> would you eliminate all male chauvinist pigs? If you could come up with some kind of spray to spray in the air and do away with them, would you? Would you do away with all scorpions and rattlesnakes, mosquitoes?' Mosquitoes are part of the ecosystem. So are male chauvinist pigs. You've got to fight them, but you don't try to exterminate them. A purifying group or system that would eliminate them all— that would be an evil force.[40]

It is an open question of whether Kesey or Percy would approve of de-aggression. Would they see it as an evil force? As a diminution of humanity? As a debasement of the phenomenological experience of living? As a corruption of our capacity for making choices? Not that we have that many choices left to make when politicians presume to know the minds of millions. During Senate hearings in 2004, New York Senator Charles Schumer (Dem) asserted, for example, that there are very few people in America "who would say that torture should never be used".[41] Which is worse: that most of us are okay with torture—or that the people who would represent us are so out of touch with reality that they think we are?

Once you answer this question for yourself, try answering the following:

> Would you consent to de-aggression?
> Would you consent to de-aggression if everyone else was guaranteed to undergo it?
> What guarantees would have to be in place for you to consent to it?

And let me know your answers.

5 It Can't Happen Here

or

Politics, Emotions, and Philip Roth's *The Plot Against America*

THE MOST BORING SUBJECT IN THE WORLD

> By being 'politicized' I mean something more telling than writing about politics or even taking direct political action. I mean . . . a daily awareness of government *as a coercive force.*
>
>   Philip Roth, in "Writing and the Powers-that-Be"

Boredom hangs in the air. Dry coughs and sotto-voce sighs drift through the half empty chamber to the accompaniment of creaking seats. Sore backs and behinds fidget in search of relief. Buried in his script, the speaker drones through another interminable address, and it is not even filibuster time. The date stamp on the TV screen differs from the day before, but C-SPAN could have been broadcasting the same footage looped back-to-back and no one would be the wiser. After all, who can tell one plenum or one subcommittee turning wine into water from another?

But—hang on a moment. Far from being boring, politics is the very stuff passions are made of. Look again at the legislative floor. Taiwanese parliamentary debates end in bloody fistfights. South Korean parliamentarians brawl over new laws. Violent scuffles roll down the legislative aisles of Ukraine, Bolivia, Turkey, Iran, Azerbaijan, Japan, Macedonia, Nigeria, Greece, Czech, and Egypt (to name a few).[1] Even the Unites States Congress has not been a stranger to dustups, not to mention bloodletting. All it took was an anti-abolitionist congressman, a cane for a bludgeon, and a headful of steam to blow.

SOUTHERN CHIVALRY — ARGUMENT versus CLUB'S.

"... Even the Unites States Congress has not been a stranger to dustups, not to mention bloodletting. All it took was an anti-abolitionist congressman, a cane for a bludgeon, and a headful of steam to blow ..."

Figure 5.1 John L. Magee's lithograph "Southern Chivalry—Argument versus Club" depicting Congressman Preston Brooks's attack on Senator Charles Sumner (1856).

Politics may be boring like a hungry termite, but only to the outsiders. At the trough tempers run so high that they frequently trump all procedural rules of conduct. Politicians are a biological anomaly—seen by the electorate as cold and calculating, their blood boils at room temperature. Few are as quickwitted about it as the former Green leader Joschka Fischer who in 1984 made Bundestag history with: "With all due respect, Mr President, you're an asshole." But, C-SPAN aside, politics may be less like watching the Appalachians erode than like watching Mount St. Helens in the month of May.

The whole dichotomy between cold calculation and volcanic emotion may be as true, in fact, as an average electoral pledge. In a paradigm shift over the last twenty years or so, emotions and feelings have finally been recognized as integral components of the machinery of thought and reason. After all, insofar as emotions are regulatory mechanisms, they are *biological* regulatory mechanisms—meaning that they could not have emerged in isolation from other life processes. Emotions are implicated, in fact, in all kinds of adaptive behaviours, from mate-seeking and aggression right down to thinking and decision making.[2]

This is not to say that emotions do the thinking or the decision making for us. But, in a head-on collision with ultra-rationalistic models of agency rooted in classical economics and political theory, contemporary neuroscience reveals how emotions play a major role in cognition. They not only laser and layer experience into the tissue of memory, but also harness this data to inform background dispositions and prioritize occurrent alternatives. In other words, they funnel the experience of urban dwellers into the same evolutionary channels as those of prehistoric hunters and foragers.

Just because emotions are underwritten by evolution, it does not mean that there is no cultural variation in how they are manifested. On the contrary, much of our emotional repertoire is mediated by communal rules of display. Also, like any other evolutionary mechanism, emotions can be adaptive in one context and not at all in another. Abetted by the sympathetic nervous system, anger or fear can help you defend your life—or else push you over the edge and earn you life in jail. But, one way or another, emotions are there for a reason, and that reason has to do with facilitating the open-ended game of survival.

When it comes to processing social information, human beings do it much too swiftly for any conscious deliberation to take place. Facial expressions, body language, and other behavioural cues to emotional states and even social standing are decoded with lightning alacrity—and astonishing reliability. This is precisely why feigned emotions often look, well, feigned. This is also why savvy campaign-trail managers sometimes feed only need-to-know information to the candidates they groom. If a campaign pledge is so much bullshit, so much better that the candidate believes it isn't, hand over the heart.

Politics is boring like hell. But those who can spin it so that it looks like it is coming straight from the heart can turn couch vegetables into political animals. Momentum, the prized quantity in any race, is nothing but a spike in the ECG of voters who until then have not connected emotionally with the candidate. Rarely does an appeal to reason quicken pulses in the course of partisan stumping. But emotional mantra can put audiences in a trance where anything seems possible—even that the clichés they are applauding aren't as shop-worn as a pole dancer's g-string.

For all his perspicacity, Descartes was in error. Thought may be the driver of human action, but it's the passions that fire up the boiler. Never mind the date stamp on the TV screen. The slogans are as generic as a dollar bill, recycled by every party and every politico who has ever played on the emotions on his fellow Americans to camouflage the fact that they are being played. But they still work:

> Fight for what's right for our country. Fight for the ideals and character of a free people.
>   (APPLAUSE)
> Fight for our children's future. Fight for justice and opportunity for all.
>   (APPLAUSE)
> Stand up to defend our country from its enemies. Stand up for each other, for beautiful, blessed, bountiful America.
>   (APPLAUSE)
> Stand up, stand up, stand up, and fight.
>   (APPLAUSE)
> Nothing is inevitable here. We're Americans, and we never give up.
>   (APPLAUSE)
> We never quit.
>   (APPLAUSE)
> We never hide from history. We make history.
>   (APPLAUSE)
> Thank you, and God bless you, and God bless America.[3]

Rationally, there is nothing here to applaud. All these banalities have been recycled enough times to get rave reviews from the environmentalists. But this is precisely the point. Spin aims not for the head but for the heart in the search of emotional contagion. It works because deep down *Homo sapiens* is an emotional animal who—C. Auguste Dupin and Hercule Poirot aside—heeds his gut feeling as much as his ratiocinating brain. Ask any campaign manager worth his fee. Or ask Joel Davitz who, in *Language of Emotion*, compiled no less than seven hundred expressions we employ to refer to emotions.

Emotions overtake reason more often than we care to admit. In 2000 Gore aced the issues; Bush aced Gore. In 1980 Mondale aced the debates; Reagan aced the votes. In 1952 Stevenson won every argument hands down; Eisenhower won at the polls. In 1940 FDR bagged the issues; Lindbergh and his antiwar crusade bagged the election—in Roth's wildly counterfactual *The Plot Against America*, that is. Political consultancy thrives precisely because the public is manipulated so much more easily by passion than by reason. The whole experience is like watching Penn and Teller: the secret is out in the open but the trick still works.

If Philip Milton Roth is right, however, all this is fertile ground for homegrown 'soft' fascism. This is not an oxymoron. In a democracy, oppression works best when it is not seen. No one knew it better than James Madison who, halfway through his peroration during the Virginia Convention to ratify the Constitution, warned that more abridgments of freedom come by silent and gradual encroachments than by *coups d'etats*. But Roth goes one step further. By means of a fictional analogue of the presidency that hijacked the nation by hijacking the emotional grief of 9/11, he shows that one type of abrogation is but a step away from the other.

NOT A POLITICAL ACT

> I write fiction and I'm told it's autobiography, I write autobiography and I'm told it's fiction, so since I'm so dim and they're so smart, let *them* decide what it is or it isn't.
>
> Philip Roth, *Deception: A Novel*

In *Ghost Writer* (1979) Roth created a middle-aged Jewish novelist who lives in rural New England, teaches liberal arts and, out of skepticism of the public world, devotes his time and energies to art. His name: E.I. Lonoff. Ever eager to fall on the sword of biographical fallacy, many critics read it as a straightforward portrait of Bernard Malamud, the writer's longtime friend. Few remarked on what Roth pointed out in interview after interview, namely that the picture was equally true of himself. No surprises there: Roth's life has always obsessively wormed itself into the counterlives of his fiction.

It is because of such profound osmosis between his art and life that the one is a valuable exponent—if never a biographical mirror—of the other. The case in point: *The Plot Against America*. It is not a coincidence that Roth's home library contains Hannah Arendt's *The Origins of Totalitarianism*, not to mention a shelf-load of political and historical monographs referenced in the note to the reader. After all, what the writer admired about the satires of Lenny Bruce is equally true of his own: life and art converging in precise social observation and extravagant fantasy.[4]

Not that Roth would easily forego his favourite role of a dissenter. Asked about the political effect of *Our Gang*, in which his president of the United States ends up running against Satan for the leader of hell, he took refuge in the myth of an artist paring his fingernails, demurring that satire cannot be judged in terms of politics. But even as he took away with one hand, he gave with the other. *Our Gang* "has teeth and claws", he boasted to *Newsweek*, "and not everybody likes that".[5] From that he went straight back to maintaining that satire is a literary, not a political act, no matter how reformist the passion of the author.

In *I Married a Communist* (1998) he even put these much quoted words in the mouth of an old-school leftist:

> Politics is the great generalizer, and literature the great particularizer, and not only are they in an inverse relationship to each other—they are in an *antagonistic* relationship.[6]

How much faith should one put in this apparent u-turn from the political course plotted in *Our Gang*, *Operation Shylock*, or *The Plot Against America*? Not much, shows one of the finer Roth critics.[7] First, the leftist is a rather predatory figure, intent on seducing the young man to whom he is pontificating, which hangs a big question mark over his credibility. Then, the antagonistic relationship is true of propaganda but not of political literature. As Roth himself remarked of the Prague writers he befriended during the 1970s, it was communism that made their art *art*.

The best reason, however, to doubt this censure of partisan involvement is that it is advanced in a novel in which politics is not a narrative wallpaper but a protagonist in its own right. From the Dewey Commission's investigation into the trumped-up charges against Trotsky in Moscow to the sycophantic bending over by the American Communist Party for Stalin, the rise of the Popular Front and the Progressive Party, and Wallace's 1948 presidential campaign—all these and other milestones that shaped the old Left get star billing alongside fictional characters.

In 1989 Tom Wolfe took Roth to task for retreating from social issues into the introspective world of fiction. No one knows how deeply Roth felt the sting, but over the next decade-and-a-half he released a series of socially and politically engagé novels, culminating in 2004 with *The Plot Against America*. His interest in political rhetoric goes back, of course, to the time when he studied Nixon's books and speeches in preparation for *Our Gang*. Yet, in a 1971 interview entitled "On Satirizing Presidents", he played the devil's advocate to Alan Lelchuk:

> Political satire isn't writing that lasts. Though satire, by and large, deals with enduring social and political problems, its comic appeal lies in the use made of the situation of the moment . . . Subtleties of wit and malice are wholly lost over the years, and we're left to enjoy the broadest, least timebound aspects of the work, and to hunt through the footnotes in order to make connections and draw inferences that are the teeth and claws of this sort of writing.

Then, to make sure no one made the political connection between fact and fiction, he appended sixty pages of straight history, politics, and biography to the end of *The Plot Against America*. Clearly Roth's artistic now-you-see-it-now-you-don't leaves a prominent excluded middle. Agitprop is not art, but from this it does not follow that 'political art' is a contradiction in terms. Literature begins where partisan proselytizing stops not because it is bereft of reformist passion but because it asks to be judged by more than a single-minded or simple-minded set of criteria.[8]

To read Roth with a view to what he intimates about the psychology and pathology of American politics is not to take anything away from his art. Slice his novels any way you like, but at the core of many of them simmers something that might be mistaken for reformist passion. That's why to separate *Our Gang* from the Nixon of Vietnam and Watergate, *Operation Shylock* from the strangulation of Palestine, or *The Plot Against America* from the Pinocchio presidency of George W. Bush, would be to emasculate his art no less than if you took every word as biographical gospel.

If Roth really affirmed nothing when he went after the social or political sacred cows of our times, then something else would have to explain the fiery opprobria that dogged his career. If *l'ecrivant terrible* is free to exercise his poetic licence to kill without minding who gets in the way of his fictive bullets, something else would have to explain Bill Kauffman's review of *The Plot Against America* as "a repellent novel, bigoted and libellous of the dead, dripping with hatred of rural America, of Catholics, of any Middle American who has ever dared stand against the war machine".[9]

Malamud, the would-be ghost writer from Roth's fiction, confided to one of his interviewers: "I prefer autobiographical essence to autobiographical history".[10] His jab was clearly aimed at the literary jaw of Muhammad Roth, but it missed its target by a country mile. Suffice it to put Roth's various incarnations of his family life side by side to know that his upbringing in Newark, New Jersey, was no more than pig iron for the artist's mill. True to form, *The Plot Against America* provides another counterpoint to a lifelong narrative fugue in which fact and fiction rub shoulders like tramway-tossed labourers on the way to work.

Seamlessly, the novel weaves in two plotlines. The first follows a Roth family sucked into the vortex of counter-historical events unfolding between June 1940 and October 1942 (punctuated by sporadic flash-forwards). The other tracks wartime America as it succumbs to a fascist makeover—and loves every minute of it. Both stories come together in the innocent-eye narration by a seven-year-old Phillie Roth, allowing the artist to refract rather than reflect the United States between 2000 and 2004 in all its consequences: tragic, comic, and grotesque.[11]

Picture yourself in the Weequahic neighbourhood in Newark where streets are named after the victorious naval commanders of the Cuban war, the same that changed the erstwhile republic into a colonial empire.[12] It is 1940 and the country goes gaga over Charles Lindbergh, Republican candidate for president and proud recipient of the Service Cross of the German Eagle conferred on him by Hitler for services to the Reich. Frenzied rhetoric chokes the national media as Lindbergh wins the popular and the electoral vote, relegating FDR to the trashbin of alternate history.

". . . It is 1940 and the country goes gaga over Charles Lindbergh, Republican candidate for president and proud recipient of the Service Cross of the German Eagle conferred on him by Hitler for services to the Reich . . ."

Figure 5.2   Charles Lindbergh accepts the Service Cross of the German Eagle from Herman Göring, second-in-command to Hitler (1936).

Politically, nothing else takes place than a democratic and constitutional change of government. Emotionally, like in the months after 9/11 when America executed a sharp turn to the right, all hell breaks loose.

Abroad, Hitler overruns Europe and hammers Russia, while Japan makes conquistadorial strides in Asia and the Pacific. Meanwhile Lindbergh goes to any length to fulfil his promise to stay out of "the Jewish war"—and then some, throwing a White House ball to a Nazi foreign minister. Having dropped a velvet curtain between the country and the world, the Republicans turn to social engineering. The new Office of American Absorption begins to 'integrate' Jews by means of programs like Just Folks that send Jewish teenagers to the Midwest to experience life in America's heartland.

The allusions to the Third Reich's programs of Aryanization, starting with their obsession with the countryside and its *Volk*, are unmistakable.[13] So are echoes of *Lebensborn*, a program set up by Himmler's SS to—among others—administer relocation programmes for children. More social engineering comes in the form of Homesteader '42, a program that relocates Jewish families from Weequahic and other New England neighbourhoods to farming and smalltown communities in the Midwest. Meanwhile, in a reverse diaspora, the Good Neighbor project resettles gentiles in the apartments vacated by the dispersed Jews.

But dark as they are, even darker shadows are cast by the ghosts of the Republican administration under Bush II, Dick Cheney, Donald Rumsfeld, Colin Powell, John Ashcroft, George Tenet, and Condoleezza Rice. In the novel it is not the Democrats but Walter Winchell, gossip columnist extraordinaire and a foe of Lindbergh, who sloganeers against the Republican razis and swastinkers in the White House. With hyperbolic spinsanity choking the airwaves and voices of reason drowning in mob chants, in no time he finds himself under attack.[14]

Nerves fray, emotionally exhausted people stagger from one false alarm to another, while the right-wing administration stokes the unrest for its own agenda. Fears reach hysterical pitch and, like Chief Bromden, some Jewish families begin to sneak across the border to the land of the free—Canada. Eventually, fanned by propaganda and disinformation, the tensions boil over. Riots erupt all over the country. Amid the bombing of synagogues and looting of Jewish stores, a hundred and twenty-two Jews are murdered during the American *Kristallnacht*.

The novel approximates the breathless, scattershot, documentary feel of its times by chopping the penultimate chapter into a montage of newsreel sections. Bad days. War. Rotting corpses. Anti-war slogans. Country split down the middle. Riots in Boston, Detroit, Louisville, Cincinnati, Pittsburgh, Youngstown, Akron, St. Louis, Buffalo, Peoria, Scranton, Syracuse. Witch hunts of individuals who stand up to the regime. Police everywhere. Winchell assassinated. Marches, rallies, demagoguery. Accusations of fascism. Counter-accusations of war mongering.

Then, a bombshell: the president's plane vanishes during one of his iconic solo flights. "Where is *Lind*-bergh?" becomes a rallying slogan for the dissenters, even as a power-hungry Republican cabal sends the army and the National Guard into the streets in the name of law and order. Commanded by the vice president, the plotters declare the country to be in peril, impose martial law and a nationwide curfew, and deploy tanks and infantry in "Jew York". Borders are sealed among an orgy of arrests of prominent statesmen and public figures, even as rumours of more secret detentions fuel mass hysteria.

And then, as suddenly as it started, it's all over. In an endgame as sly as provocative, America gets back on its feet. Led by Lindbergh's wife, who escapes detention from a mental hospital, the political and emotional assault on the nation is exposed for what it is. America shakes off its infatuation with fascism, the usurpers are arrested, FDR returns to power, Japan torches Pearl Harbor (a year later than in reality), and history settles back onto its familiar course. All that remains is a multitude of theories trying to make sense of what *really* happened. According to one of them, the Republican president wasn't even such a monster, just a stooge for his Veep. . .

For some, Roth's endgame might seem to deflate the reality of the putsch. America's democratic traditions are resilient enough, it seems to say, to overcome a potential assault from within.[15] For others, it is a fitting climax to a scenario that, albeit counterfactual, seems almost factual at times. After all, only a year before Roth went after homegrown repression, another writer made waves with what many had thought in the run-up to the invasion of Iraq, but dared not say aloud. "The US is really beyond reason now", pointed out Harold Pinter. "There is only one comparison: Nazi Germany".

Released in 2004, *The Plot Against America* also went bare-knuckled after a fascist Republican presidency. It captured the spirit of the days when, conditioned with countrywide social engineering in the form of the Patriot Act—which violated sections of the Bill of Rights, i.e., the Constitution itself—dissident voices were shouted down.[16] When wearing a 'Peace on Earth' t-shirt in public got you arrested and jailed. When peace-marchers on Washington under the banner of "One Nation Under Surveillance" were told by Rumsfeld that they "should have more trust in the government".

". . . When peace-marchers on Washington under the banner of 'One Nation Under Surveillance' were told by Rumsfeld that they 'should have more trust in the government' . . ."

Figure 5.3   When the Democrats rolled over, artists stepped into the breach with anti-Patriot Act fliers.

Against this political canvas, Roth uses some of his tenderest brushstrokes to bring to life the victims of the plot against America.[17] The Roths, their cousins, and neighbours do not so much pick their way by the compass of reason as by gut instinct and feeling. The family trip to Washington, D.C., during which Herman Roth staggers from red fury to blanched shock to black fear as he rages against the regime, is only the beginning. In another emotional climax, young Alvin runs off to fight Hitler, only to return home without a leg. From then on, foreboding and tears take up permanent residence in the Roth house.

If a novelist doesn't persuade by what he is trying to say but by a sense of fictional authenticity, then Roth is very persuasive, indeed. Look no further than his Lindbergh. Like Picasso's single-line sketch of a dachshund, he is drawn with the economy that allows all Americans to project their hopes and fears onto him. Such is Roth's narrative power that the president looms like one of Albert Speer's architectural monuments: at once larger-than-life and a proof that if the lie is big enough, it will be believed. He is, quite simply, a stand-in for another war-fixated Republican president.

Ironically, as Bush was pursuing his second war in Asia, Roth created a White House dead set against sending America to fight. The contrast could not be harsher. Historically, WWII is regarded as a good war which the U.S. fought in defense of democracy, if not the world itself. The neo-colonial grab of Iraqi oil, on the other hand, was shot through with lies that conned Americans reeling from the emotional agitation of 9/11 into believing that it had something to do with retributive justice—or, later on, nation building. How much the country was taken for a ride is divulged by George W. Bush himself:

> I don't think our troops ought to be used for what's called nation building. I think our troops ought to be used to fight and win war. I think our troops ought to be used to help overthrow a dictator when it's in our best interests. But in this case, it was a nation-building exercise . . . And it was not very successful.[18]

Bush's attack on nation building in Haiti took place less than three years before his about-face about nation building in Iraq.

How did he get away with it? Conditioning the country with phony terror alerts and nonexistent WMDs, his administration exploited a key evolutionary feature of emotions: in the presence of a powerful impulse, they grab the wheel. There's a time to reason and there's a time to act, and when emotions take over, that time is now. Mobilizing chemically minds and bodies, emotions tunnel our vision so that it fixates on the immediate context regardless of consequences.

That is why myths and fictions, so long as they are emotionally satisfying, often prevail over sober fact. Problem is, inflationary alarmism exhausts itself and the populace in the long run. With each successive jolt, the returns diminish as the emotional needle settles on the baseline. To get a rise again, the stimulus has to be sharper, the threat greater, the message louder. But, if sustained over a prolonged period, the escalation may erode the effectiveness of the whole policy, sometimes to the point of turning it into a force more destabilizing than any potential threat.

A good model of this process is a dollar auction proposed by game theorist Martin Shubik. Starting at $1, players bid in one-dollar increments for a twenty-dollar bill. But there is a catch: while the winner takes the prize, the second-highest bidder also has to pay up. Typically the bidding races up to $20, whereupon two top players enter a ruthless and senseless war of attrition. After all, as soon as they make the opening bid, they are trapped in an arms race. Perversely, the higher the bids—and the higher the losses—the more incentive there is to go on playing and losing. *In for a penny, in for a pound*, indeed.

Best strategy? Don't play. Otherwise, even when you win, you lose, as the price of this pyrrhic victory outweighs the gain. Vietnam is the textbook example of a fear of loss fuelling escalating commitment. So is the current escalation of commitment euphemized as surges. At the beginning of 2008 there were twenty-six thousand American troops in Afghanist'nam. Bush II's "quiet surge" brought the total to under fifty thousand. Early in 2009 another three thousand soldiers—ordered by Bush but sent by Obama—were shipped over. In February, this time on his own, Obama dispatched another seventeen thousand. At the end of 2009, another thirty thousand troops were sent.

Ask yourself: why are we raping foreign countries buried in the deserts and mountains of Asia Minor whose people did us nothing wrong and pose no credible threat to the United States? Why are we bombing the bejesus out of their civilians, fuelling hatred for the invaders? Non-combatant casualties always inflict the deepest wounds on the national psyche. In World War II, the same that Lindbergh tries to stay away from at all costs, the British suffered fewer than seventy thousand civilian deaths. The French suffered more than two hundred and fifty thousand. Germany 1.8 million. Poland 5.5 million. The USSR more than 11 million. China more than 16 million.

Compare this to American civilian losses. In both World Wars, which took some one hundred million lives worldwide, the United States lost fewer than two thousand civilians. In other words, American folks did not have to suffer carnage, annihilation, firestorms, pogroms, deprivation, starvation, cannibalism. Perhaps as a consequence—if you discount Israeli or British hawks—America today is the only prosperous nation in the world that exalts the military. Anything that might be construed as lack of respect or support for combat troops is political suicide, if not sedition.

The U.S. economy and politics are addicted to war. Every year *half* of the discretionary budget goes to war and only 0.0006 percent to peacekeeping ops.[19] And to paraphrase the words of one of Nixon's henchmen, with the military economy holding the United States by the balls, the country's minds and hearts follow. This is why American soldiers are still pacifying Afghanistan under 'good guy' Obama. This is why planning for the military occupation of Iraq began years before Bush II's accession to power. This is why planning for the plot against America began before Lindbergh.

PASSION PLAY

> Only the most outrageous demagogue would contrive to arouse the passions of the mob.
>
> Philip Roth, *The Plot Against America*

In the final days of the Clinton presidency, Tracfone, a prepaid cellphone service, ran a television ad that spliced documentary footage of American presidents. First up was Richard Nixon, choking on his sincerity as he proclaimed that he was not a crook. Next came Bush the Father, asking his fellow Republicans to read his lips in an unequivocal promise of no new taxes. Finally, there was Bill Clinton waving his finger at the camera and enunciating that he did not have sexual relations with that woman, Ms. Lewinsky. Tracfone's sales pitch? "Talk is cheap".

From a schoolboard superintendent to the president of the United States, every candidate for office promises a clean sweep. As far as campaign promises go, few could make it more apparent that we chronically elect the worst possible aspirant. After all, with so many sweepers shaking their brooms at the Augean stables, by now there should be nothing left to sweep. Instead, every time it is more of the same, from pork-barrel earmarks to political simony. The former Illinois governor Rod Blagojevich, who solicited bids for Obama's vacant Senate seat, made only one mistake: he got caught.

But, against reason, we want to believe. That's why in November 2008 we succumbed to a mass delusion by sending a 47-year-old senator from Illinois to the White House. Cynics are by and large failed romantics, and many saw in him if not a saviour, then at least a redeemer. Democratic candidate, then presidential candidate, then president-elect promised to act swiftly and boldly. No dithering, no pandering to lobbyists. Just do the right thing and do it now. After hearing the same spiel from every would-be president since the beginning of the American presidency, voters took him at his word.[20]

Politicians will promise anything to get people to get into bed with them, and campaigns are bad harbingers of things to come. Obama the president is not Obama the stumping firebrand. He promised to be swift: now he has fallen behind with everything, starting with closing Guantanamo. He promised change. Now he copycats Dubya by increasing military budgets, escalating wars in Asia, muzzling the release of photos of dead soldiers' coffins, short-changing education, and bailing out Big Banks and Big Businesses with little people's money. No wonder that in November 2010 his party got slapped (and loud) with a mid-term reality check.

Some people remain so hung up on change, however, that they cannot see past the historic image of a half-black man in the White House. As E.O. Wilson put it in *On Human Nature*, people often "would rather believe than know" (562). Not that it is always wrong to put belief ahead of reason. A false belief may even have a greater survival value than the truth. The morale of an occupied nation may hinge on a baseless belief in a quick liberation which can, however, stave off collapse. The same with charisma. In rational terms, it may be so much hot air, but hot air can sometimes uplift the nation.

Quite simply, the adaptive value of a belief cannot be measured strictly by its referential veracity. This is why emotional harmonics—whether in the form of personal charisma or national mythology—are capable of instilling psychological cohesion, offering solace in times of trouble, or even eliciting self-sacrifice. Not every president can get away with telling a hundred and eighty million people to ask not what their country can do for them, but what they can do for their country. But charismatic leaders who know how to move the masses can move the masses to move mountains.

Charisma—or, more mundanely, the voter's perception of the candidate's character—is the cornerstone of political campaigns. The reformists' endeavours to refocus debates on issues and away from personalities fly in the face of history which dictates that the latter usually carry the day. This is exactly why the whole machinery of political management is geared towards the idea of 'the candidate'. People connect with people rather than with bullet-point manifestos, quite apart from the fact that the judgment of character is one of the few decisions still left in the hands of otherwise powerless voters.[21]

Once in office, a candidate can change his platform, but he cannot change his nature. Issues facing contemporary societies are complex, oftentimes requiring specialist knowledge and time-consuming deliberation. But we are all equipped by evolution to automatically evaluate clues transmitted by faces, gestures, and social contexts. We are equipped to detect cognitive and even emotional states of others and, in this way, to detect cheaters. We are, in short, equipped to judge character—notwithstanding the fact that, like every piece of equipment, ours can sometimes give false readings.

Every national myth marks a triumph of emotion over reason. Myth, if you like, is emotional credit that can be spent when the political account dips into the red. After all, people want to believe and, in that sense, they want to be deceived. As with any religion, voluntary indoctrination is easy. All it takes is emotionally stirring incantations from the head priest, some symbolic pageantry, and a lot of faith. Supported by iconography, such as physical elevation or the swearing of the oath of allegiance, they redirect kinship affiliation onto the non-genetic political entity.

The American presidency is such a secular religion, eliciting reverence for what is, after all, just a non-tenured administration job. The vestal colouration of the White House enhances the imagery of the head priest dwelling in a sacred temple. Relics of its past occupants, from Lincoln's canopy bed to Hayes's *Resolute* desk, consecrate the hallowed grounds. State functions are liturgical communions of the power emanating from the Office. Rounding up the picture, Washington's house—piously visited by the Roths in *The Plot Against America*—is a shrine to the American Adam, the father of the nation.

Meanwhile, once inside the White House, every First Lady becomes Eve *immaculata*. Roth taps into this prelapsarian imagery when, leading the resistance to the coup, Lindberg's wife is revered as "Our Lady of the White House" (319). Indeed, while lay-religious symbolism permeates every state address that directs God to bless America, the theological presidency of Bush the Younger kicked it into overdrive. Just recall the iconic overtones of Bush's descent from on high onto the deck of the *Abraham Lincoln* to deliver his 'Mission Accomplished' sermon to the saluting disciples, before rising up to heaven again.[22]

The theatricality of the pageant was enhanced by the use of a jet fighter, utterly unnecessary as the carrier was well within the range of Bush's helicopter. But thanks to it, the military commander got his picture taken in the apostolic gear. Not that there is anything new about it. From ancient times, every regime tried to convert military success into political capital: victory on the battlefield was interpreted as a sign of divine protection and favour.

". . . While lay-religious symbolism permeates every state address that directs God to bless America, the theological presidency of the younger Bush kicked it into overdrive. Hence the iconic overtones of Bush's theatrical descent from on high onto the deck of the Abraham Lincoln to deliver his 'Mission Accomplished' sermon to the saluting disciples, before rising up to heaven again . . ."

Figure 5.4 Explaining the missionary position: George W. Bush stepping down on the deck of the carrier *Abraham Lincoln* (1 May, 2003) / The carrier returns to port under the "Mission Accomplished" banner (2 May, 2003).

Conversely, when the all-too-human and all-too-fallible occupants of the temple strip it of its gloss, the shock among the believers belies the fact that, far from saviours, America's leaders are only its top bureaucrats. And yet there is this shibboleth, chimes in Roth, "respect for the office of the Presidency—as though there were no distinction between the man who holds and degrades the office and the office itself".[23] To be sure, many presidents suffer from acute shortage of moral fibre, not to mention intelligence, but that's not how Camelot is spun. From George Washington on, every POTUS is an Arthur, every policy wonk a Galahad.

Able as a commander of the revolutionary militia, as a president, however, Washington was a political dupe, unable to grasp that the legislative floor was far more treacherous than any battleground. In the role that required the vigilance of an East German Berlin Wall sentry, he was slipshod and gullible. Still, the myth trumps historical fact. Washington continues to be revered as one of the greatest presidents of the United States, with every greenback reinforcing the lay faith by overlaying the trust in the father of the nation with the trust in the divine father (in a country that constitutionally separates the State and the Church).

Trust—or if you like, faith—is indeed the key. Insofar as securing votes is the lifeline of any politician, they make promises right and left as long as there is a chance they will be believed. But stump promises can be a double-edged sword. There is always the risk they might backfire if they are seen to have been unkept. Most presidential campaign promises have, in fact, been broken. When Wilson vowed to keep America out of the war in Europe, few believed him even though the Germans had not yet torpedoed the *Lusitania*. When FDR pledged in the 1941 inaugural that this country was not going to war, few believed him even though Nagumo had not yet sneaked up on Pearl Harbor.[24]

Still, when their survival instincts are primed by war, Americans tend to rally behind their leaders instead of taking them to task for breach of trust. From time to time they do it even in times of peace. LBJ pledged to eliminate poverty, even though no nation in history has succeeded in doing so. Reagan promised to eliminate illicit drugs. His successor vowed to engineer America into a kindler and gentler nation. Never meant to be kept, all these covenants had, however, a certain emotional decorum. They were presidential—not to say utopian—in ambition.

In this they differed from those that could have been kept, but weren't. In 1968 Nixon promised everything to everybody, beginning with ending the Vietnam War with all possible dispatch. He lied. Bush I tethered his electoral campaign to the promise of no new taxes. Once in office, he reneged on his word to tackle deficits run up, among others, by the first war in Iraq.

Such flagrant nose-thumbing at the constituents is not, however, as widespread as it might seem. Cartoonists may draw politicians as slimeballs, but when politicians lie they rarely leave tracks. Much of the time they operate in the comfort zone between truth and falsehood, praying on the unwary with emotion and hyperbole. This is in keeping with perhaps the most effective tactic used to bamboozle voters: holding them hostage to emotions.

The textbook example comes from Bush's 2001 tax relief plan. Mindful not to repeat his father's error, once in office Dubya got the Republican Congress to whittle the top income tax rate down to 35 percent (after World War II it stood at 90 percent). When the opposition contested that it mainly benefited the rich, Bush countered that the bottom of the economic ladder would receive the biggest savings: "Six million families, one out of every five families with children, will no longer pay federal income taxes at all".[25]

So, here is how you cheat on taxes president-style by wringing every drop out of emotionally—not to say evolutionarily—charged terms such as family and children. Take a 'nucular' low-income American family of four, with income of twenty-six grand a year. Under Bush's plan, they received a monster one-hundred-percent reduction in taxes. But in real terms they netted all of . . . $20. That's right: twenty bucks, or the value of their entire annual income tax. The president's promise of relieving six million families with children from paying up was a federal three-card Monte.

In fact, if you rake up all the money from Bush's tax-relief plan into one big pile, the top one percent of the richest folks in the United States pocketed almost *half* of the total. The top twenty percent pocketed almost three-quarters. On the other hand, the bottom 40 percent received only a shade over four percent of that pile. The poorest 20 percent—supposedly the category that benefitted the most—received less than one percent of the total. Twelve million lowest-income families saw no benefits whatsoever because they had zero income-tax liability.[26]

Another part of Bush's plan was to rescind the estate tax. Only, instead of calling it by its rightful name, he glazed it over with emotion. "To keep family farms in the family", announced the president, "we're going to get rid of the death tax."[27] According to the IRS, however, there is *not a single case* of farms being repossessed because of the estate tax (which kicks in only for estates worth over a million). But emotionally loaded correlatives such as 'family' and 'death' became rhetorical magnets to attract support from the masses for the tax breaks for the rich.

Rhetorical gambits can conjure up different emotions even when they refer to one and the same thing.[28] Compare Obama and McCain's tax credits from their 2008 campaign trail. Tax credits differ from tax cuts in that they are measured in absolute (dollar) terms—which means that you can qualify even if you didn't pay any tax at all. Obama tabled a number of refundable tax credits to low- and middle-income workers, for example $500 for those making less than $75,000 a year. Immediately, the Republicans tagged it as 'welfare' since some Americans who paid no taxes would still qualify.

The thing is, McCain also proposed a refundable tax credit of up to $2,500 for individuals, or up to $5,000 for families, as part of his health care plan. Only instead of smearing his own proposal as 'welfare', he extolled it as tax 'reform'. Different terms, tagging essentially the same initiative, carried different emotional connotations for the public. For most taxpayers, 'reform' comes bundled up with the eutopian subtexts of improvement and progress. 'Welfare', on the other hand, is stereotyped as the mother of social parasitism and the child of special interests.

Emotion-laden stereotypes sustain many political myths, including knee-jerk charges that liberal policies punish hard-working Joes by sponsoring welfare. In 2008 the issue shot to nationwide eminence during the third McCain-Obama debate, acquiring emotional resonance from the presence of Joe the Plumber. Remember him? A few days earlier, Joe pooh-poohed Obama's economic plan during a rally in Ohio. Now, cameras rolling, McCain ripped Obama for wrecking Joe and other regular guys who "all of these years, worked ten, twelve hours a day" to buy a small business in their bid "to realize the American Dream".[29]

If only. The facts in the case—which caused no end of embarrassment to McCain, who implicitly staked his credibility on this rhetorical salvo—flipped the script. Not only did Joe turn out not to even have a plumbing licence, but he could not have earned the capital he implied to have earned to open a plumbing business and realize his American dream. And the punchline? If he opened a plumbing shop, he would benefit more from Obama's plan which lowered taxes for small businesses (raising them only for the top two percent).

Politicians and lobbyists spend big on promo gurus whose job it is to spin and typecast. Of course, most stereotypes are checks that could never be cashed out. The GOP is alleged to be the standard bearer for fiscal accountability, small government, and non-interventionist free market. Yet when the chips are down, it is anything but. When a conservative administration, headed by a former Texan oilman and a Wall Street investment banker, touched off the 2008 mortgage and financial meltdown, it showed its true colours by bailing out or buying out banks and businesses left and right. Eugene Debs would be proud.

The Democrats, on the other hand, are tagged not only as big spenders but as wasteful spenders. Looking at the post-World War II years, however, the Demublicans are, by and large, indistinguishable from one another. All throw money out of the Oval Office window by the fistful. In fact, the only president in the last half-century to balance the books was Clinton, a Democrat. Ur-conservatives Reagan and Bush II, on the other hand, clocked the biggest deficits. Tell that on Fox, however, and you'll be tagged as a demagogue. Tell that to the Tea Party and you'll be tagged as a Leninist Hitlerite.[30]

Another way to lead voters by the nose can be summarized with one word: microtrends. Campaign bosses identify a population niche, in some cases less than one percent of the electorate, and then target it with a tailor-made media blitz to corral votes for their candidate. It is here that politics becomes indistinguishable from advertising, embedding in consumers values they never suspected they had. This is because identification of electoral microtrends can be tendentious, creating 'ecological' subgroups—such as soccer moms—by the very act of identifying them.

On a larger scale, the very ascendancy of political consultancy erodes the power of voting in the United States. Why? Because focus-group research means that more and more frequently voter preferences can be elicited without the need for a vote. The problem is that polls open themselves to easy manipulation. Push polls, selective polls, tendentious interpretation or outright suppression of results that do not advance the candidate's cause are common tactics.

What is waiting at the end of this process? Direct non-invasive mind-reading of political content, the forerunners of which are already being tested today. Monitoring subjects' MRI scans while displaying campaign commercials on the insides of their goggles, political consultants clearly try to put more science in political science. Instead of asking voters to identify their partisan leanings or to comment on the efficacy of campaign spin, they aim to read those off the monitor. One study has, indeed, identified differences in the blood flow in the brains of registered Democratic and Republican voters when exposed to campaign attack ads.[31]

A brave new world, indeed, that has such people in't.

The vulnerability of reason to spin is often most pronounced in attack ads. Exhibit A? The negative spot sponsored recently by the conservative American Issues Project. Entitled "Every Single Day", it pillories Obama and his stimulus bill for fiscal profligacy. Golf carts for everyone, piles of cash for the remodelling of federal offices, neon signs for Vegas, butterfly gardens, Frisbee golf courses, a dog park, a levitating train—in other words, federal pork by the barrel, guaranteed to rile regular folks, few of whom will check the facts. Which is too bad, since all the above claims are either wildly exaggerated or downright false.

For one, it is not true that the bill subsidizes golf carts. It simply sets aside $300 million for fuel-efficient vehicles, like those widely used on military bases.[32] Funds for the alleged remodelling of offices are to upgrade them to 'green' status through better insulation and more efficient lighting. As for butterfly gardens and other frivolities, the bill makes no provisions for them whatsoever. As it happens, Obama's leviathantine stimulus package does smuggle in a number of earmarks, in addition to cloaking highly speculative projections about its efficacy as facts. But the inflationary pressures of partisan campaigns demand not sober analysis but rhetorical flaming.

THE WAY WE FEEL OUR WAY THROUGH LIFE

> You put too much stock in human intelligence, it doesn't annihilate human nature.
>
> Philip Roth, *American Pastoral*

Writing on human nature, David Hume contended that reason is—and *ought* to be—the slave of the passions. Yet for centuries we have lionized rational calculus at the expense of emotions. Getting emotional was disparaged as a sign of weakness, if not evidence of malfunctioning cognitive circuitry. Logic was the reigning monarch and the principal yardstick by which to measure human actions and motives. Given their low place on the totem pole, it is no surprise that, of all mental phenomena, emotions and feelings remain to this day the least understood in neurobiological and evolutionary terms.

Policies that govern public life depend on the institutional models of social relations. These models, in turn, depend on our understanding of human nature which, as is now apparent, must incorporate a better understanding of the way in which we feel our way through life—the way we feel thoughts. Our social lives are, after all, coloured daily by pride, shame, admiration, anger, frustration, desire, and a bevy of other passions. And to the extent that politics forms a part of our social life, it is subject to the same evolutionary machinery that governs emotions and feelings.

In evolutionary terms, emotions predate thought. This is why, triggered by the appropriate context, they can take over, stimulating us to avoid danger, pursue success, fall in love—in short, to engage in behaviours that benefit survival and reproduction. Unthinking they may be but, tried and tested by natural selection, emotions can be quite intelligent. They had better, for, whether by innate design, by learning, or both, human beings "react to most, perhaps all, objects with emotions, however weak, and subsequent feelings, however feeble".[33]

Once again, this is not to deny that on occasion emotions and feelings can be grossly maladaptive. Much as it might be desirable to rid ourselves of certain passions, however, it is not possible. Emotions and feelings form a control system for body and mind, and hence the core of our being. They funnel and hierarchize experiences and, as such, far from being an afterthought, are indispensable even to learning and cognition.

This is precisely why it is astonishing to find Skinner, a lifelong student and professor of learning, dismiss them in *Beyond Freedom and Dignity* with a curt: "feelings are at best by products".[34] In *Walden Two* his disdain for emotions is even more pronounced. "We don't need them any longer in our struggle for existence," proclaims Frazier.[35] "We all know that emotions are useless", concurs Castle.

So there you go. Four billions years of terrestrial evolution, a quarter billion of mammalian evolution, fifty-five million years of primate evolution, two million years of human evolution, and now at a stroke you can fix nature by getting rid of the 'redundant' emotional subprograms. Clearly, Skinner put little stock in the wisdom of ages encapsulated in the old Chinese proverb: *Man's heart controls everything.*

Contradicting behaviourist engineers, the experience of Waldenite groups highlights the role of emotions in social affairs. Any pretense to a utopia at Lake Village vanished when, time and again, passions threw a choke-hold on rational debate. At Twin Oaks seasoned planners would be shouted down irrespective of their credentials—sometimes by other planners. Incidents of this nature were too common to be bracketed off as anomalies. It would take contemporary research in cognitive and evolutionary psychology, however, to confirm the adaptive primacy of affect over logic.[36]

Many of our decisions, it turns out, owe to swift emotional judgments that are only then rationalized and deliberated. Here, mirror neurons again show their hand insofar as emotions are often shared without mediation. A mere perception of someone else's joy, grief, or fear can activate the same areas of the cortex as when we ourselves experience these states. Voters and jurors beware: a tearful politician betters his odds of getting away with a slap on the wrist simply because you may be contaminated by his shame and contrition (assuming it is genuine—or well acted out).

Human capacity for affective cognition—for feeling thoughts, if you will—is phylogenetically and developmentally prior to the capacity for propositional thought. That's why propaganda may be less effective as an instrument of agitation than as a controller of already agitated minds. When one's cognitive faculties function sub-optimally, especially in emergency or under stress, actions are frequently undertaken on the basis of emotional rather than rational calculus. In these kinds of situations we are primed to think in feelings. We shoot first and ask questions later.

If the first casualty of war is truth, this is as true of a war of words as of any other. *The Plot Against America* assembles a masterful picture of propaganda wars in which emotional orators grab you by the lapels and pull you so close that your nose is flattened against their rhetoric. It is natural that writers should be attuned to the ways words are forged into weapons, and Roth's novel is replete with examples of verbal sniping and hyperbolic overkill. With Winchell on the far left, the Bundists on the far right, and America caught in the crossfire, everyone has a slogan to grind.

The Bundists sport "Keep America Out of the Jewish War" buttons and "Wake up America—Smash Jewish Communists!" banners (176). Winchell rants "Fascism! Fascism!" against the Republican government's "Hitlerite plot against America" (260). In turn, the *Detroit Times* smears him as the "Jewish demagogue whose aim from the outset had been to incite the rage of patriotic Americans with his treasonous rabble-rousing" (266). On the other end of the spectrum, *PM*, the left-wing tabloid religiously read by Herman Roth, flaunts its own slogan: "*PM* is against people who push other people around" (18).

In the wake of the Hawaii Understanding—whereby Lindbergh joins the German-Japanese axis of evil in all but name—joyful Americans take to the streets, chanting "No war, no young men fighting and dying ever again!" (55). Lindberg's own catchphrase, hammered no less than fifteen times in his State of the Union, proclaims: "An independent destiny for America" (84). Earlier on, he secures his election with an even catchier slogan: "Vote for Lindbergh or vote for war" (31). FDR pulls all rhetorical stops by haranguing: "The only thing we have to fear. . . is the obsequious yielding to his Nazi friends by Charles A. Lindbergh" (178).

This inundation with slogans, buzzwords, catchphrases, and taglines is all too familiar to us, victims of extreme journalism. As the internet, television, and newspapers fight for the American public's scant time and attention, gone are the old-fangled notions of objective stenography of events. Today's news media inundate voters with a googolplex of ever-more flashy headlines and story breaks in an attempt to crowd one another out of the already saturated market. Jamming people's radar with inflationary quantities of facts and factoids, political spin may be changing, however, not only the rules of the game but the game itself.[37]

More and more, the basis of forming a decision lies not in separating good information from the bad, but in finding the good in the haystack. We live, after all, in the age of infoglut that has willy-nilly turned all of us into infogluttons. The overall proportion of accurate to total information may not have changed, but multiplying both a million-fold has the effect of burying it as if it wasn't there at all. You can be pretty sure of finding ten good books in a thousand. But you will never find ten million good books in a billion—or, by the same token, wrap your head around the tides of political communication beating daily at the door.

So, how to stave off the paralysis potentiated by the deluge of spots, casts, blogs, posts, vids, and tweets? Once again, this is where emotions come in handy. Exercising algedonic (pleasure-pain) control over the process of reasoning, they often help us narrow the information band to manageable proportions. The whole process is largely automatic, being active already at birth or not long thereafter. As such, prompts Antonio Damasio, it shows "little or no dependence on learning, although as life continues learning will play an important role in determining *when* the devices are employed".[38]

In practice, most consumers preselect their news channels by tagging them as good or bad. As a consequence, the bulk of information they are exposed to tends to reflect and, at the same time, reinforce their point of view. Ironically, most of the news from the rival camp is discounted as being tainted with partisan bias. In short, identification with one's political 'tribe' employs emotional filters to the detriment of adversarial or even non-partisan news sources. The latter, in fact, frequently end up being attacked as ideologically and informationally suspect by *both* camps.

Notwithstanding the massive variability of human languages and cultures, we express ourselves—and thus activate behavioural clues—with a fairly narrow set of emotions. Every person uses essentially the same basic repertoire of facial expressions, body language, and vocalizations. Whether in downtown St. Louis or in the jungle of Papua New Guinea, limp shoulders, lowered gaze, hangdog face, and plaintive tones convey appeasement and submission rather than domination and anger. This is precisely why internet emoticons are instantly recognizable all over the world.

"... Every person uses essentially the same basic repertoire of facial expressions, body language, and vocalizations. Whether in downtown St. Louis or in the jungle of Papua New Guinea, limp shoulders, lowered gaze, hangdog face, and plaintive tones convey appeasement and submission rather than domination and anger. This is precisely why internet emoticons are instantly recognizable all over the world ..."

Figure 5.5   Six dwarves: Grumpy, Happy, Bashful, Startled, Music-Head, and Lovey-Drooly.

That emoticons—and, more to the point, emotions—can be activated regardless of environmental or cultural specifics has significant ramifications for campaign rhetoric. At their bottom campaigns are attempts to 'brainwash' voters into thinking and feeling what the candidate wants them to. Emotional invariance offers, therefore, a clearcut pathway to the voters' hearts and, downstream, their heads. Ironically, as one eminent political analyst complained,

> despite the fact that the formal study of rhetoric is twenty-five hundred years old, despite the fact that during all this time it has been an important element of the school

curriculum, despite the fact that the best students of politics from Gorgias and Aristotle to Machiavelli and Madison have themselves been skilled rhetoricians as well as thoughtful commentators on rhetoric—despite all this we have no general systematic knowledge, only a vast accumulation of examples, classified and reclassified in a myriad ways.[39]

Yet, much as knowledge of evolutionary psychology can allow controllers to better manipulate the electorate by better manipulating their emotions, that same knowledge can lead to a more systematic understanding of campaign rhetoric.

Let us bring adapted human nature into the picture. What would evolutionary sciences advise a candidate running for office? First of all, go negative. Clever attack ads rarely fail to transform snores into roars. These days, when apathy and disenchantment routinely keep almost two thirds of the electorate at home, one surefire way to get their attention is to aim for the gut—or, better still, a few inches below. Poll after poll, confirms John Geer in *In Defense of Negativity* (2006), the American public condemns negativity but continues to fall under its spell.

Next, go tribal. Boost your own in-group identity by denouncing outsiders. Marginalize your challenger or, better still, brand him as a traitor to the group. Meanwhile, hammer home your own tribal credentials, if need be by assuming the identity of Mr. Average. In American terms, this means: drive a domestic vehicle, go to church, choke down a few hot dogs, wash them down with lite beer, and give a hard time to intellectuals. Once you're done with the jugular, go for the heart. Ham it up with the family, community, and country (in that order) like there was no tomorrow. Remember: emotion keeps your campaign in motion.

Pack your message with adaptively charged referents like survival, power, and unity, but above all keep it simple. In politics, when you're explaining, you're losing. Do like Reagan did. Don't get entangled in debates; instead, simplify even the most complex issue to an emotionally satisfying victory of the good guys over the bad. People's moral judgments are, by and large, too swift to be the outcome of deliberation and self-reflection envisaged by moral philosophers. Hume was right: sentiment is frequently the primary mover, while reason is only the translator of sentimental decisions into the moral lexicon.

Go easy on numbers. Research with unexpected arithmeticians like crows or speakers of Warlpiri or Anindilyakawa (Aboriginee languages with very few number words) suggests that limited numeracy may be inborn. But outside that, literacy precedes numeracy. So pitch a slow numberless ball at your constituents, perhaps garnished up *á la* Ross Perot with a few pie charts. During the Gore–Bush debates, Gore was mostly making sense while Bush was mostly talking nonsense, but whenever the audience heard a mouthful of statistics they heard a policy wonk and switched off. Most people want just the slogans, not the facts, ma'am.[40]

A Stevenson or a Mondale can orate as much as he likes, but if there are no emotions riding on the issues, few people care and few care to care. Why are so many low-income Americans today against the government and for health-insurance providers that, as Michael Moore jeered in *Sicko*, routinely deny them claims and cancel policies? Because emotional harmonics blind them to reason and to their own interests. Republican propaganda stokes their resentment against Democratic elitism, with the result that many of America's poorest defend social policies that serve the interests of the rich.

Voluntary indoctrination is, indeed, the cornerstone of democracy. This is why, as John Dos Passos intimated it already seven decades before Roth, American-style abrogation of civil liberties will not announce itself with a platoon of hobnailed boots crashing through doors in the dead of night. Instead, it will be designed by public relations mavens, koshered by mainstream media, vetted by Congress, and executed by the White House. In other words, it will be as patriotic, democratic, and autocratic as the soft fascism that blanketed the United States in the wake of September 2001.

After all, no one jammed a handgun to the collective temple of America's congressional representatives and ordered them to contravene the Constitution—the same Constitution that is forever trotted out as the rhetorical last word on what constitutes political right and wrong. Instead, the House and the Senate rushed of their own free will to pass the Patriot Act which abrogated sections of the Bill of Rights. No less freely, Congress divested itself of its solemn right to wage war by granting Bush II a military *carte blanche* in Iraq. Dissenters to this mass surrender of legislative power to the executive would not fill a Fiat Pinto.

There were no mass protests when the administration gave itself the power to obtain personal information about citizens without public acknowledgment. Its Terrorism Information and Prevention System legalized nationwide spying on the American populace in the name of homeland security. Its successor, the Pentagon surveillance system known as TIA (Total Information Awareness) was even more Orwellian. For years now it has been intercepting data in cyberspace about every American. Phone, email, internet, library, school, medical, travel, and credit-card records are decrypted, stored in a database, and tagged for biometric analysis.[41]

To enumerate the gamut of these totalitarian policies would be superfluous in the wake of a library of monographs devoted to the ins and outs of the Bush administration.[42] When it comes to a literary correlative, however, there are none to equal Roth's artful evocation of homegrown fascism. When *The Plot Against America* landed in bookstores across the country on the eve of the 2004 election, it must have been hard for readers to refrain from pinching themselves—Roth's half-hearted disclaimers against interpreting it as a *roman à clef* notwithstanding.

How could readers not think of the Patriot Act when stung by Winchell's rants at the suppression of the Bill of Rights? How could they not think of phony WMDs and America's illegal wars when confronted with Herman Roth's plaints: "How can this be happening in America? How can people like these be in charge of our country?" (196). How could Roth think that his readers would not think of Bush II when he asked them: "How long will Americans remain asleep while their cherished Constitution is torn to shreds by the fascist fifth column of the Republican right marching under the sign of the cross and the flag?" (230).

The simple answer is—he couldn't. That's why it's not a coincidence that Lindbergh's approval ratings of 80–90 percent are a perfect match of Bush's in the wake of 9/11 and the war on

Afghanistan.[43] That's why the war-mongers insinuate a ridiculous threat of a WMD attack by . . . Canada. That's why the Republicans spinners assure the public that the president—the plain speaking, aviator-attired president—is not a dictator but a democratically elected leader. Add the false alerts, the diversions, and the hysteria, and it is clear that under no circumstances should any of this be taken to bear any resemblance to real-life events or persons, dead or alive.

THE HISTORY OF THE FUTURE PAST

> It can't happen here? It *is* happening here.
>
> Philip Roth, *The Plot Against America*

History, in spite of what is taught at school, is not primarily about facts and dates, although facts and dates are essential to good history. History is about the stories we tell each other about the past that was once our present. Some of these stories are disseminated in textbooks approved for use in America's classrooms while others are found in literature, film, or journalism. Some are narrated with much attention to veracity. Others borrow from history in order to fashion any number of national myths. Others still set out to challenge the very foundations of the national myths.

But one way or another—as Roth is at pains to point out in a novel that won him the Sidewise Award for Alternate History and the Best Historical Fiction prize from the Society of American Historians—history matters. Not, as he puts it, the kind of history that children memorize in school, "harmless history, where everything unexpected in its own time is chronicled on the page as inevitable" (114). But real history, the kind that does not lose sight of what happens to real people as they interact in a myriad ways to produce the macroeffects later footnoted as the rise or fall of this or that 'ism'.

It is in this profound sense of history that *The Plot Against America* is both a Jewish and an American novel. Significantly, with the Second World War as his background, Roth does not say even one word about the Holocaust. Instead, he approaches the essence of the Jewish experience historically, via their struggles to assimilate into whatever culture they had had the misfortune to find themselves outside of. Few ethnic groups make it more apparent that moral codes are biased in favour of harmonizing in-group attitudes than history's ultimate outsiders: the Jews.

Even love-thy-neighbour Christians would regularly go after Jews with a vengeance. Among accusations of murdering Jesus, the Catholic church—starting with many of its saints, such as Augustine—fomented pogroms and inquisitions for much of its two-thousand-years-long history. Lindbergh only updates anti-Semitism for the twentieth century by redrawing the battle lines in evolutionary terms of segregating the 'aliens' from the in-group:

> *We* cannot blame *them* for looking out for what *they* believe *their* own interests, but *we* must also look out for *ours*. *We* cannot allow the natural passions and prejudices of *other* people to lead *our* country to destruction.[44]

But *The Plot Against America* describes the experience of more than just one ethnic group. Roth hardly needs to point out that within-you-without-you life, isolated from Main Street not so much by ghetto walls but by social and cultural discrimination, has been the lot of most immigrant groups in the promised land: the antinomians, the niggers, the krauts, the micks, the wops, the pollacks, the pakis, the wetbacks, and all other hyphenated Americans.

Most wanted only to get on with their lives, so they accepted whatever society and industry tossed their way, hoping their docility would count in their favour. A few took up political and even armed struggle in order to enforce their constitutional rights. But all too often both groups ended up in the footnotes of the kind of history in which 'economy' is a synonym for 'profit'. Still, armed with better data and better analytic techniques, we may be overdue for a change in the ways we think about economic development. That, at least, is the message from Alan Blinder, vice-chairman of the Federal Reserve System under Clinton. His new monograph, *The Quiet Revolution*

(2004) brings out into the open what most of us have known anyway.

Social engineering in the form of free trade, deregulation, and austerity measures is far from always good. Social engineering in the form of interventionism, protectionism, debt relief, and minimum wage is far from always bad. It is a modern-day American tragedy that it takes a federal banker to propose that social good, be it an improvement in collective decision-making or a decline in immigrant alienation, is not measured in GNP or per-capita dollars. But the American republic has little use for history-mindful writers or even historians themseves.

It's not even that America forgets its history. More like, it never learned it in the first place. And, if the Texas Education Board will have its way, it never will. The board, dominated by Christian conservatives, voted in 2010 to adopt a new curriculum in all state primary and secondary schools. With more than five million schoolchildren, Texas wields disproportionate influence over the country. Instead of spending scarce resources on developing their own teaching materials, other states may find it easier to follow its standards, with the result that national history could get a facelift more thoroughgoing than any of Michael Jackson's.

Among others, the new and improved curriculum is going to:

- drop Jefferson from the list of enlightenment thinkers in the world-history curriculum
- drop references to the late Ted Kennedy
- adopt an even more laudatory stance toward Reagan
- require students follow conservative leaders and organizations such as the NRA, the Heritage Foundation, and Moral Majority
- minimize the coverage of minority leaders such as Cesar Chavez or liberal Supreme Court Justices like Thurgood Marshall
- portray the country as a Constitutional Republic and not democracy
- question or eliminate references to the separation of Church and State

- teach the benefits of US-style free-market economics and how government taxation can harm economic progress
- teach that the United Nations threatens American liberty, freedom, and sovereignty

One proposal that was debated but eventually voted down was to rename the slave trade "Atlantic triangular trade". A lost opportunity. At a stroke of a pen slavery could have been put to rest as a minor episode in the kaleidoscope of economic development that made the United States what it is today. But no matter. If not this time around, then the next we will succeed in twisting history's rubber arm to make it conform to the utopian vision of a city on the hill, with liberty and justice for all.

Notes

NOTES TO THE INTRODUCTION

1. In Avery, 145–146.
2. *Newsweek* [2009].
3. Psychologist Howard Gardner identified no less than seven types of intelligence: linguistic, logical-mathematical, bodily-kinaes-thetic, spatial, musical, social- interpersonal, introspective-in-trapersonal (later he added two more: natural and existential).
4. Ruddick's introduction to the novel offers an excellent analysis of its political, eugenic, social engineering, and evolutionary dimensions; for background on social engineering in the early twentieth century, see Jordan.
5. On modelling and thought experiments in literature, see Swirski, *Of Literature and Knowledge*, Chapters 2 through 4.
6. Stillman, 11.
7. For example, Freese.
8. Ironically, Mendel's studies between 1856–1871 predate *On the Origin of Species* which came out in 1859 (*Descent of Man* in 1871).
9. Tooby and Cosmides [1992], 104.
10. See Hamilton; Irons, esp. 257; Betzig.
11. Carroll [2005], 92.
12. For a critical reassessment of this utopian anthropology, see Freeman; also Ekman; Brown.

NOTES TO CHAPTER 1

1. Vargas, v–vi. For reappraisals of Skinner's work, see Todd and Morris; Richelle.
2. Pages 81–82; 84–85.
3. For a contemporary defense of behaviourism along the same lines, see Stout.

4. Page 99.
5. Page 257; all subsequent references are to *Walden Two* unless otherwise indicated.
6. It is quite imprecise, if not wholly inaccurate, to speak of behaviourism *tout court*; just like psychiatry had a number of founding fathers—Freud, Jung, Adler—there are various schools and types of behaviourism.
7. Bjork, 51.
8. *Science and Human Behavior* [1953].
9. H.A.L., 655; next quote, Williams [1949], 357.
10. Poore, 6; *Fortune* quote by Jessup, 193 (see also his "The Newest Utopia"); Rand, 137.
11. Wallerstein, 1. Belying the critiques, more than a dozen utopian studies have appeared since the late 1980s, among them Morris and Koss; Armytage. For other major anthologies, see Carey; Kelly; Claeys and Sargent; see also Segal; Kumar.
12. Bjork (146) documents Skinner's youthful readings about the Shakers and the Mormons and his visit to Oneida, the site of one of the more successful American utopian communities. In contrast to the Hutterites, *Walden Two* has no religion; instead, it 'religiously' follows the precepts of operant conditioning which—in a sharp contrast to the Hutterites, whose treatment of those who strayed from their credo could be punitive—mandates only positive reinforcement. For background on the Amish and the Hutterites, see Peter; Hostetler; Kraybill and Olshan.
13. Letter dated 14 November, 1803. For background on urbanization, see Swirski, *All Roads Lead to the American City.*
14. Ironically, Skinner's behaviourist paradise fits seamlessly with RAND's contingency plans for a nuclear holocaust which called for dispersing the American populace from cities to self-sufficient small communities trained in practical survival skills.
15. For example, Klaw; Elms.
16. Page 191.
17. Pages 106 and 181.
18. For adaptive food aversions during pregnancy see Tierson et al; Fessler. For sexual adaptations, see Trivers; Clutton-Brock; Alcock; Wiederman; Hrdy. The attitude of "wed early and thereby solve sexual problems" is actually early Victorian.
19. Jessup, "Utopia Bulletin", 191.
20. In Komar, 10.
21. "*Walden Two* Revisited", ix.
22. For background and analysis, see Swirski, *Ars Americana, Ars Politica* and *I Sing the Body Politic.*

23. Simon, 1665.
24. On aggression, see Wrangham and Peterson; Buss [2005]; Bourke.
25. Kuhlman [2005], 10. Parts of this section appeared previously in Swirski, "When Biological Evolution and Social Revolution Clash".
26. See Harlow; Symons; Pinker; Tooby and Cosmides [1992].
27. In Kuhlmann, 195.
28. See the classics works by Williams; Dawkins.
29. Daly, et al. [1997]; Daly and Wilson; Mackey and Daly [1995]; more generally, for a cultural difference in emotional display rules, see Matsumoto.
30. See Fernald; Fernald and Mazzie; Malloch; Mithen, esp. 72–74; for background, Kuhl.
31. For this and related issues from the Bolshevik 1920s and 1930s, see Goldman; Stites (esp. Chapters 6 and 10); Fitzpatrick; in the socio-literary context, Cooke.
32. All quotes in this paragraph from Kuhlmann, 105.
33. In Kuhlmann, 182. A prescient formulation of this nested triad, which anticipates contemporary research into altruism, can be found in Hume, 397.
34. In Kuhlmann, 175; next quote 119.
35. See also David Sloan Wilson [2007]; for hierarchy in primates, Kinzey.
36. Price, et al.; Shinada and Yamagishi; Boehm.
37. Kuhlmann, 109; see also 201; 204.
38. This and the following quote in Kuhlman, 126.
39. See also the classic study by Allport and Postman which came out a year before Skinner's utopia; and Dunbar [1998].
40. For different contexts of ToM, see Wellman; Tomasello; Baron-Cohen; Dunbar [2004]; Swirski [2009]; on intentional stance, see Dennett.
41. See also Bhugra; Mathes; Daly et al; Clanton and Smith.
42. Notable recent studies of envy are DeSteno and Salovey; Feather. See also Frank on passions with which we measure successes or failures relative to others.
43. See Williams; Axelrod and Hamilton; Axelrod; Sober and Wilson.
44. Miller and Feallock, 74.
45. In Kuhlmann, 204.
46. In Kuhlmann, 64.
47. Kinkade, 404.
48. See Parker for survey and analysis of utopian governments.
49. Besides the classic studies by Kuhn and Merton, see Cole; Shapin and Schaffer.
50. See Kumar; next quote, Kuhlmann, 96.

51. In Kuhlmann, 96.
52. In Kuhlmann, 182.
53. Page 215; see also the description of municipal takeover on 217.
54. In Kuhlmann, 211.
55. "Walden (One) and Walden Two", 2. In 1970 Skinner boasted: "In *Walden Two* there are very few automobiles, food is not purchased in small packages, tins and bottles to be thrown away, consumption does not require much heavy industry, a few copies of papers suffice for many readers, and so on. The citizens are not taking much out of nature nor are they putting much waste back in" (in Bjork, 147).
56. See Kuhlmann, 108.
57. See Heyman, 49; Ruth, 58; for background, see Kuhlmann [2001].
58. In Kuhlmann, 190.
59. In Kuhlmann, 224. In his own article, Ulrich is equally adamant: "There is no Walden Two nor will there ever be", 39.
60. Webb, 254.
61. Outside the biological disciplines, the so-called standard social-scientific model (SSST) still assumes cultural determinism to the exclusion of evolutionary factors.

NOTES TO CHAPTER 2

1. For the history of ECT and its effectiveness, see Shorter and Healy.
2. Faggen, 70. In his youth Kesey was an avid reader of the Tarzan adventures of Edgar Rice Burroughs and the Westerns of Zane Grey, both of whom feature lone heroes involved in a Manichean contest between sharply defined good and evil.
3. Kesey claimed never to have seen the film which he consistently disparaged.
4. All subsequent references are to *Cuckoo's Nest*, unless indicated otherwise. For readings of the ward as a microcosm of America, see the critical edition of Kesey; Searles; Tanner. Despite becoming an instant hit, the first honour for the novel came only in 1988 when the Western Literature Association gave Kesey their annual Award for Distinguished Achievement in Writing.
5. For reappraisals of Skinner's work, see Todd and Morris; Richelle; O'Donohue and Ferguson.
6. Thompson, 399.
7. *Beyond Freedom*, 99.
8. For a typically accusatory reference in Kesey's context, see Kerr, 458.

9. Tellingly, as new photographic evidence emerged in May 2009 of Americans torturing Iraqi prisoners, Obama u-turned on his promise of transparency and suppressed their release.

10. See Marks; Bindman; Foreman; Klein; Thomas.

11. For definition and discussion of democide, see Rummel.

12. In Steiner, 149; on perversions of the enlightenment rationality, see Saul.

13. King Leopold II of Belgium, despotic and democidal owner and ruler of the Congo Free State, averred that the "degeneracy" of the Congolese was an inherited condition. Lombroso's theories were not exactly new; for a review of classical and Islamic physiognomic theories, see Swain.

14. See Annas for background and discussion.

15. See Whitaker.

16. See Swirski [2007], Chapter 1, on the illustrative role of literature.

17. On the secret CIA's LSD trials, see Lee and Shlain; Marks. As if on cue, on the day I wrote this paragraph, BBC reported on CIA's frequent lies to the Congress.

18. See Swirski, *All Roads Lead to the American City*.

19. Leslie Fiedler twists the scene out of recognition by claiming that Mac attempts to rape the Nurse.

20. Faggen, 77. Far from blaming the Combine, however, Kesey makes clear that it is the evil in the hearts of men—and women—that combines into the system we know. For key references to the Combine in the novel, see pages 38, 109, 153, 203, 208–209, 227–228, 255, 292; for discussion, see Wallis.

21. Hubner, 87.

22. In a constitutional first (and so far last), the 18th "Prohibition" Amendment was repealed by the 21st.

23. Chapter 3, "The Types of Legitimate Domination," 215; see also, Calvert.

24. Whenever there are more than two candidates—when there are only two, plurality is as good a system as any (if fact, they are equivalent).

25. For the analysis of numerous other problems with the American electoral and political systems, see Swirski, *Ars Americana, Ars Politica*.

26. For background and analysis, see Poundstone's brilliant primer on voting theory and praxis, *Gaming the Vote*; for a critique of range voting, see Tideman.

27. Los Horcones, 43.

28. See Swirski [2009].

29. See Poundstone (pages 291–292) for addresses of political offices to be contacted to lobby for voting reform.

30. Strictly speaking, Switzerland is a semi-direct democracy.
31. For more on "sister republics", see Huston.
32. The Swiss secession, organized by Catholic cantons, took place in 1847 and the war lasted only twenty-six days. For analysis of Swiss democracy from the perspective of multiculturalism, see Linder.
33. In a still surviving type of popular assembly (*Landsgemeinde*), townsfolk assemble to receive face-to-face reports from their political representatives, to elect them, and to vote on new initiatives by a public show of hands.
34. Vestiges of the power to the people allow citizens in twenty-one states to propose state legislation by means of the popular initiative, and in 16 states to "recall" public officials from office. For a contemporary (January 2010) example in Oregon, see *The Economist*. On direct democracy in the United States, see Zimmerman; Waters; Schmidt; Cronin.
35. Sabato [2007].
36. Not only on the federal level; the same goes for the cantonal governments, called State Councils.
37. The so-called half-cantons (Basel city and Basel county) have only a half-vote, versus a full vote for full cantons; for background, see Church; Hughes.
38. On the question of literacy in the context of Michael Moore and George W. Bush, see Swirski, *Ars Americana, Ars Politica*, Chapter 5.
39. See the empirical work of Bruno S. Frey at Switzerland's Center for Research in Economics Management and the Arts.
40. See Faggen, 79.
41. See Howard on the political dimensions of homosexuality in the United States.
42. BBC News online [2009].
43. See Paul, esp. 133.

NOTES TO CHAPTER 3

1. Page 3–4; all subsequent references are to *God's Grace*, unless indicated otherwise.
2. In reality, for morphological and anatomical reasons, apes cannot vocalize like humans do.
3. See Garchik, "Malamud's Sense of Despair"; Swirski [2007], Chapter 5.
4. For Malamud's verbatim restatement, see Lasher, 7.
5. An autobiographical sketch of his life and work can be found in Malamud [1985]; for a full biographical account, see Davis; Malamud Smith (the writer's daughter).

6. For typical reviews, see Leonard and Lelchuk; the latter's confusion of baboons with chimps and chimps with gorillas, respectively, puts such reviews in perspective. For a critical exception to the rule, see Siegel.

7. In Lasher, 38; see also 112. For Malamud's comments on his indebtedness to Chaplin, see Rothstein.

8. In Lasher, 132.

9. Based on a considerably better 1963 novel by Pierre Boulle. Through Miranda's memorable line from *The Tempest*, Malamud also alludes to *Brave New World*; for that matter, even his *The Tenants*, in which a Jew and a Black play out their racial hatreds in the "accursed island" of their tenement, prefigures this allegorical fantasy.

10. *Consilience*, 224.

11. In McCombs, 202.

12. In Lasher, 68; also Lasher, 113.

13. Better known as a 1984 feature with Robert Redford; see Lasher, 62 and 131.

14. In Lasher, 132.

15. BBCNews [2008].

16. Both on 212. The 'golden rule' is expressed by Jesus in Matthew 7:12; cf. also Paul in Romans 13: 9–10, "Love your neighbours as yourself".

17. Wershba, 7.

18. Page 198. See Brandt [1996], 78–79, for a comparative discussion of the earliest versions of the moral code in ancient Attica. For Malamud's remarks on constitutional ideals, see *Talking Horse*, 145–146.

19. Hutton online; see also Johnston; Swirski, *Ars Americana, Ars Politica*.

20. Eastern Iranian ethno-linguistic group; today the language of Pashtuns is found mostly in Afghanistan and some provinces of Pakistan.

21. Wilson, [2000], 249.

22. Gene-culture coevolution is also known as Double Inheritance Theory (DIT).

23. For cultural ratcheting, see Tomasello; Tomasello et al.; Tomasello and Rakoczy. Of course, chimps and bonobos have some culture: for example, they teach youngsters how to use tools to crack nuts (though they don't keep tools but get new ones each time) and they also hunt cooperatively and exchange sex for monkey meat. However, they display almost no shared intentionality.

24. Research on mirror neurons in simians predates that on humans; see di Pelligrino et al.

25. Rizolati and Sinigaglia, 124; for "triadic" semiotics, see Percy [1975]; for more on indicated structures, see Swirski, *Literature, Analytically Speaking.*
26. Mirror neurons, reports Giacomo Rizzolatti, operate "by feeling not by thinking"; in Blakeslee online.
27. See de Waal [2006].
28. See de Waal [2006].
29. Swirski [2007].
30. In actuality there were two theorems.
31. Book of Proverbs, 1:3.
32. Ghiselin repulsed what is known as the Veneer Theory of human morality with this ironic summary of its tenets: "Scratch an 'altruist' and watch a 'hypocrite' bleed" (247).
33. Christian, Cordry, Gray, Hart, Jensen, Mertvago, Mieder, Owomoyela, Scarborough, and Stone in the bibliography.
34. Paraphrase of an obscure and long original; see Owomoyela.
35. See Mieder [2001].
36. For details, see Newberg, d'Aquili, and Rause.
37. See Gregory Paul.
38. For more on evolution and religion, see edited collections by Bulbulia et al.; Voland and Schiefenhovel; Feierman.

NOTES TO CHAPTER 4

1. Page 99; the terms comes from Trivers [1971]. Moralistic aggression is not uniquely human since it occurs in nonhuman primates as well; see, de Waal [1996], 89; also Trivers [1985].
2. Following Lorenz, I refer to aggression as intraspecies violence rather than as violence committed by one species against another (predation).
3. The word can also be translated as sign, omen, warning or even remembrance; for analysis in the context of human violence, see Wertham.
4. Page 146; see also Alexander. Although accused by de Waal [2006] of subscribing to the Vaneer Theory—whereby morality in humans is merely a matter of cultural overlay rather than of an evolutionarily deep-seeded suite of behaviours—Wright's approach is more nuanced, as exemplified by the cited passage. Wilson [1978] states: human behaviour "is the circuitous technique by which human genetic material has been and will be kept intact. Morality has no other demonstrable ultimate function" (167).
5. Keeley, esp. 28.
6. Page 191; all subsequent references are to *The Thanatos Syndrome* unless indicated otherwise.

7. See Richardson's studies of war statistics (casualties) and their distributions. Richardson focused on the period 1820–1949 because pre-1820 data at his disposal was scant (he died in 1953); altogether he tagged 108 wars in the world during that period. For contemporary databases of war statistics, see the comprehenaive study by Smith (esp. 43); Hayes.
8. In 1991 a posthumous collection of his essays appeared as *Signposts in a Strange Land.*
9. In Lawson and Kramer [1985], 300; see also Lawson and Kramer [1993], 193.
10. On narrative continuities between Percy's two More novels, see Lawson.
11. In Lawson and Kramer [1993], 136.
12. A similar range of intellect-enhancing symptoms was posited by Disch in *Camp Concentration.*
13. See Bugliosi for a legal case in the prosecution of George W. Bush for murder.
14. In Scheflin and Opton, 338.
15. In Lawson and Kramer [1993], 200. Percy derived much of the material relating to Weimar eugenetic practices from Wertham.
16. Percy, *Signposts*, 300–301.
17. In Marks, 140.
18. See Swirski [2009], Chapter 2.
19. For background, see Lemov; Adjibolosoo.
20. In *Looking for Spinoza* Antonio Damasio's research leads him to argue that we "should seek joy, by reasoned decree, regardless of how foolish and unrealistic the quest may look", 271. See Gilbert for a recent influential study of happiness.
21. Johns and Ormerod, 20.
22. For a particularly sinister Cold War example, see Marks, 130.
23. Bowart, 258. Symbolically perhaps, the 1949 Nobel Prize in medicine was shared by Walter Rudolf Hess for his work on electric brain stimulation and by neurologist Egas Moniz, the inventor of lobotomy.
24. See, for example, Park and Wieser [2000].
25. Graham-Rowe [2003], online.
26. In Phillips online [2004].
27. BBC, "Brain Chips Could Help Paralyzed" [2004]; next quote in Nagel, "Brain Chip Reads Man's Thoughts" [2005]; see also BBC "Mind Power Moves Paralyzed Limbs" [2008].
28. Begley, 10; see also Kerri Smith [2008].
29. BBC, "A Step Closer to Reading the Mind" [2009].
30. Setiathome (Sci-Tech News) [2009].
31. Sacks, 157–158.

32. In Wall, online.
33. Such sympathetic harmonics, however, are strongest in direct contact between individuals; see Hatfield, et al.
34. In Levin's novel the treatment, called LPK, is based on lithium. Much revised herein, the remainder of this section appeared in my *The Art and Science of Stanislaw Lem.*
35. Barrow and Tipler furnish a host of precise arguments debunking the deterministic, teleological, and anthropic assumptions thought to establish that, as individuals or species, we may be predetermined (less than free) in our states and actions.
36. See Swirski, *Of Literature and Knowledge.*
37. In Tooze, 11. For social Darwinism in the context of American robber-baron tactics, see Hofstadter, 45–46.
38. *Between Literature and Science* [2000].
39. In Klaw, 45.
40. In Faggen, 80.
41. Quoted in Pruden; for background see Smith.

NOTES TO CHAPTER 5

1. See Mackay.
2. For a distinction between emotions—affects expressed as somatic effects—and feelings—mental representations of emotions—see Damasio [2003]. For the biological nature of emotional universals, see Izard; Ekman; Wallbott and Scherer; Plutchik; Nesse; Zajonc; Damasio [1994].
3. The finale of John McCain's 2008 Republican nominee acceptance speech; a superb selection of American political speeches until 2006 can be found in Widmer.
4. See Searles, 39. Cf. Shechner: "Roth has strip-mined his own life for the stony ore of his books" (18); and Roth's "own experience has been the basis for much of his storytelling" (21). For example, "My True Story" section in *My Life as a Man* is written with such fidelity that it can be read as Roth's memoir; on life and art in Roth, see Posnock (esp. 19).
5. Searles, 41; see also Searles, 51.
6. Page 224; see Swirski, *Ars Americana, Ars Politica.*
7. See Rampton [2009]; Posnock also deflates Roth's protestations of art-for-art's sake.
8. See Swirski, *From Lowbrow to Nobrow,* and *Ars Americana, Ars Politica.*
9. For counterbalance, see reviews by Berman; Yardley; Morrison.
10. In Lasher, 65; see also Shechner, 18.

11. This is only the second time, after *Operation Shylock* [1993], that Roth's character bears his own name.
12. For more on American empire, see Swirski, "The Historature of the American Empire".
13. More subtle, perhaps, are the echoes of FDR's real-life Civilian Conservation Corps which countrified a number of rural boys in the 1930s.
14. The real Winchell turned into a McCarthyite in the 1950s.
15. See Kauffman; Pinter in Chrisafis and Tilden.
16. Reviewing Roth's novel, West calls the Patriot Act a "lifesaver"; for "t-shirt", see McConnell; Rumsfeld quote in Scott-Tyson.
17. For Posnock—who treats *Plot* only in the prefaratory section and only as an afterthought—the novel is largely a failure insofar as it fails to build narrative momentum and lacks character development (31); in reality, *The Plot* simply refuses to fit his thesis of Roth as a rude writer.
18. Bush [2000].
19. US Department of Defense, "FY 2003". On advanced planning of the current Iraq war, see Swirski, "The Historature of the American Empire".
20. For a refreshingly fact-based critique of Obama's legislative record which documents him not as a demon but just another Washington pol, see Freddoso.
21. See Hitchens.
22. The words "mission accomplished" were crossed out from the draft of Bush's speech by Rumsfeld.
23. In Searles, 50.
24. Many historians argue that, rather than Tojo, Yamamoto, and Nagumo, it was Roosevelt who took America into World War II; see, for example, Alsop; for background, Alterman.
25. Bush, "Remarks."
26. Data from Corn, 79–92.
27. In Woolley and Peters, online.
28. For detailed analysis of Obama's vs McCain's tax policies, see FactCheck "Obama's 'Welfare'".
29. CBCNews, online.
30. BBCNews [2010], online.
31. Tierney.
32. Known as NEVs, or neighbourhood electric vehicles; see Factcheck.org.
33. Damasio [2003], 93.
34. Page 25.
35. Page 92.
36. On psychology of emotion, see Frank; Zajonc; Greene; Bargh and Chartrand; Kahneman and Sunstein.

37. See Swirski, *Ars Americana, Ars Politica*, Chapter 4.
38. Damasio [2003], 34.
39. Riker, 4–5.
40. See Westen.
41. As exposed by *The Washington Post* in July 2010, this system is now so unwieldy that no one knows its true costs or size.
42. The interested reader may start with three who served under Bush: Bartlett; Suskind; Greenspan. For more on political *roman à clef* in the American context, see Swirski, *Ars Americana*, Chapter 3.
43. At the end of 2003, with the Iraq war raging long after Bush declared (in May 2003) that it was over, his popularity rating was still 63 percent, the highest of any president at the corresponding stage in their tenure (Johnson's rating of 74 percent in December 1963 was a one-off bump following Kennedy's assassination).
44. Page 13, my emphasis.

Bibliography

Adjibolosoo, Senyo. *Developing Civil Society: Social Order and the Human Factor.* San Diego: Ashgate, 2006.

Alcock, John. *Animal Behavior.* 5th ed. Sunderland, MA: Sinauer, 1993.

Alexander, Richard D. *The Biology of Moral Systems.* Hawthorne, NY: Aldine de Gruyter, 1987.

Allport, G.W., and L. Postman. *The Psychology of Rumor.* New York: Holt, 1947.

Alsop, Joseph. *FDR, 1882–1945: a Centenary Remembrance.* New York: Washington Square Press, 1982.

Alterman, Eric. *When Presidents Lie: A History of Official Deception and Its Consequences.* New York: Viking, 2004.

Annas, George J. "At Law: One Flew Over the Supreme Court." *Hastings Center Report* 20.3 (May/June 1990): 28–30.

Armytage, W.H.G. *Heavens Below: Utopian Experiments in England, 1560–1960.* London, New York: Routledge, 2006.

Avery, Evelyn. "Remembrances of Malamud: 1972–1986." In Lasher, Lawrence M., ed. *Conversations with Bernard Malamud.* Jackson, MI: University Press of Mississippi, 1991. 145–151.

Ayllon, Teodoro, and Nathan H. Azrin. *The Token Economy: a Motivational System for Therapy and Rehabilitation.* New York: McGraw-Hill/Appleton and Lange, 1968.

Axelrod, Robert. *The Evolution of Cooperation.* New York: Basic, 1984.

Axelrod, Robert, and William D. Hamilton. "The evolution of cooperation." *Science* 211 (1981): 1390–1396.

Bargh, John A., and T.L. Chartrand. "The Unbearable Automaticity of Being." *American Psychologist* 54 (1999): 462–479.

Barrow, John, and Frank J. Tipler. *The Anthropic Cosmological Principle.* Oxford: Oxford University Press, 1986.

Barsness, John A. "Ken Kesey: The Hero in Modern Dress." In Kesey, Ken. *One Flew Over the Cuckoo's Nest. Text and criticism.* Ed. John Clark Pratt. New York: Penguin, 1996. 431–439.

Bartlett, Bruce. *Impostor: How George W. Bush Bankrupted America and Betrayed the Reagan Legacy.* New York: Doubleday, 2006.

Batson, C. Daniel. *The Altruism Question: Toward a Social Psychology Answer.* Hillsdale, NJ: Lawrence Erlbaum Associates, 1991.

BBCNews World Edition (online): US & Canada. "Tea Party Activists Fund Sign Linking Obama to Hitler." July 14 (2010). http://www.bbc.co.uk/news/world-us+canada-10636746

BBCNews World Edition (online). "Uganda Fear over Gay Death-penalty Plans." December 22 (2009). http://news.bbc.co.uk/2/hi/africa/8412962.stm

BBCNews World Edition (online). "DNA Computer Solves Logic Queries." August 5 (2009). http://news.bbc.co.uk/go/pr/fr/-/2/hi/technology/8184033.stm

BBCNews World Edition (online). "CIA 'Often Lied to Congressmen.'" July 9 (2009). http://news.bbc.co.uk/2/hi/americas/8143081.stm

BBCNews World Edition (online). "A Step Closer to Reading the Mind." March 12 (2009). http://news.bbc.co.uk/2/hi/health/7937926.stm

BBCNews World Edition (online). "Mind Power Moves Paralyzed Limbs." October 15 (2008). http://news.bbc.co.uk/2/hi/health/7669159.stm

BBCNews World Edition (online). "Marine Threw Himself onto Grenade." March 30 2008. http://news.bbc.co.uk/go/pr/fr/-/2/hi/uk_news/england/west_midlands/7321647.stm

BBCNews World Edition (online). "Brain Chips Could Help Paralyzed." April 17 (2004). http://news.bbc.co.uk/2/hi/health/3632855.stm

Begley, Sharon. "Mind Reading Is Here." *Newsweek* February 4 (2008): 10.

Bellamy, Edward. *Looking Backward: 2000–1887.* New York: Dover, 1996. [Orig. 1888]

Berman, Paul. "The Plot Against America." *The New York Times* 3 October (2004). http://www.nytimes.com/2004/10/03/books/review/03BERMAN.html

Berreby, David. *Us and Them: Understanding Your Tribal Mind.* New York: Little Brown, 2005.

Betzig, Laura. *Despotism and Differential Reproduction: A Darwinian View of History.* Hawthorne, NY: Aldine de Gruyter, 1986.

Betzig, Laura. "Not Whether to Count Babies, but Which." In Crawford, Charles, and Dennis L. Krebs, eds. *Handbook of Evolutionary Psychology: Ideas, Issues, Applications.* Mahway, NJ: Lawrence Erlbaum Associates, 1998.

Bhugra, D. "Cross-cultural Aspects of Jealousy." *International Review of Psychiatry* 5 (1993): 271–280.

Bindman, Stephen. "Brainwashing Victims to Get $100,000." *The Montreal Gazette,* November 18 (1992): A1.

Bjork, Daniel W. *B.F. Skinner: A Life*. New York: HarperCollins, 1993.

Blakeslee, Sandra. "Cells That Read Minds." *New York Times*, January 10 (2006). http://www.nytimes.com/2006/01/10/science/10mirr.html

Blinder, Alan S. *The Quiet Revolution*. Yale: Yale University Press, 2004.

Boehm, Christopher. *Hierarchy in the Forest: The Evolution of Egalitarian Behavior*. Cambridge, MA: Harvard University Press, 1999.

Bourke, Joanna. *An Intimate History of Killing: Face to Face Killing in 20th-Century Warfare*. New York: Basic, 1999.

Bowart, Walter. *Operation Mind Control*. New York: Dell, 1978.

Boyd, Brian. *On the Origin of Stories:, Evolution, Cognition, and Fiction*. Cambridge, MA: Belknap, 2009.

Boyers, Robert. "Porno-Politics." In Kesey, Ken. *One Flew over the Cuckoo's Nest. Text and Criticism*. Ed. John Clark Pratt. New York: Penguin, 1996. 445–451.

Brandt, R.B. *Facts, Values and Morality*. Cambridge: Cambridge University Press, 1996.

Broom, Donald M. *The Evolution of Morality and Religion*. Cambridge: Cambridge University Press, 2003.

Brown, D.E. *Human Universals*. New York: McGraw-Hill, 1991.

Bugliosi, Vincent. *The Prosecution of George W. Bush for Murder*. Cambridge, MA: Vanguard, 2008.

Bulbulia, Joseph, Richard Sosis, Russell Genet, Cheryl Genet, Erica Harris, and Karen Wyman, eds. *The Evolution of Religion: Studies, Theories, and Critiques*. Santa Margarita, CA: Collins Foundation Press, 2008.

Bush, George W. "Remarks on Transmitting the Tax Relief Plan to the Congress". In Woolley, John T., and Gerhard Peters. *The American Presidency Project*. Santa Barbara, CA. February 8, 2001. http://www.presidency.ucsb.edu/ws/index.php?pid=45937

Bush, George W. "Bush vs Gore, Second Presidential Debate October 11." http://www.fas.org/news/usa/2000/usa-001011.htm

Buss, David M. *The Dangerous Passion: Why Jealousy Is as Necessary as Love and Sex*. New York: Free Press, 2000.

Buss, David. *The Murderer Next Door: Why the Mind is Designed to Kill*. New York: Penguin, 2005.

Calvert, Randall. "Leadership and Its Basis in Problems of Social Coordination." *International Political Science Review* 13 (1992): 7–24.

Camus, Albert. "Albert Camus, The Nobel Prize in Literature 1957: Banquet Speech." (1957). http://nobelprize.org/nobel_prizes/literature/laureates/1957/camus-speech-e.html

Carroll, Joseph. "Human Nature and Literary Meaning: A Theoretical Model Illustrated with a Critique of *Pride and Prejudice*." In

Gottschall, Jonathan, and David Sloan Wilson, eds. *The Literary Animal: Evolution and the Nature of Narrative.* Forewords by E.O. Wilson and Frederick Crews. Evanston IL: Northwestern University Press, 2005.

Carroll, Joseph. *Evolution and Literary Theory.* St. Louis: University of Missouri Press, 1994.

Carey, John, ed. *The Faber Book of Utopias.* London: Faber and Faber, 1999.

CBC News/*New York Times* poll, November 18–21 (2004), reported by American Scientific Affiliation. www.asa3.org/ASA/topics/Evolution/index.html

CBCNews: Politics. "Transcript: Final Presidential Debate." October 16 (2008). http://www.cbsnews.com/stories/2008/10/16/politics/2008debates/main4525254.shtml

Christian, John. *Behar Proverbs.* London: Kegan Paul, Trench Trübner & Co., 1891.

Church, Clive H. *The Politics and Government of Switzerland.* Basingstoke: Palgrave Macmillan, 2004.

Claeys, Gregory, and Lyman Tower Sargent, eds. *The Utopias Reader.* New York: New York University Press, 1999.

Clanton, G., and L.G. Smith. *Jealousy.* 3rd ed. New York: University Press of America, 1998.

Clutton-Brock, T.H. *The Evolution of Parental Care.* Princeton, NJ: Princeton University Press, 1991.

Cole, Stephen. *Making Science: Between Nature and Society.* Cambridge, MA: Harvard University Press, 1992.

Cooke, Brett. *Human Nature in Utopia: Zamyatin's We."* Evanston, IL: Northwestern University Press, 2002.

Cordry, Harold V. *The Multicultural Dictionary of Proverbs.* Jefferson, NC: McFarland & Co., 1997.

Corn, David. *The Lies of George W. Bush: Mastering the Politics of Deception.* New York: Crown, 2003.

Cosmides, Leda, and John Tooby. "Cognitive Adaptations for Social Change." In Barkow, Jerome, Leda Cosmides, and John Tooby. *The Adapted Mind.* New York: Oxford University Press, 1992.

Couch, Richard W., et al. "Some Considerations of Behavior Analysts Developing Social Change Interventions." *Behavior Analysis and Social Action* 5.1–2 (1986): 9–13.

Cronin, Thomas E. *Direct Democracy: The Politics of Initiative, Referendum, and Recall.* Cambridge, MA: Harvard University Press, 1989.

Daly, Martin, et al. "Kinship: the conceptual hole in psychological studies of social cognition and close relationships." In Simpson, J.A., and D.T. Kendrick, eds. *Evolutionary social psychology.* Mahwah, NJ: Lawrence Erlbaum Associates, 1997. 265–296.

Daly, Martin, et al. "Male Sexual Jealousy." *Ethology and Sociobiology* 3 (1982): 11–27.

Daly Martin, and Margo Wilson. *Sex, Evolution, and Behavior.* Boston: Willard Grant, 1983.

Daly, Martin, and Margo Wilson. "Discriminative Parental Solicitude and the Relevance of Evolutionary Models to the Analysis of Motivational Systems." In Gazzaniga, M.S., ed. *The Cognitive Neurosciences.* Cambridge, MA: MIT Press, 1995.

Damasio, Antonio. *Descartes' Error: Emotion, Reason, and the Human Brain.* New York, Putnam, 1994.

Damasio, Antonio. *Looking for Spinoza: Joy, Sorrow, and the Feeling Brain.* Orlando: Harcourt, 2003.

Davis, Philip. *Bernard Malamud: A Writer's Life.* Oxford: Oxford University Press, 2007.

Davitz, Joel R. *The Language of Emotion.* New York: McGraw Hill, 1969.

Dawkins, Richard. *The Selfish Gene.* New York: Oxford University Press, 1976.

Dennett, Daniel C. *The Intentional Stance.* Cambridge, MA: MIT Press, 1989.

DeSteno, D.A., and P. Salovey. "Jealousy and Envy." In Manstead, A.S.R., and M. Hewstone, eds. *The Blackwell Encyclopedia of Social Psychology.* Oxford: Blackwell, 1995.

Deutsch, Albert. *The Shame of the States. Mental Illness and Social Policy: The American Experience.* Manchester, NH: Ayer, 1948.

Deutsch, Albert. *The Mentally Ill in America: A History of Their Care and Treatment from Colonial Times.* New York: Columbia University Press, 2007. Orig. 1937.

de Waal, Frans. *Good Natured.* Cambridge, MA: Harvard University Press, 1996.

de Waal, Frans, and Robert Wright, Christine M. Korsgaard, Philip Kitcher, Peter Singer. *Primates and Philosophers: How Morality Evolved.* Princeton; Oxford: Princeton University Press, 2006.

di Pellegrino, G., L.Fadiga, L. Fogassi, V. Gallese, and G. Rizzolatti. "Understanding Motor Events: A Neurophysiological Study." *Experimental Brain Research* 91 (1992): 176–180.

Disch, Thomas M. *Camp Concentration.* New York: Vintage, 1999. [1968]

Donnelly, Ignatius. *Caesar's Column: A Story of the Twentieth Century.* Ed. Nicholas Ruddick. Middletown, CN: Wesleyan University Press, 2003.

Dunbar, Robin. "Theory of Mind and the Evolution of Language." In Hurford, J.R., M. Studdert-Kennedy, and C. Knight, eds. *Approaches to the Evolution of Language.* Cambridge: Cambridge University Press, 1998. 92–110.

Dunbar, Robin. *The Human Story*. London: Faber and Faber, 2004.

Dunbar, Robin. *Grooming, Gossip, and the Evolution of Language*. London: Faber & Faber, 1996.

Ekman, Paul, ed. *Darwin and Facial Expression: A Century of Research in Review*. New York: Academic Press, 1973.

Ekman, Paul. "Expression and the Nature of Emotions." In Scherer, K., and Paul Ekman, eds. *Approaches to Emotion*. Hillsdale, NJ: Lawrence Erlbaum Associates, 1984.

Elms, Alan C. "Skinner's Dark Year and *Walden Two*." *American Psychologist* 36 (May 1981): 470–479.

Emerson, Ralph Waldo. "Self Reliance." Ed. Gene Dekovic. St. Helena, CA: Illuminations Press, 1975.

FactCheck.org. "GOP Stimulus Myths." February 24 (2009). http://www.factcheck.org/politics/gop_stimulus_myths.html

FactCheck.org. "Stimulus Bill Bravado." February 20 (2009). http://www.factcheck.org/politics/stimulus_bill_bravado.html

FactCheck.org. "Obama's 'Welfare.'" October 20, 2008. http://www.factcheck.org/elections-2008/obamas_welfare.html

Faggen, Robert. "Ken Kesey: The Art of Fiction CXXVI." *The Paris Review* 36 (Spring 1994): 58–94.

Feather, N.T. "Attitudes toward Achievers and Reactions to Their Fall: Theory and Research Concerning Tall Poppies." *Advances in Experimental Social Psychology* 26 (1994): 1–73.

Feierman, Jay R., ed. *The Biology of Religious Behavior: The Evolutionary Origins of Faith and Religion*. Santa Barbara, CA: Praeger, 2009.

Fernald, Anne. "Intonation and Communicative Intent in Mother's Speech to Infants: Is the Melody the Message?" *Child Development* 60 (1989): 1497–1510.

Fernald, Anne. "Prosody in Speech to Children: Prelinguistic and Linguistic Functions." *Annals of Child Development* 8 (1991): 43–80.

Fernald, Anne, and C. Mazzie. "Prosody and Focus in Speech to Infants and Adults." *Developmental Psychology* 27 (1991): 209–221.

Fessler, D.M.T. "Reproductive Immunosuppression and Diet." *Current Anthropology* 43 (2002): 19–38.

Fiedler, Leslie. *The Return of the Vanishing American*. New York: Stein and Day, 1968.

Fitzpatrick, Sheila, and Yuri Slezkine, eds. *In the Shadow of Revolution*. Princeton, NJ: Princeton University Press, 2000.

Fordham Foundation. "Good Science, Bad Science: Teaching Evolution in the States." September 1 (2000): Figure 1. www.dexcellence.net

Foreman, Judy. "How the CIA Stole Their Minds." *Boston Globe* 30 October (1998): 77.

Forrey, Robert. "Ken Kesey's Psychopathic Savior: A Rejoinder." *Modern Fiction Studies* 21 (1975): 222–230.

Frank, Robert H. *Passions within Reason: The Strategic Role of the Emotions.* New York: Norton, 1988.

Freddoso, David. *The Case against Barack Obama: The Unlikely Rise and Unexamined Agenda of the Media's Favorite Candidate.* Washington: Regnery Publishing, 2008.

Freeman, Derek. *Margaret Mead and Samoa: The Making and Unmaking of an Anthropological Myth.* Cambridge, MA: Harvard University Press, 1983.

Freese, Peter. "Surviving the End: Apocalypse, Evolution, and Entropy in Bernard Malamud, Kurt Vonnegut, and Thomas Pynchon." *Critique* 36.3 (1995): 163–177.

Freud, Sigmund. *Beyond the Pleasure Principle.* New York: Norton, 1990.

Frey, Bruno S. *Inspiring Economics: Human Motivation in Political Economy.* Cheltenham: Edward Elgar, 2002.

Frey, Bruno S. *Happiness: A Revolution in Economics.* Cambridge, MA: MIT, 2008.

Gallup News Service. "Public Favorable to Creationism." February 14 (2001). http://poll.gallup.com/content/default.aspx?ci=2014&pg=1

Garchik, Leah. "Malamud's Sense of Despair." In Lasher, Lawrence M., ed. *Conversations with Bernard Malamud.* Jackson, MI: University Press of Mississippi, 1991. 119–122.

Gardner, Howard. *Frame of Mind: The Theory of Multiple Intelligences.* New York: Basic, 1993.

Geer, John G. *In Defense of Negativity: Attack Ads in Presidential Campaigns.* Chicago: Chicago University Press, 2006

Ghiselin, Michael. *The Economy of Nature and the Evolution of Sex.* Berkeley: University of California Press, 1974.

Gilbert, Daniel. *Stumbling on Happiness.* London: Harper, 2007.

Goldberg, Lewis R. "From Ace to Zombie: Some Explorations in the Language of Personality." In Spielberger, Charles, and J. Butcher, eds. *Advances in Personality Assessment.* Hillsdale, NJ: Lawrence Erlbaum Associates, 1982. 203–234.

Goldman, Wendy Z. *Women, the State and Revolution: Soviet Family Policy and Social Life, 1917–1936.* Cambridge: Cambridge University Press, 1993.

Goldman, Wendy Z. "Working-class Women and the "withering away" of the Family: Popular Responses to Family Policy." In Fitzpatrick, Sheila, Alexander Rabonowitch, and Richard Stites, eds. *Russia in the Era of NEP.* Bloomington, IN: Indiana University Press, 1991. 125–143.

Goodwin, Barbara, ed. *The Philosophy of Utopia.* London/New York: Routledge, 2001.

Gottschall, Jonathan, and David Sloan Wilson, eds. *The Literary Animal: Evolution and the Nature of Narrative.* Forewords by E.O. Wilson and Frederick Crews. Evanston IL: Northwestern University Press, 2005.

Gould, Stephen Jay. *Ethology: The Mechanisms and Evolution of Behavior.* New York: Norton, 1982.

Graham-Rowe, Duncan. "World's First Brain Prosthesis Revealed." *NewScientist.com* (March 2003). www.newscientist.com/news/news.jsp?id=ns99993488

Gray, James. *Ancient Proverbs and Maxims from Burmese Sources.* London: Trubner & Co, 1886.

Greene, Joshua. "Emotion and Cognition in Moral Judgment: Evidence from Neuroimaging." In Changeux, Jean-Pierre, Antonio Damasio, W. Singer, and Y. Christen, eds. *Neurobiology of Human Values.* Berlin: Springer, 2005. 57–66.

Greenspan, Alan. *The Age of Turbulence: Adventures in a New World.* New York: Penguin, 2007.

H.A.L. "*Walden Two.*" *Journal of Philosophy* 46.20 (September 29, 1949): 654–655.

Hamilton, William D. "The Genetical Evolution of Social Behavior." *Journal of Theoretical Biology* 7 (1964): 1–52.

Hart, Henry H. (translator). *Seven Hundred Chinese Proverbs.* Stanford, CA: Stanford University Press, 1947.

Hatfield, Elaine, J.T. Cacioppo, and R.L. Rapson. "Emotional Contagion." *Current Directions in Psychological Science* 2 (1993): 96–99.

Hayes, Brian. "Statistics of Deadly Quarrels." *American Scientist Online* (January/February 2002). www.americanscientist.org/template/AssetDetail/assetid/14426

Healy, David. *Mania: A Short History of Bipolar Disorder.* Baltimore: Johns Hopkins University Press, 2008.

Healy, David. *Let Them Eat Prozac: The Unhealthy Relationship Between the Pharmaceutical Industry and Depression.* New York: New York University Press, 2006.

Healy, David. *The Antidepressant Era.* Cambridge, MA: Harvard University Press, 1999.

Healy, David. *Before Prozac: The Troubled History of Mood Disorders in Psychiatry.* New York: Oxford University Press, 2008.

Herrnstein, R.J. "The Evolution of behaviorism." *American Psychologist* 32 (1977): 593–603.

Hernstein, R.J. "Doing What Comes Naturally. A Reply to Professor Skinner." *American Psychologist* 32 (1977): 1013–1016.

Heyman, Ken. "Skinner's Utopia: Panacea, or Path to Hell?" *Time* (September 20, 1971): 47–53.

Hitchens, Christopher. *No One Left to Lie To: The Values of the Worst Family*. London/New York: Verso, 1999.

Hobbes, Thomas. *Leviathan*. Cambridge: Cambridge University Press, 1991.

Hofstadter, Richard. *Social Darwinism in American Thought*. New York: Brazillier, 1969. [1944].

Hostetler, John Andrew. *Amish Society*. Baltimore: Johns Hopkins University Press, 1993.

Howard, John. *Concentrations Camps on the Home Front: Japanese Americans in the House of Jim Crow*. Chicago: University of Chicago Press, 2008.

Howard, John. *Men Like That: A Southern Queer History*. Chicago: University of Chicago Press, 2001.

Hrdy, Sarah B. *Mother Nature: Natural Selection and the Female of the Species*. New York: Pantheon, 1999.

Hübner, Zygmunt, and Daniel Gerould. "Interview: Directing in Poland: A Confrontation with History: Zygmunt Hübner." *Performing Arts Journal* 5.2 (1981): 81–90.

Hughes, Christopher. *Switzerland*. New York: Praeger, 1975.

Hughes, Harold. "The Man behind the *Fixer*." In Lasher, Lawrence M., ed. *Conversations with Bernard Malamud*. Jackson, MI: University Press of Mississippi, 1991.

Hume David. *A Treatise on Human Nature*. London: Penguin, 1985.

Huston, James H. *The Sister Republics*. Washington: Library of Congress, 1991.

Hutton, Will. "Why America's Richest Love Taxes." *Observer* Febrary 25 (2001). http://observer.guardian.co.uk/comment/story/0,6903,442671,00.html

Huxley, Aldous. *Brave New World*. New York: Harper and Brothers, 1946.

Irons, William. "Cultural and Biological Success." In Chagnong, Napoleon A., and William Irons, eds. *Evolutionary Biology and Human Social Behavior*. North Scituate, MA: Duxbury Press, 1979.

Izard, C.E. *Human Emotions*. New York: Plenum Press, 1977.

Jefferson, Thomas. *The Writings of Thomas Jefferson: Memorial Edition*. Lipscomb, Andrew A., and Albert E. Bergh, eds. 20 vols. Washington, DC: Thomas Jefferson Memorial Association, 1903–1904.

Jensen, Herman. *A Classified Collection of Tamil Proverbs*. London: Kegan Paul, Trench Trübner & Co., 1897.

Jessup, John K. "The Newest Utopia." *Life* (June 28, 1948): 38.

Jessup, John K. "Utopia Bulletin." *Fortune* (October 1948): 191–196.

Johns, Helen, and Paul Ormerod. *Happiness, Economics and Public Policy.* London: Institute of Economic Affairs, 2007.

Johnson, Paul. *Modern Times: The World from the Twenties to the Eighties.* New York: Harper and Row, 1983.

Johnston, David Cay. "Corporate Wealth Share Rises for Top-Income Americans." *New York Times* January 29 (2006): 1:22.

Jordan, John M. *Machine-age Ideology: Social Engineering and American Liberalism, 1911–1939.* Chapel Hill: University of North Carolina Press, 1994.

Kahneman Daniel, and C.R. Sunstein. "Cognitive Psychology and Moral Intuitions." In In Changeux, Jean-Pierre, Antonio Damasio, W. Singer, and Y. Christen. Berlin: Springer, 2005. 91–105.

Kassiola, Joel. "Political Values and Literature: The Contribution of Virtual Experience." In Whitebrook, Maureen, ed. *Reading Political Stories: Representations of Politics in Novels and Pictures.* Lanham, MD: Rowman and Littlefield, 1992.

Kauffman, Bill. "Heil to the Chief." *The American Conservative* 27 September (2004). http://www.amconmag.com/article/2004/sep/27/00028/

Keeley, Lawrence H. *War Before Civilization.* New York: Oxford University Press, 1996.

Kelly, Catriona, ed. *Utopias: Russian Modernist Texts 1905–1940.* London: Penguin, 1999.

Kerr, Walter. ". . . And the Young Flew Over the Cuckoo's Nest." In Kesey, Ken. *One Flew over the Cuckoo's Nest. Text and criticism.* Ed. John Clark Pratt. New York: Penguin, 1996. 455–459.

Kesey, Ken. *One Flew over the Cuckoo's Nest. Text and Criticism.* Ed. John Clark Pratt. New York: Penguin, 1996.

Kinkade, Kathleen. "Power and the Utopian Assumption." *Journal of Applied Behavioiral Science* 10.3 (1974): 402–414.

Kinzey, Warren G., ed. *The Evolution of Human Behavior: Primate Models.* Albany, NY: State University of New York Press, 1987.

Klaw, Spencer. "Harvard's Skinner: The Last of the Utopians." *Harper's Magazine* (April 1963): 45–51.

Klein, Naomi. *The Shock Doctrine.* London: Penguin, 2007.

Klinkowitz, Jerome. "McMurphy and Yossarian as Politicians." In Searles George, ed. *A Casebook on Ken Kesey's* One Flew Over the Cuckoo's Nest." Albuquerque, NM: University of New Mexico Press, 1992.

Komar, Ingrid. *Living the Dream: A Documentary Study of Twin Oaks Community.* Louisa, VA: Twin Oaks, 1989.

Kraybill, Donald B., and M.A. Olshan. *The Amish Struggle with Modernity.* Hanover, NH: University Press of New England, 1994.

Kuhl, Patricia K. "Perceptions of Speech and Sound in Early Infancy." In *Handbook of Infant Perception: Volume 2*. New York: Academic Press, 1987.

Kuhlmann, Hilke. *Living Walden Two: B.F. Skinner's Behaviorist Utopia and Experimental Communes*. Champaign, IL: University of Illinois Press, 2005.

Kuhlmann, Hilke. "The Illusion of Permanence: Work Motivation and Membership Turnover at Twin Oaks Community." In Goodwin, Barbara, ed. *The Philosophy of Utopia*. London/New York: Routledge, 2001. 157–171.

Kuhn, Thomas S. *The Structure of Scientific Revolutions*. Chicago: University of Chicago Press, 1970.

Kumar, Krishan. "The Utopia of 'Behavioral Engineering': B.F. Skinner and *Walden Two*." In *Utopia and Anti-Utopia in Modern Times*. Oxford: Blackwell, 1991. 347–378.

Kumar, Krishan. *Utopianism*. London: Taylor&Francis, 1991.

Laing, Ronald D. *The Politics of Experience, and, The Bird of Paradise*. Harmondsworth: Penguin, 1965.

Laing, Ronald D. *The Divided Self: An Existential Study in Sanity and Madness*. Harmondsworth: Penguin, 1965.

Lasher, Lawrence M., ed. *Conversations with Bernard Malamud*. Jackson, MI: University Press of Mississippi, 1991.

Lawson, Lewis A., and Victor A. Kramer, eds. *Conversations with Walker Percy*. Jackson: University Press of Mississippi, 1985.

Lawson, Lewis A., and Victor A. Kramer, eds. *More Conversations with Walker Percy*. Jackson: University Press of Mississippi, 1993.

Lawson, Lewis A. "Tom More: Walker Percy's Alienated Genius." *South Central Review* 10 (1993): 34–54.

Lee, Martin A., and Bruce Shlain. *Acid Dreams: The Complete Social History of LSD*. New York: Grove, 1985.

Lelchuk, Alan. "Malamud's Dark Fable." *New York Times* August 29 (1982): A1.

Lelchuk, Alan. "On Satirizing Presidents." In Searles, George J., ed. *Conversations with Philip Roth*. Jackson, MI: University Press of Mississippi, 1992.

Lemley, Brad. "Future Tech: Really Special Forces." *Discover.com*. February 2002. Discover Magazine Online. www.discover.com/feb_02/feattech.html

Lemov, Rebecca. *World as Laboratory: Experiments with Mice, Mazes, and Men*. New York: Hill and Wang, 2005.

Lenin, Vladimir I. "The Tasks of the Youth Leagues." *On Youth*. Moscow: Progress Publishers, 1967.

Leonard, John. *God's Grace*. By Bernard Malamud." *New York Times* August 23 (1982): C18.

Levin, Ira. *This Perfect Day.* New York: Random House, 1970.

Linder, Wolf. *Swiss Democracy: Possible Solutions to Conflict in Multicultural Societies.* New York: St. Martin's, 1994.

Lipow, Arthur. *Authoritarian Socialism in America: Edward Bellamy and the Nationalist Movement.* Berkeley, CA: University of California Press, 1982.

Longstreth, T. Morris. "Utopia with Low Ceiling." *The Christian Science Monitor* June 24 (1948): 15.

Lorenz, Konrad. *On Aggression.* New York: Harcourt, Brace and World, 1966.

Los Horcones. "Personalized Government: A Governmental System Based on Behavior." *Behavior Analysis and Social Action* 7.1 (1989): 42–47.

Lumsden, Charles. "The Next Synthesis: 25 Years of Genes, Mind, and Culture." In Lumsden, Charles J., and Edward O. Wilson. *Genes, Mind, and Culture.* Hackensack, NJ: World Scientific, 2005. 2nd ed.

Mackay, Robert. "When Legislators Attack: 10 Political Brawls Caught on Tape." *The New York Times* July 22 2009. http://thelede.blogs.nytimes.com/2009/07/22/when-legislators-attack/

Mackey, W.C., and Daly R.D. "A Test of the Man–Child Bond: The Predictive Potency of the Teeter-totter Effect." *Genetic, Social, and General Psychology Monographs* 121 (1995): 424–444.

Malamud, Bernard. *Talking Horse.* Cheuse, Alan, and Nicholas Delbanco, eds. New York: Columbia University Press, 1997.

Malamud, Bernard. *Long Work, Short Life.* Hoosick Falls, NY: Bennington College, 1985.

Malamud, Bernard. *God's Grace.* New York: Avon, 1982.

Malamud Smith, Janna. *My Father Is a Book.* New York: Houghton Mifflin, 2006.

Malloch, S.N. "Mothers and Infants and Communicative Musicality." *Musicae Scientiae* (Special Issue 1999–2000): 29–57.

Malinowski, Bronislaw. *Crime and Custom in Savage Society: An Anthropological Study of Savagery.* Littlfield: Adams, 1966. [1926].

Marks, John D. *The Search for the Manchurian Candidate: The CIA and Mind Control: The Secret History of the Behavioral Sciences.* New York: Norton, 1979.

Mathes, E.W. *Jealousy: The Psychological Data.* New York: University Press of America, 1991.

Matsumoto, D. "Cultural Similarities and Differences in Display Rules." *Motivation and Emotion* 14 (1990): 195–214.

McCain, John. "Text: McCain's Speech." *The New York Times,* September 5 (2008). http://www.nytimes.com/2008/09/05/world/americas/05iht-05mccainspeech.15915360.html?pagewanted=1&_r=1

McCombs, Phil. "Century of Thanatos: Walker Percy and His Subversive Message." In Lawson, Lewis A., and Victor A. Kramer, eds. *More Conversations with Walker Percy.* Jackson: University Press of Mississippi, 1993. 189–207.

McConnell, Terry. "Liberty Is Dealt Another Blow." *The Edmonton Journal*, March 9 (2003): D2.

Merton, Robert K. *The Sociology of Science: Theoretical and Empirical Investigations.* Chicago: University of Chicago Press, 1979.

Mertvago, Peter. *Dictionary of 1000 French Proverbs with English Equivalents.* New York: Hippocrene Books, 1996.

Mieder Wolfgang. *Proverbs from Around the World.* Paramus, NJ: Prentice Hall, 1998.

Mieder, Wolfgang. "Do Unto Others as You Would Have Them Do Unto You": Frederick Douglass's Proverbial Struggle for Civil Rights." *Journal of American Folklore* 114. 453 (2001): 331–357.

Miller, Kenneth R. *Only a Theory: Evolution and the Battle for America's Soul.* New York: Viking, 2008.

Miller, L. Keith, and Richard Feallock. "A Behavioral System for Group Living." In Ramp, Eugene, and George Semb. *Bahavior Analysis: Areas of Research and Application.* Englewood Cliffs, NJ: Prentice-Hall, 1975. 73–96.

Mithen, Steven. *The Singing Neanderthals: The Origins of Music, Language, Mind and Body.* Cambridge, MA: Harvard University Press, 2006.

Morris, James M., and Andrea L. Koss. *Historical Dictionary of Utopianism.* Lanham, MD: Scarecrow, 2004.

Morrison, Blake. "The Relentless Unforeseen." *The Guardian*, October 2 (2004): 9.

Myrdal, Gunnar, Richard Sterner, and Arnold Rose. *An American Dilemma: The Negro Problem and Modern Democracy.* New York: Harper, 1944.

Nagel, Matthew. "Brain Chip Reads Man's Thoughts." BBCNews World Edition (online). March 31, 2005. news.bbc.co.uk/2/hi/health/4396387.stm

Negley, Glen, and J. Max. Patrick. *The Quest for Utopia: An Anthology of Imaginary Societies.* 1952.

Nesse, R.M. "Evolutionary Explanation of Emotion." *Human Nature* 1 (1990): 261–189.

Newberg, Andrew, Eugene d'Aquili, and Vince Rause. *Why God Won't Go Away: Brain Science and the Biology of Belief.* New York: Ballantine, 2001.

Newsweek, August 24 (2009): 9.

O'Donohue, William, and Kyle E. Ferguson. *The Psychology of B.F. Skinner.* Thousand Oaks, CA: Sage, 2001.

One Flew Over the Cuckoo's Nest. Dir. Milos Forman, 1975.

Owomoyela, Oyekan. *Yoruba Proverbs*. Lincoln, NE: University of Nebraska Press, 2005.

Pardalos, Panos M., and Jose Principe. *Biocomputing*. Dordrecht: Kluwer, 2002.

Park, Dean, and John Wieser. "Summary of Field Studies Evaluating the Efficacy of Bio-Bond®, a Porous Polymer Sheath, on Radio Frequency Identification (RFID) Transponders to Prevent Migration from a Known Implant Site." 2000.www.animal-id.com.au/report.html

Parker, Martin. *Utopia and Organization*. Oxford: Blackwell, 2002.

Paul, Gregory. "The Chronic Dependence of Popular Religiosity Upon Dysfunctional Social Conditions." *Evolutionary Psychology* 7.3 (2009): 398–441.

Paul, Ron. *The Revolution*. New York, Boston: Grand Central Publishing, 2008.

Percy, Walker. *Signposts in a Strange Land*. New York: Farrar, Straus, and Giroux, 1991.

Percy, Walker. *The Thanatos Syndrome*. New York: Picador, 1987.

Percy, Walker. *Lost in the Cosmos: The Last Self-Help Book*. New York: Farrar, Straus & Giroux, 1983.

Percy Walker. *Love in the Ruins: The Adventures of a Bad Catholic at a Time Near the End of the World*. New York: Farrar, Straus, and Giroux, 1971.

Percy, Walker. *Message in the Bottle: How Queer Man Is, How Queer Language Is, and What One Has to Do With the Other*. New York: Farrar, Straus & Giroux, 1975.

Peter, K.A. *The Dynamics of Hutterite Society: An Analytical Approach*. Edmonton: University of Alberta Press, 1987.

Pew Research Center Pollwatch. "Reading the Polls on Evolution and Creationism." http://people-press.org/commentary/display.php3?AnalysisID=118

Phillips, Helen. "Brain Prosthesis Passes Live Tissue Test." *New Scientist*, October 25 (2004). http://www.newscientist.com/article/dn6574-brain-prosthesis-passes-live-tissue-test.html

Pinker, Steven. *How the Mind Works*. New York: Norton, 1997.

Pinker, Steven. *The Bank Slate: The Modern Denial of Human Nature*. New York: Penguin, 2003.

Plutchik, R. "Emotions and Evolution." *International Review of Studies on Emotions* 1 (1991): 37–58.

Podgorecki, Adam, John Alexander, and Rob Shields, eds. *Social Engineering*. Ottawa: Carleton University Press, 1996.

Poore, Charles. "Tour of an Almost Perfect Utopia." *New York Times Book Review*, June 13 (1948): 6.

Posnock, Ross. *Philip Roth's Rude Truth: The Art of Immaturity*. Princeton/Oxford: Princeton University Press, 2006.

Poundstone, William. *Gaming the Vote: Why Elections Aren't Fair (and What We Can Do About It)*. New York: Hill and Wang, 2008.

Price, M.E., et al. "Punitive Sentiment as an Anti-free-rider Psychological Device." *Evolution and Human Behavior* 23 (2002): 203–231.

Proctor, R.W., and D.J. Weeks. *The Goal of B.F. Skinner and Behavior Analysis*. Heidelberg/New York: Springer, 1990.

Pruden, Wes. "Drawing a Line in the Water." *Jewish World Review*, February 15 (2008). http://www.jewishworldreview.com/cols/pruden021508.php3

Rampton, David. "Stupidity's Progress: Philip Roth and Twentieth-Century American History." In Swirski, Peter, ed. *I Sing the Body Politic: History as Prophecy in Contemporary American Literature*. Montreal/London: McGill-Queen's University Press, 2009.

Rand, Ayn. *Philosophy: Who Needs It?* New York: Signet, 1984.

Reynolds, Vernon, Vincent Falger, and Ian Vine, eds. *The Sociobiology of Ethnocentrism: Evolutionary Dimensions of Xenophobia, Discrimination, Racism and Nationalism*. Athens, GA: University of Georgia Press, 1986.

Richards, Janet Radcliffe. *Human Nature after Darwin: a Philosophical Introduction*. London/New York: Routledge, 2000.

Richardson, Lewis Fry. *Statistics of Deadly Quarrels*. In Quincy Wright and C.C. Lienau, eds. ????????????. Pittsburgh: Boxwood Press, 1960.

Richardson, Lewis Fry. *Arms and Insecurity: a Mathematical Study of the Causes and Origins of War*. Eds. Nicolas Rashevsky and Ernesto Trucco. Pittsburg: Boxwood Press, 1960.

Richelle, Marc N. *B.F. Skinner: A Reappraisal*. Hove, East Sussex: Lawrence Erlbaum Associates, 1993.

Richerson, Peter J., and Robert Boyd. *Not By Genes Alone: How Culture Transformed Human Evolution*. Chicago: University of Chicago Press, 2005.

Ridley, Matt. *The Origins of Virtue*. London: Viking, 1996.

Riker, William H. *The Strategy of Rhetoric: Campaigning for the American Constitution*. Edited by Randall L. Calvert, John Mueller, and Rick K. Wilson. New Haven/London: Yale University Press, 1996.

Rizzolatti, Giacomo, and Corrado Sinigaglia. *Mirrors in the Brain: How Our Minds Share Actions and Emotions*. Oxford: Oxford University Press, 2008.

Roemer, Kenneth. "Mixing Behaviorism and Utopia: The Transformations of *Walden Two*." In Eric Rabkin et al., eds *No Place Else: Explorations in Utopian and Dystopian Fiction*. Carbondale: Southern Illinois University Press, 1983. 125–146.

Roth, Philip. *The Plot Against America*. Boston: Houghton Mifflin, 2004.

Roth, Philip. *I Married a Communist*. London: Jonathan Cape, 1998.

Roth, Philip. *The Ghost Writer*. New York: Farrar, Straus & Giroux, 1979.

Roth, Philip. *Our Gang (Starring Tricky and His Friends)*. New York: Random House, 1971.

Rothstein, Mervyn. "Bernard Malamud, Author, Dies at 71." *New York Times*, March 20 (1986): D26.

Rummell, Rudolph J. *Death by Government*. New Brunswick, NJ: Transaction, 1994.

Ruth, David. "The Evolution of Work Organization at Twin Oaks." *Communities: Journal of Cooperative Living* 35 (Nov–Dec 1975): 58–60.

Sabato, Larry. *A More Perfect Constitution: 23 Proposals to Revitalize Our Constitution and Make America a Fairer Country*. New York: Walker and Company, 2007.

Sacks, Oliver. *Musicophilia*. New York, Toronto: Knopf, 2007.

Saul, John Ralston. *Voltaire's Bastards: the Dictatorship of Reason in the West*. New York: Free Press, 1992.

Scarborough, W. *A Collection of Chinese Proverbs*. Changsha: China, 1926; New York: Paragon, 1964.

Scheflin, Alan W., and Edward M. Opton. *The Mind Manipulators*. New York: Paddington Press, 1978.

Schell, Jonathan. "The Unfinished Twentieth Century: What We Have Forgotten About Nuclear Weapons." *Harper's Magazine* (January 2000): 41–56.

Schell, Jonathan. *The Fate of the Earth*. New York: Knopf, 1982.

Schmidt, David D. *Citizen Lawmakers: The Ballot Initiative Revolution*. Philadelphia: Temple University Press, 1898.

Scott-Tyson, Ann. "Rumsfeld: Moral Warrior." *The Edmonton Journal*, January 4 (2003): A12.

Searles, George J., ed. *Conversations with Philip Roth*. Jackson: University Press of Mississippi, 1992.

Searles, George J., ed. *A Casebook on Ken Kesey's* One Flew Over the Cuckoo's Nest." Albuquerque, NM: University of New Mexico Press, 1992.

Segal, Howard P. *Technological Utopianism in American Culture*. Chicago: University of Chicago Press, 1985.

Setiathome (Sci-Tech News). "DNA Computer Solves Logic Queries." (2009). http://setiathome.berkeley.edu/forum_thread.php?id=54789

Shapin, Steven, and Simon Schaffer. *Leviathan and the Air-pump: Hobbes, Boyle, and the Experimental Life*. Princeton, New Jersey: Princeton University Press, 1985.

Shechner, Mark. *Up Society's Ass, Copper: Rereading Philip Roth.* Madison: University of Wisconsin Press, 2003.

Shinada, M., and T. Yamagishi. "Punishing Free Riders: Direct and Indirect Promotion of Cooperation." *Evolution and Human Behavior* 28.5 (2007): 330–339.

Shorter, Edward, and David Healy. *Shock Therapy: The History of Electroconvulsive Treatment in Mental Illness.* Piscataway, NJ: Rutgers University Press, 2007.

Shubik, Martin. "The Dollar Auction Game: A Paradox in Noncooperative Behavior and Escalation." *Journal of Conflict Resolution* 15.1 (1971): 109–111.

Siegel, Lee. "*Bernard Malamud: A Writer's Life*, by Philip Davis." *New York Times*, December 9 (2007): Section 7, page 12.

Simon, Herbert A. "A Mechanism for Social Selection and Successful Altruism." *Science* 250 (1990): 1665–1668.

Skinner, B.F. *Walden Two.* Indianapolis, IN: Hackett, 2005. [1948]

Skinner, B.F. "The Phylogeny and Ontogeny of Behavior." *Science* 153 (1966): 1205–1213.

Skinner, B.F. *Science and Human Behavior.* New York: Free Press, 1965. [1953]

Skinner, B.F. *Beyond Freedom and Dignity.* New York: Bantam/Vintage, 1987. [1971]

Skinner, B.F. "Walden (One) and Walden Two." *Thoreau Society Bulletin* 122 (Winter 1973): 1–3.

Skinner, B.F. *About Behaviorism.* New York: Knopf, 1974.

Skinner, B.F. "Walden Two Revisited." *Walden Two.* Indianapolis, IN: Hackett, 2005.

Skinner, B.F. "Herrnstein and the Evolution of Behaviorism." *American Psychologist* 32 (1977): 1006–1012.

Skinner, B.F. *A Matter of Consequences: Part Three of an Autobiography.* New York: Knopf, 1983.

Skinner. B.F. "News From Nowhere, 1984." *The Behavior Analyst* 8.1 (1985): 5–14.

Skinner, B.F. "The Place of Feelings in the Analysis of Behavior." *Recent Issues in the Analysis of Behavior.* Columbus, OH: Merrill, 1989.

Smith, Adam. *The Theory of Moral Sentiments.* Edinburgh: 1759.

Smith, David Livingstone. *The Most Dangerous Animal: Human Nature and the Origins of War.* New York: St. Martin's Griffin, 2007.

Smith, Kerri. "Mind Reading with a Brain Scan." *Nature*, March 5 (2008). www.nature.com/news/2008/080305/full/news.2008.650.html.

Sober, Elliott, and David Sloan Wilson. *Unto Others: The Evolution and Psychology of Unselfish Behavior.* Cambridge, MA: Harvard University Press, 1999.

Sokoloff, Boris. *Jealousy: A Psychological Study*. London: Carroll and Nicholson, 1948.

Steiner, Gary. *Anthropocentrism and its Discontents: The Moral Status of Animals in the History of Western Philosophy*. Pittsburg, PA: University of Pittsburgh Press, 2005.

Stillman, Peter G. "'Nothing is, but what is not': Utopias as Practical Political Philosophy." In Goodwin, Barbara, ed. *The Philosophy of Utopia*. London/New York: Routledge, 2001. 9–24.

Stites, Richard. *Revolutionary Dreams: Utopian Vision and Experimental Life in the Russian Revolution*. Oxford: Oxford University Press, 1989.

Stone, Jon R. *The Routledge Book of World Proverbs*. London/New York: Routledge, 2006.

Stout, Rowland. *The Inner Life of a Rational Agent: In Defence of Philosophical Behaviourism*. Edinburgh: Edinburgh University Press, 2006.

Sulzer-Azaroff, Beth. "Is Back to Nature Always Best?" *Journal of Applied Behavior Analysis* 25.1 (Spring 1992): 81–82.

Suskind, Ron. *The Price of Loyalty: George W. Bush, the White House, and the Education of Paul O'Neill*. New York: Simon and Schuster, 2004.

Suskind, Ron. "Without a Doubt." *New York Times Magazine*, October 17 (2004): 44–51; 64; 102; 106.

Swain, Simon. *Seeing the Face, Seeing the Soul: Polemon's "Physiognomy" from Classical Antiquity to Medieval Islam*. Oxford: Oxford University Press, 2007.

Swirski, Peter. *Ars Americana, Ars Politica: Partisan Expression and Nobrow American Culture*. Montreal/ London: McGill-Queen's University Press, 2010.

Swirski, Peter. *Literature, Analytically Speaking: Explorations in the Theory of Interpretation, Analytic Aesthetics, and Evolution (Cognitive Approaches to Literature and Culture Series)*. Austin: University of Texas Press, 2010.

Swirski, Peter, ed. *I Sing the Body Politic: History as Prophecy in Contemporary American Literature*. Montreal/ London: McGill-Queen's University Press, 2009.

Swirski, Peter. "The Historature of the American Empire: Joseph Heller's *Picture This*." In *I Sing the Body Politic: History as Prophecy in Contemporary American Literature*. Montreal/ London: McGill-Queen's University Press, 2009.

Swirski, Peter. "When Biological Evolution and Social Revolution Clash: Skinner's Behaviorist Utopia." In Andrews, Alice, and Joseph Carroll, eds. *The Evolutionary Review: Art, Science and Culture*. New York: State University of New York Press, 2009. 46–58.

Swirski, Peter. *All Roads Lead to the American City.* Hong Kong/London: Hong Kong University Press, 2007.

Swirski, Peter. *Of Literature and Knowledge: Explorations in Narrative Thought Experiments, Evolution, and Game Theory.* London/New York: Routledge, 2007.

Swirski, Peter, ed. *The Art and Science of Stanislaw Lem.* Montreal/London: McGill-Queen's University Press, 2006.

Swirski, Peter. "Bernard Malamud: *God's Grace.*" *Beacham's Encyclopedia of Popular Fiction.* Ed. Kirk Beetz. Osprey, FL: Beacham Publishing, 1998. Vol. 9. 5592–5601.

Symons, Donald. *The Evolution of Human Sexuality.* Oxford: Oxford University Press, 1979.

Symons, Donald. "On the Use and Misuse of Darwinism in the Study of Human Behavior." In Barkow, Jerome, Leda Cosmides and John Tooby, eds. *The Adapted Mind: Evolutionary Psychology and the Generation of Culture.* New York: Oxford University Press, 1992.

Tanner, Stephen L. *Ken Kesey.* Boston: Twayne, 1983.

Tideman, Nicolaus. *Collective Decisions and Voting: The Potential for Public Choice.* Aldershot, England: Ashgate, 2006.

Tierney, John. "Using M.R.I.'s to See Politics on the Brain." *New York Times,* April 20 (2004). http://www.nytimes.com/2004/04/20/science/20SCAN.html

Tierson, F.D., et al. "Influence of Cravings and Aversions on diet in pregnancy." *Ecology of Food and Nutrition* 17 (1985): 117–129.

Tiger, Lionel, and Joseph Shepher. *Women in the Kibbutz.* New York: Harcourt Brace Jovanovich, 1975.

The Economist. "The Pendulum Swings Back. Oregon's Tax Referendums." *The Economist* January 30 (2010): 39–40.

Thomas, Gordon. *Journey into Madness.* New York: Bantam, 1989.

Thompson, Travis. "Retrospective Review: Benedictus Behavioral Analysis: B.F. Skinner's Magnum Opus at Fifty." *Contemporary Psychology* 33 (1988): 397–402.

Thoreau, Henry David. *Walden and Civil Disobedience.* New York: Penguin, 1983.

Tocqueville, Alexis de. *Democracy in America. Democracy in America.* New York: Penguin, 1955. [1835].

Todd, J.T., and E.K. Morris. "Case Histories in the Great Power of Steady Misrepresentation." *American Psychologist* 47 (1992): 1441–1453.

Tomasello, Michael. *Origins of Human Communication.* Cambridge, MA: MIT Press, 2008.

Tomasello, Michael, et al. "Understanding and Sharing Intentions: The Origins of Cultural Cognition." *Behavioral and Brain Sciences* 28 (2005): 675–735.

Tomasello, Michael, and H. Rakoczy. "What Makes Human Cognition Unique? From Individual to Shared to Collective Intentionality." *Mind and Language* 18 (2003): 121–147.

Tomasello, Michael. "The Human Adaptation for Culture." *Annual Review of Anthropology* 28 (1999): 509–529.

Tomasello, Michael, et al. "Cultural Learning." *Behavioral and Brain Sciences* 16 (1993): 495–552.

Tooby, John, and Leda Cosmides. "The Psychological Foundations of Culture. In *The Adapted Mind: Evolutionary Psychology and the Generation of Culture.* New York: Oxford University Press, 1992.

Tooze, Adam. *The Wages of Destruction: The Making and Breaking of the Nazi Economy.* New York: Viking, 2007.

Trahair, Richard C.S., ed. *Utopias and Utopians: An Historical Dictionary of Attempts to Make the World a Better Place and Those Who Were Involved.* London: Fitzroy Dearborn, 1999.

Trivers, Robert L. "The Evolution of Reciprocal Altruism." *Quarterly Review of Biology* 46 (1971): 35–57.

Trivers, Robert L. "Parental Investment and Sexual Selection." In Campbell, B., ed. *Sexual Selection and the Descent of Man: 1871–1971.* Chicago: Aldine, 1972. 136–179.

Trivers, Robert. *Social Evolution.* Menlo Park, CA: Benjamin Cummings, 1982.

Ulrich, Roger. "Some Moral and Ethical Implications of Behavior Modification." In *Rites of Life: A Book about the Use and Misuse of Animals and Earth.* Kalamazoo, Mich.: Life Giving Enterprises, 1989. 36–49.

USA TODAY online. "*USA TODAY*/Gallup Poll Results." June 9 (2007). http://www.usatoday.com/news/politics/2007–06–07-evolution-poll-results_N.htm?csp=34

US Department of Defense. "FY 2003 International Affairs Request—Summary." In *State Department Budget.* 2003. http://www.state.gov/s/d/rm/rls/iab/2003/7807.htm

Vargas, Julie S. "Foreword." In O'Donohue, William, and Kyle E. Ferguson. *The Psychology of B.F. Skinner.* Thousand Oaks, CA: Sage, 2001. v–vii.

Voland, Eckart, and Wulf Schiefenhovel, eds. *The Biological Evolution of Religious Mind and Behavior.* Dordrecht: Springer, 2009.

Wall, Judy. "Mind Control with Silent Sounds and Super Computers." *AboveTopSecret.com* 18 June (2004). http://www.abovetopsecret.com/forum/thread59992/pg1

Wallbott, H.G., and K.R. Scherer. "How Universal and Specific is Emotional Experience? Evidence from 27 Countries on Five Continents." In Scherer, K.R., ed. *Facets of Emotion: Recent Research.* Hillsdale, NJ: Erlbaum, 1988.

Wallerstein, Immanuel Maurice. *Utopistics: Or Historical Choices of the Twenty-first Century.* New York: New Press, 1998.

Wallis, Bruce E. "Christ in the Cuckoo's Nest: Or, the Gospel According to Ken Kesey." *Cithara* 12 (1972): 52–58.

Walsh, Chad. *From Utopia to Nightmare.* New York: Harper & Row, 1962.

Ward, Mary Jane. *The Snake Pit.* New York: Random House, 1946.

Washington Post. "Top Secret America." July 19 (2010). http://projects.washingtonpost.com/top-secret-america/

Waters, M. Dane. *The Battle Over Citizen Lawmaking.* Durham, NC: Carolina Academic Press, 2001.

Watson, John B. *Psychological Care of Infant and Child.* New York: Norton, 1928.

Webb, George E. *The Evolution Controversy in America.* Lexington: The University Press of Kentucky, 1994.

Weber, Max. *Economy and Society.* Trans. Ephraim Fischoff et al. Eds. Guenther Roth and Claus Wittich. Berkeley: University of California Press, 1978. [1914].

Wellman, H. *The Child's Theory of Mind.* Cambridge, MA: MIT Press, 1990.

Wershba, Joseph. "Not Horror but Sadness." In Lasher, Lawrence M., ed. *Conversations with Bernard Malamud.* Jackson: University Press of Mississippi, 1991. 3–7.

Wertham, Fredric. *A Sign for Cain: An Exploration of Human Violence.* New York: Warner, 1973. [1966].

West, Diana. "The Unnerving Plot." *Townhall.com* October 11 (2004). http://townhall.com/columnists/DianaWest/2004/10/11/the_unnerving_plot

Westen, Drew. *The Political Brain: The Role of Emotion in Deciding the Fate of the Nation.* New York: Public Affairs, 2007.

Whitaker, Robert. *Mad in America: Bad Science, Bad Medicine, and the Enduring Mistreatment of the Mentall Ill.* 2nd ed. New York: Basic, 2010.

Widmer, Ted. *American Speeches: Political Oratory from the Revolution to the Civil War.* New York: Library of America, 2006.

Wiederman, M.W. "Evolved Gender Differences in Mate Preferences: Evidence From Personal Advertisements." *Ethology and Sociobiology* 14 (1993): 331–352.

Williams, Donald C. "The Social Scientist as Philosopher and King." *Philosophical Review* 58.4 (July 1949): 345–359.

Williams, George C. *Adaptation and Natural Selection: A Critique of Some Current Evolutionary Thought.* Princeton, NJ: Princeton University Press, 1966.

Wilson, David Sloan. *Darwin's Cathedral: Evolution, Religion, and the Nature of Society.* Chicago: University of Chicago Press, 2002.

Wilson, David Sloan. *Evolution for Everyone: How Darwin's Theory Can Change the Way We Think about Our Lives*. New York: Delacorte, 2007.

Wilson, David Sloan, and Edward O. Wilson. "Rethinking the Theoretical Foundation of Sociobiology." *The Quarterly Review of Biology* 82.4 (2007): 327–348.

Wilson, Edward O. *Sociobiology: the New Synthesis*. Cambridge, MA: Belknap, 2000.

Wilson, Edward O. *Consilience: The Unity of Knowledge*. New York: Knopf, 1998.

Wilson, Edward O. *On Human Nature*. Cambridge: Harvard University Press, 1978.

Woolley, John, and Gerhard Peters. "George W. Bush. Remarks at the Swearing-In Ceremony for Ann M. Veneman as Secretary of Agriculture. March 2, 2001." *The American Presidency Project [online]*. http://www.presidency.ucsb.edu/ws/index.php?pid=45736

Wrangham, Richard W., and Dale Peterson. *Demonic Males: Apes and the Origins of Human Violence*. Boston: Houghton-Mifflin, 1996.

Wright, Robert. *The Moral Animal*. New York: Pantheon, 1994.

Yardley, Jonathan. "Homeland Insecurity." *Washington Post,* October 3 (2004): BW02.

Zajonc, Robert B. "Feeling and Thinking: Preferences Need No Inferences." *American Psychologist* 35 (1980): 151–175.

Zajonc, Robert B. "On the Primacy of Affect." *American Psychologist* 39 (1984): 117–123.

Zimmerman, Joseph F. *The Initiative: Citizen Law-Making*. Santa Barbara, CA: Praeger, 1999.

Index